SERVICE LEARNING

Ninety-sixth Yearbook of the
National Society for the Study of Education

PART I

Edited by

JOAN SCHINE

Editor for the Society

KENNETH J. REHAGE

Distributed by THE UNIVERSITY OF CHICAGO PRESS • CHICAGO, ILLINOIS

The National Society for the Study of Education

Founded in 1901 as successor to the National Herbart Society, the National Society for the Study of Education has provided a means by which the results of serious study of educational issues could become a basis for informed discussion of those issues. The Society's two-volume Yearbooks, now in their ninety-sixth year of publication, reflect the thoughtful attention given to a wide range of educational problems during those years. Each year the Society's publications contain contributions to the literature of education from scholars and practitioners who are doing significant work in their respective fields.

An elected Board of Directors reviews proposals for Yearbooks, selects the proposals that seem suitable for a Yearbook, and appoints an editor, or editors, to oversee the preparation of manuscripts for the projected volume.

The Society's publications are distributed each year without charge to members in the United States, Canada, and elsewhere throughout the world. The Society welcomes as members all individuals who desire to receive its publications. Information about current dues and a listing of its publications that are still in print may be found in the back pages of this volume.

This volume, *Service Learning*, is Part I of the Ninety-sixth Yearbook of the Society. Part II, published at the same time, is entitled *The Construction of Children's Character.*

Library of Congress Catalog Number: 96-72098
ISSN: 0077-5762

Published 1997 by
THE NATIONAL SOCIETY FOR THE STUDY OF EDUCATION

5835 Kimbark Avenue, Chicago, Illinois 60637

First Printing

Printed in the United States of America

Board of Directors of the National Society for the Study of Education

(Term of office expires March 1 of the year indicated.)

Contributors to the Yearbook

JOAN SCHINE, Editor, Center for Advanced Study of Education, Graduate School, City University of New York

GEORGE A. ANTONELLI, University of North Carolina
GENE R. CARTER, Association for Supervision and Curriculum Development
JAMES P. COMER, M.D., Yale University
DONALD J. EBERLY, National Service Secretariat
DWIGHT E. GILES, JR., Peabody College, Vanderbilt University
NORRIS M. HAYNES, Yale University
MORRIS T. KEETON, University of Maryland
PETER KLEINBARD, DeWitt Wallace-Reader's Digest Fund
DONNA KOPPELMAN, Edenton (North Carolina) Public Schools
MADELEINE M. KUNIN, U.S. Department of Education
RICHARD K. LIPKA, Pittsburgh (Kansas) State University
WINIFRED PARDO, Shoreham-Wading River (New York) Public Schools
PETER C. SCALES, Search Institute
BARRY G. SHECKLEY, University of Connecticut
SUZANNE TARLOV, Funds for the Community's Future
JANIE VICTORIA WARD, Simmons College
ALLEN WUTZDORFF, Lowcountry Aids Services
SHEPHERD ZELDIN, Funds for the Community's Future

Foreword

Service is the rent each of us pays for living.

Marian Wright Edelman

The last fifteen or twenty years of the 20th century in America have seen a modest growth of interest in "service learning" along with an intense and almost rabid enthusiasm for additional "academic learning." *A Nation at Risk*, published in 1983, has become the Bible of academic learning, and its shrill rhetoric pervades every corner of almost every schoolhouse. This call to worshipers sets forth the virtues of the major academic disciplines as the lessons to be mastered—lessons seen primarily as weapons to beat other nations in economic competition. This highly individualistic, competitive emphasis on learning is verified by standardized tests to sort out its students.

Definitions of "Service Learning" vary widely but none of them draws on *A Nation at Risk*. An author in this volume provides a useful starting point: "The term 'service learning' can be loosely defined as an educational activity, program, or curriculum that seeks to promote student learning through experiences associated with volunteerism or community service." This somewhat wordy statement might be summarized into: Service learning emerges from helping others and reflecting on how you and they benefited from doing so. A still briefer statement might go back to the Bible: "Love thy neighbor" and learn from doing it.

Whatever you choose as the banner to carry for service learning, it will be quite different from most academic learning; and it is worth thinking about those differences. They require the learner to be engaged directly with other people—both those providing services and those being served. These engagements constitute a significant learning process because they bring new experiences. Here are some examples: (1) working together in a group to plan and carry out service activities; (2) adjusting these activities to fit the tastes and needs of people who are often very different from the learner—different in age, cultural background, and viewpoints about daily living; (3) opportunity for reflection on the meaning of these activities in the lives of both the server and the served; (4) the chance to develop effective habits of performance in joint endeavors and to assume growing responsibilities in such relationships; (5) emphasis on helping others in ways that develop "habits of the heart," which cannot be measured with standardized tests.

This list could go on and on, but these five examples will suffice to back up the assertion that service learning is a significant element in the educational process at all levels—school, college, and beyond. It has more to do with becoming a mature adult than any academic exercise; and it is at least the equal of academic effort in building an understanding of others, the capacity to be an effective citizen, and the promise of leading a balanced life in an increasingly complex world.

If these potential outcomes of service learning have any validity, and there is beginning to be research evidence that they do, then the next century will have to change the balance between service learning and academic learning that has characterized American schools in recent years. Service learning will have to become an integral part of the school curriculum rather than the extracurricular activity it too often is. The chapter in this book by Haynes and Comer carries a succinct and powerful message to this effect:

> Service to others, particularly those who are in need and less fortunate, and service to the larger community through unselfish acts of caring and kindness are defining characteristics of a great and compassionate nation. But because of the increasing pluralism in our society, uncertainty about the future, and skepticism surrounding services to the poor and the most needy members of society, there sometimes seems to be a retreat by many from the altruism and compassion which have helped to make this nation great. Many educators recognize that service learning in schools . . . should be an important and integrated component of students' educational experience to prepare them for life and for service in the larger community.

If this argument appears to be saying that typical academic learning is narrow, individualistic, and excessively competitive, while service learning stresses working cooperatively with others in a morally meaningful way, there is some truth in that interpretation, at least to the extent that traditional modes of teaching still dominate most academic classrooms. These classrooms in both schools and universities are dominated by a passive learning process. Teachers and professors stand before a class and tell the students what they should know or they assign reading to convey it. Then to demonstrate their learning the students are asked to parrot back what they have been told or what they have read. Many classrooms neglect in-depth discussion, student responsibility for the learning of others, and efforts to relate what is studied to their own lives and the world they live in.

Successful service learning avoids this dry and unimaginative process. It is based on active learning, which is characterized by very different behaviors on the part of both teachers and students. Both are engaged in planning what is to be done and how; both carry it out together, often outside the classroom in the world of reality—families, communities, groups with particular needs, institutions with inadequate resources and dependent on volunteer assistance; both get together to evaluate what has been accomplished and to suggest changes that will produce better service.

The sad fact of this disparity between academic study and service learning is that it does not have to exist. Academic learning can adopt the strategies of active learning on which service learning is based. A well-known Chinese proverb explains this possibility:

> I hear and I forget.
> I see and I remember.
> I act and I understand.

This rubric holds the potential of a revolution in academic learning. A few schools and colleges in America are moving in the direction implied by it. Some professional schools are quite successful with it because they have at hand the realities of a profession to stimulate experience. To change from passive to active learning, however, is very difficult for both students and teachers because the ruts they are in are familiar and comfortable. The development of a healthy element of service learning in a school or college will help to open the doors to change, particularly if the service activities are followed up by well-planned reflection on their meaning.

The many authors of this book light up the varied facets of service learning—its background, its sources of initiative from the Peace Corps to the nursery school, its internal struggles for time and support in traditional institutions, its need for more research on its outcomes and effectiveness. For the reasons outlined here it seems to me a valuable element in the American effort to improve education.

Harold Howe II
Formerly U.S. Commissioner of Education
and Vice President of the Ford Foundation
for Education and Public Policy

Editor's Preface

The decision of the Board of Directors of the National Society for the Study of Education to include a volume on service learning in its distinguished series of Yearbooks is testimony to the growing importance of the field at this time of "education reform." Whether viewed primarily as an element in the social studies curriculum, as enrichment within a variety of disciplines, citizenship education, or a teaching methodology, service learning has attracted support from practitioners, policymakers, researchers, government at all levels, and from the broader community. That support is not unanimous, but with encouragement at the federal level through the National and Community Service Trust Act of 1993, and the backing of distinguished leaders in education and youth development, service learning is finding a place in the program and planning of an increasing number of schools and school districts. Forty-seven states have established state commissions on national service under the National and Community Service Trust Act. Estimates of the number of schools that involve their students in service vary, but there is no doubt that their numbers are growing.

Service learning is scarcely a new arrival on the scene, but only lately has it come into its own as a significant element in schooling. As some of the authors of this volume point out, there was a time not long ago when young people—even the very young—were active participants in the household, when the family's work was centered near or in the home, and all members had a contribution to make. Inevitably, the young learned as they worked. Not only in the family setting, but as members of closely knit communities, they practiced some of the skills they would need as adult workers; they learned to collaborate with others, to plan, to see a task through from beginning to end. And they were valued for their work.

School-based service learning can, to some extent, compensate for the disappearance of those naturally occurring opportunities. Some independent schools, reflecting a religious orientation or the school's underlying philosophy, have long incorporated service to the community (though not necessarily service learning) in their programs. While debate over values education consumes thousands of words in meetings of local school boards and in the media, few people question the propriety of imbuing students with a sense of responsibility and a desire to contribute to the society.

But even though supporters of service learning share common ground, differences remain. Vocabulary can become an obstacle to understanding and collaboration. For example, even a hyphen may become a matter for dispute. Readers will note that some authors use service-learning as one word, and present a rationale for this usage; others believe that the two words, though interdependent, represent distinct elements. We believe (and hope) that as the field matures, the players will arrive at some agreement over terminology. We have not, however, tried to achieve uniformity in the chapters in this volume, leaving the choice to each writer.

Similarly, until quite recently the terms "community service" and "service learning" were often used interchangeably; this still occurs among those who are relatively new to the field. The distinction is implicit in every essay in this volume. Community service is in itself a worthy pursuit, but it may or may not include an element of learning. Service learning, as the term (with or without a hyphen) implies, always embodies both.

Other issues will continue to be debated, and indeed it is entirely likely that unanimity will never be achieved, even among the proponents of service learning. A case in point is the ongoing discussion of mandatory versus voluntary participation in service learning. Proponents of required service like to point out that we do not hesitate to require students to learn mathematics, because we have determined that mathematical knowledge is necessary for a productive life in today's world; equally, they say, a knowledge of the community and the skill and will to serve are needed for survival of both the individual and a democratic society. Opponents of mandatory participation, on the other hand, are equally vehement in arguing that only if participation in service is voluntary will the young truly comprehend the meaning of commitment to community and internalize the values of altruism and unselfishness that service should teach.

The essays in this Yearbook address a wide variety of the issues that educators, policymakers, and all of us must explore as we seek to expand our understanding of the burgeoning field of service learning. More issues will arise, as thoughtful individuals delve deeper into its goals and outcomes. It is the hope of the editor and the authors that the reader will find some answers in this volume, and will at the same time be inspired to ask more questions and to seek more answers.

I wish to thank the following people, all of whom gave valuable assistance by providing or verifying information for this volume: Dale Baker, Pennsylvania Learn and Serve Coordinator; Saul Benjamin and Diana Phillips in the Office of the Deputy Secretary, USOE; Calvin Dawson, Corporation for National and Community Service; Suzanne Goldsmith, American Alliance for Rights and Responsibilities; Barbara Gomez, Council of Chief State School Officers; Stan Hanson, New York State Department of Education; Nancy Rhodes, director of Campus Compact; Marilyn Wallister, Oregon Department of Education, and the staff of the National Helpers Network.

JOAN SCHINE
January, 1997

Acknowledgments

Joan Schine, editor of this volume, has had a long and close relationship with the rapidly developing movement for service learning. A devoted advocate for the concept of joining service with learning in schools and colleges, Ms. Schine maintains a balanced view of the place of service learning in current efforts for school reform. Her wide acquaintance among leaders in the service learning movement has enabled her to assemble essays for this volume from authors with broad experience with service learning in different settings. The Society is grateful for the wisdom she has shown in planning the volume as well as for her tireless effort at every stage of the project.

The Society also appreciates the contributions of each of the authors. Their work has enabled us to bring out a volume that not only places service learning in a historical perspective but also provides enormous help to teachers and administrators interested in investigating the possibilities for service learning in their schools.

Margaret Early of the University of Florida at Gainesville and a former member of the Society's Board of Directors has again devoted many hours to a critical reading of all the manuscripts for this volume, as she has done for all our Yearbooks in recent years. Her comments and suggestions are invaluable as each of the chapters is prepared for publication.

Jenny Volpe, assistant in the NSSE office, prepared the name index and assisted with many other tasks as this work was brought to completion.

KENNETH J. REHAGE
Editor for the Society

Table of Contents

CHAPTER I

Youth Participation: Integrating Youth into Communities

PETER KLEINBARD

In this chapter I describe a particular form of service learning—Youth Participation—that was developed by the National Commission on Resources for Youth, Inc. (NCRY), which operated from 1967 to 1986 as a not-for-profit agency based in New York City. A small group of prominent educators and business people created NCRY and served as its Board of Directors. They were led by Mary Conway Kohler, a dynamic woman who had served previously as a judge in the juvenile courts of San Francisco. Their goal was to increase awareness among all Americans, and especially in government and among youth professionals, of the need to integrate youth, especially adolescents, into the wider community and to propose strategies for doing so. They coined the term "Youth Participation" to describe several program elements which, when taken together, represented their idea of what the best youth development programs should offer.

Helped by the agency's clear focus, Youth Participation programs were implemented widely, and great gains were made during the 1970s and early 1980s in building understanding and acceptance of the idea of youth involvement. The program designs for Youth Participation brought together the experience of practitioners with the findings of research and the perspectives of thoughtful academics. Consistent with the plan of its founders, the NCRY staff dissolved the organization after nineteen years. This reflected the Board members' conviction that the idea would prove itself over time and would become widely accepted. NCRY's legacy is apparent today in the broad national interest in service learning and in other program efforts that stress active community roles for youth.

Youth Participation is similar in concept and practice to service learning: active roles for young people and reflection are essential to

Peter Kleinbard was on the staff of the National Commission on Resources for Youth from 1971 to 1981. In 1984, he established the Young Adult Learning Academy in New York City, a school devoted to school dropouts. Currently, he is a Program Officer at the DeWitt Wallace-Reader's Digest Fund in New York City.

both. In Youth Participation, however, leadership and decision making by youth receive great emphasis. Thus, political activities might qualify as Youth Participation, provided other components are in place. Both concepts are broad and relatively inclusive, however, and little is gained by stressing fine distinctions.

The National Commission on Resources for Youth: People and Strategies

Most of NCRY's founders, having grown up in the early part of the twentieth century, were struck by the changes that they saw in the 1960s and 1970s, above all by the reduction of opportunities for young people to interact with adults and to assume responsibility for themselves and others. Ralph W. Tyler, one of the founders of NCRY, summarized its mission as follows:

> The National Commission on Resources for Youth was established because of the increasing difficulty young people find today in making the transition from adolescence to constructive adult life. In earlier periods, the home, the local community, and the place of employment furnished a variety of opportunities for youth to work, to make helpful contributions to family and community, and to associate in other ways with adults. As they grew older, this enabled them to participate more and more in adult activities and to assume an increasing degree of responsibility. In this way, they both gained competence and assurance that they were moving successfully into adulthood.[1]

Several of the founding members of NCRY had met while serving on a committee that advised President John F. Kennedy on youth employment issues. They had agreed to continue their work, but to address a wider range of youth development issues.

Mary Kohler took the lead and devoted her energies to NCRY and to the promotion of its cause from its founding in 1967 until she died in 1986. Born in California in 1902, she attended Stanford Law School in the 1920s, an extraordinary accomplishment for a woman at that time. She became a juvenile probation officer in San Francisco in 1929 and a short time later she was appointed "Referee" in the juvenile court in San Francisco. As Referee, she sat with the judges and heard all cases involving juveniles. In 1951, with her three children she moved to New York City, where she served on the Tweed Commission for the Reform of the Juvenile Court System, on the New York City Board of Education, and helped to initiate the Neighborhood Youth Corps. In 1959, she spent time abroad looking at youth issues. In England, she met Alec Dickson, who had created the Overseas Volunteer Services through which English youth could volunteer for human services between their high school and college years. The two remained lifelong friends, influencing each other's professional achievements. Her travels resulted in the publication of a popular article in the *Saturday Evening Post* of November 7, 1959, "Why Does Europe Have Less Delinquency?" Insisting on the need for a broad range of positive activities for young people in America, she cited examples from Eastern Europe of youth operating a railroad and performing many other essential roles in their communities.

Kohler remained NCRY's director until 1979 when she retired to become Board Chairperson. The Commission's work continued until 1986, when the core organization closed, spinning off what was to become the National Center for Service Learning in Early Adolescence. That Center was directed by Joan Schine, who had worked with Kohler for many years.

While remaining a small organization with rarely more than eight employees, NCRY undertook to change how Americans perceive adolescents. Toward this end, Kohler and her staff designed and disseminated Youth Participation models and identified exemplary programs developed by others. Two of the programs they established, Youth Tutoring Youth and Day Care Youth Helper, will be described in detail later in this chapter. Perhaps most important, Kohler herself, a tireless and passionate spokesperson for youth, reached the élite and the deprived alike with her message that the young can contribute to their communities and gain in maturity and compassion by doing so.

NCRY did contract work for nearly every major federal agency concerned with youth: the Office of Juvenile Justice and Delinquency Prevention, the Department of Labor, and the Department of Education within the then Health, Education, and Welfare Department. The target populations ranged from the gifted and talented, to school dropouts, and to incarcerated youth. In each case, Youth Participation was brought to the forefront of the agency's agenda and as a result, each agency began to apply Youth Participation criteria in developing and assessing its own programs. Several federal programs made Youth Participation part of their program guidelines, the largest being the Youth Employment Demonstration Project Act in the Department of Labor. Success in securing the commitment of federal agencies as well as local program operators can be attributed to several factors. One was NCRY's dissemination of proven, high-quality examples. Kohler's single-mindedness and skills as a salesperson were important. Most of all, the idea itself had power: people could understand at an emotional level the yearning of youth to make a difference and the need of communities to engage the best energies of their youth.

The Case for Youth Participation

In arguing for Youth Participation, NCRY's Board and staff developed an analysis of the changes in society and its institutions that affected the maturation of young people during the first sixty years of the century.[2] At the beginning of the twentieth century, collaboration and contact between youth and adults were far more common than today. Mothers stayed home; fathers worked in or near the home. More people lived on farms or in small communities where young people were included in the family's economic effort. The need to contribute to the household income brought them together with family members.

Today few workplaces are in or near residential neighborhoods. In an urbanized nation, most farm jobs for youth have been eliminated. Youth work in today's cities but rarely in ways that connect them with adults they know. They often work for nationally franchised "fast food" outlets where even the local managers have limited personal knowledge of their young employees. Often their work is not a priority for them or their families. The separation of youth and adults is further exacerbated by the loss of extended families and by the fact that both parents work. It is difficult to identify activities which young people and adults can share and that both groups perceive as essential. They may watch television together, but they are not likely to be involved together in activities that are productive economically.

Limited interaction with adults other than teachers has reduced informal educational opportunities for young people. Thus, while they spend more time at school in formal study, they spend far less time in activities that affect others or in informal hands-on learning. Overall, there are fewer resources outside of school to foster learning.[4] Not long ago, community institutions such as clubs or churches offered an arena in which young people could get together, learn from adults, and do things in an organized way with other youth, but today with fewer such resources they are likely to spend their after-school hours and school holidays unsupervised either at home alone or on the streets. At home, the "informal educational resources" usually means television, and on the streets, their equally unsupervised peers.[5] All these problems impact far more powerfully on poor youth whose working parents may not be able to provide alternative means of supervision.

Another consequence of the separation of youths and adults is the adults' loss of control of socializing resources. The peer group and the media have become major influences on the development of young people. Parents have no influence over television programming and little influence over peer groups that their children may join. The great stretches of unsupervised time that youth spend with their peers present dangerous possibilities, especially in a culture marked by widespread availability of drugs and guns and easy sex with its threat of HIV and other infections.

Parents sometimes encourage watching television in order to keep children "safe" at home. But television's fantasy world of easily acquired possessions, violence, and simplistic contrasts of good and evil hardly offers a positive educational environment. Moreover, television frees young people from taking responsibility for entertaining themselves. This lack of responsibility for one's own well-being was of great concern at NCRY because without taking responsibility for oneself it is difficult to develop the belief that one can take responsibility for others.

Schools offer youth few opportunities for taking responsibility. Although young people today spend more time in school than youth did during the first part of this century, schooling is often passive, requiring long hours of sitting and listening to adults, wise or not.[6] Drawing on the work of John Dewey and Jean Piaget, NCRY's staff stressed that the teacher's responsibility is to create an environment where learning occurs, not to impart knowledge. Fortunately, among today's school reformers there is a similar recognition of the need to make learning more like "work" and the instructor more like a "coach" instead of imitating the passive absorption promoted by television.[7] NCRY programs fostered activities such as peer counseling and tutoring in order to link academic learning with making a difference to others. Projects like Computer Car Pooling (described on p. 8) provide contexts in which what is studied in school can be related to needs and problems in the community.

During the 1970s when it seemed that everyone was trying to change the schools, NCRY sought to provide leaders of alternative schools and other experimenters with the concepts of Youth Participation. Having little patience with the romantic educational philosophies of the 1970s that were epitomized in common interpretations of A. S. Neill's *Summerhill*, they stressed the need to enhance existing academic objectives through structured hands-on projects. A good example of this effort was their promotion of *Foxfire*,[8] *The Fourth Street I*, and other school publications that offer opportunities to study the community (social studies), to read and write (language arts), and in some cases to become involved with the economic side (mathematics) through activities like maintaining sales records. Producing a publication means that there are deadlines to meet with copy that communicates clearly to an audience who can choose whether or not to read it.

NCRY's leaders had been influenced by the progressive education movement. They saw in schools and in community organizations the potential to affect all aspects of youngsters' lives and prepare them to be active, participating members of a democracy. The extent and quality of citizen involvement were of profound concern. Unlike some progressives, however, NCRY's staff stressed the need to get out into the community rather than to simulate the community in the school. While working with schools, NCRY maintained its involvement with community youth organizations representing informal educative resources, such as the Boys Clubs and 4-H. They looked for opportunities to bring the experiences of these groups to the schools, maintaining always the perspective that valuable learning can occur either in school or out.

Kohler made "caring" an explicit theme in many of her speeches and publications.[9] Like Kohler, many Americans were deeply troubled by well-publicized incidents in which people failed to help others in dire circumstances even when the opportunity existed. As a consequence, Youth Participation emphasized ways to prepare young people to be more caring. Peer counseling programs especially offered a programmatic strategy to encourage caring behavior. Students trained in listening and helping skills made themselves available to their peers. Some programs had formal group meetings led by trained adults and students. Others worked primarily through informal contacts among students. Students were trained as counselors and staffed "help lines" and other emergency referral services.

In recent years, caring once again has commanded the attention of those concerned with youth development and healthy communities. In 1989 the Lilly Endowment launched a Research Program on Youth and Caring, the first concentrated effort focusing on caring as a field of inquiry. An interdisciplinary and exploratory effort, the Research Program provided small grants for research projects that would begin to investigate issues relating to the concept of caring and its role in the lives of young people. In the first phases of the Program, the Endowment funded more than thirty-five research projects on the effects on youth of caring and being cared for, on the nature of caring organizations, and on measures of caring behaviors and attitudes. The promise of these initial explorations has led the Endowment to fund dissemination efforts in order to bring the values and findings of this nascent field to a larger audience of practitioners, parents, and other concerned adults.

Definition of Youth Participation

Observations of many youth programs led NCRY's staff to try to define clearly what distinguished Youth Participation from other approaches. They developed the following definition:

> The involvement of youth in responsible, challenging action that meets genuine needs with opportunity for planning and/or decision making affecting others in an activity whose impact or consequences extends to others, i.e., outside or beyond the youth participants themselves. Other desirable features are provision for critical reflection on the participatory activity and the opportunity for group effort toward a common goal.[10]

In this definition, the stress is upon *action* in situations that require young people to extend themselves intellectually or physically as a result of a personal commitment. Youth Participation programs are not to be created for the benefit of the youth; rather, they should be designed to address a problem or need outside of the young people who are doing the work. (Many internship or apprenticeship programs do not meet this criterion.) The "planning and/or decision making" referred to in the definition means that the action involved is part of a process in which youth must consider and choose among alternative approaches to a problem. The emphasis on "group effort toward a common goal" reflects the importance that the NCRY staff attached to experiences that are part of a larger community effort—experiences that are rare in the lives of young people.

The importance of reflection in Youth Participation programs cannot be overstated. Reflection usually means structured discussion, often led by adults, about the experience and its meaning to the participants. Journal writing and other forms of documentation such as video also serve as a means of reflection. Since experience by itself does not produce learning automatically and can be "mis-educative," reflection is essential.[11] Serving in a home for the elderly, for example, where a young person might witness death and illness, creates a need to discuss observations with others. Undigested, such experiences can become overwhelming and cause a youth to avoid future involvement of this kind. Without discussion, the significance of the experience may never be put into perspective.

Adults have an important role in facilitating the work of young people and in assuring that reflection occurs. In most cases, adults manage the institution in which the project takes place, raise funds, and train new cohorts of youth participants. The adults are admonished not to "take over" from youth but not to abandon their adult roles.

A prevalent misconception of adults who work with teenage youth is that they themselves must act like teenagers. This is a particularly misleading notion for adults who work in programs of youth participation—young people need adult models. They need to work with adults who take themselves seriously as adults. Likewise, they need adults who take young people seriously—who believe in the capacity of young people. These characteristics rather than "personality," "popularity," or "charisma" make for effective adult supervision.[12]

Examples of Youth Participation Projects Identified by NCRY

The conception of Youth Participation described here represented an ideal. Although not all these components would be found in every good youth project, the conceptualization provided a standard that was helpful in identifying and developing projects. The following examples of projects that NCRY identified in schools and community agencies during the period from 1971 to 1975 illustrate how closely related the Youth Participation models of twenty years ago are to current service learning programs.[13]

Students in the Advanced Computer Class at George Washington High School in Denver, Colorado, responding to the gasoline shortage of the mid-seventies, devised a Computer Car Pooling plan that was adopted by their city. The young people made the plan available to help large firms in the Denver area organize their employees into car pools. It should be noted that this project occurred well before computers were widely and comfortably used in schools.

The West High School Ecology Club in Manchester, New Hampshire, was formed in 1971 when a group of students began a campaign to clean up the Merrimack River. One student discovered that the discharge from a local meat packing plant was turning the Merrimack into "Blood River." He and his classmates documented the pollution and through their investigation helped bring legal action against the culprit. West High ecology students also designed ecology lessons and taught them to elementary school children, petitioned for environmental testing equipment, and showed teachers and students from all over New England how to use it.

Junior high and elementary school students at the Open Living School in the mountain town of Evergreen, Colorado, interned with community adults through the school's Apprenticeship Program. "Apprentices" from the ages of nine to fifteen carried out responsible duties at an educational television station, at day care centers, and at a nearby zoo. The internships were selected not just because they offered work experience, but because they offered young people some level of decision making in the work activities. Each week the youth met to discuss their experiences.

Students at Berkeley (California) East Campus High School established a Career Center in which the students were trained and paid (or received school credit) to locate paying jobs for fellow students, learned the requirements for various vocations, and then counseled their schoolmates who sought information and job placements. The students also learned job-seeking skills which they then passed on to other students who came to the center.

New York City's Cityarts Workshop Inc., which is still in operation as of this writing, involves young people in making public works of art for their neighborhoods. A professional artist from Cityarts helps the young people decide on a theme for a mural, design it, and transfer it to a large exterior wall; then they put up scaffolding and paint it.

The Fourth Street I, a community magazine, was operated entirely by young people on the Lower East Side of New York City. The young people used their magazine as a voice for poor residents of various ethnic groups by interviewing local artists and crafts people and by printing poetry and art work by people who live in the community. The young people who published the magazine interviewed, edited, translated, took photographs, and did all the production work.

The Gloucester Experiment in Gloucester, Massachusetts, began when a resident sculptor saw in a colonial cemetery, vandalized and overgrown with weeds, an opportunity to use the talent and energy of young people. The sculptor recruited a group of local youth who did everything from manual labor, including landscaping, clearing brush, and straightening headstones, to research and historical documentation. Eventually the high school in Gloucester agreed to grant students academic credit for their work.

The High School Archaeology Project in Cobb County, Georgia, began because a Pebblebrook High School student discovered that his school was located on a 2,000 year old Indian site which was about to be destroyed by a construction project. With the help of an archaeologist from the University of Georgia and other experts, students began an emergency dig. They unearthed pottery fragments, stone tools and bones and, in the process, learned geography, ecology, and history.

Public high school students at New City School, an alternative school in St. Paul, Minnesota, used video tape as an instrument to inform the public and influence decisions on important municipal issues. In one project, representatives from the Minneapolis and St. Paul Tenants' Unions asked students from New City's Public Service Video Workshop to help make a tape on renters' rights. The unions supplied the legal information and the students furnished the technical know-how and the talent. For each tape they did research, scripting, directing, interviewing, narrating, and editing.

About twenty students in each of three Marin County, California, high schools were involved in Shoulders, a peer counseling program. Students attended a thirteen-week after-school training program in which they learned counseling, communications, and utilization of community resources. Then they counseled peers referred to them by guidance counselors and administrators, participated in seminars in which they practiced advanced counseling techniques, shared problems encountered in counseling, and organized outreach activities.

In rural Adams, Minnesota, high school students spent their study halls and lunch hours giving physical therapy and companionship to handicapped children whose special education class met in the high school. Students began this Teens Who Care project and they felt they needed additional training. They traveled with the children to the Mayo Clinic to talk to specialists and to learn how to carry out individual therapy prescriptions.

Two Demonstration Programs from NCRY

The NCRY staff conducted two major demonstration programs, Youth Tutoring Youth (YTY) and the Day Care Youth Helper Program (DCYH). YTY was designed to provide opportunities for youth to learn and develop by teaching younger children. The NCRY model stressed that the primary benefits were to the tutor. "While it may be uncertain that people *receiving* help are always benefited, it seems much clearer that the people *giving* the help are profiting from their role."[14]

YOUTH TUTORING YOUTH

The idea for YTY was borrowed from the experiences of earlier pilots at Mobilization for Youth and elsewhere.[15] In descriptions of the program, the NCRY staff stressed the early history of learning through teaching, going back to the Romans.

YTY was piloted in Newark and Philadelphia in the summer of 1967, using federal Neighborhood Youth Corps funds. Two hundred tutors whose average age was 14.4 years were all behind academically. They were paid $1.25 per hour for twenty-two hours each week, sixteen hours in tutoring and six in training. (In Newark, an additional six hours were set aside for remedial instruction of the tutors). In both pilots, paraprofessional staff, including the parents of students and/or members of the community, were involved, often supervising the tutors. While the pilots differed in focus, the central idea was "confidence in the tutors as able to teach and learn." Evaluation results were positive. For example, during the summer program, Newark tutors showed an average reading gain of 3.7 years. While clearly gratified by these results, NCRY's leadership, wary of exaggerated claims, did not emphasize them in arguing for the program. "No one expects that the Newark tutors really did gain 3.5 years in reading maturity in a mere six weeks."

Why did NCRY staff and evaluators not stress the dramatic reading gains, but instead placed more emphasis on the quality of the process? "Although some of the gains may have been genuine, there are many explanations—such as test familiarity and pressures for improvement—for the startling rise."[16] They were concerned to promote the program based on benefits that they believed would be replicated in other settings. "Basically, YTY was set up to give tutors a sense of potency, . . . to foster a sense of personal effectiveness through a work experience, . . . (and) to give meaningful job responsibilities through the task of tutoring."[17]

The formal report of the pilot programs on tutoring pointed to what the staff considered to be evidence of the following benefits:

> the care and excitement with which a tutor led a tutee through a challenging lesson . . .;
>
> the tutors' sustained interest and participation (only seven of two hundred tutors left the program . . .);
>
> the increased literacy skills of the tutors and tutees, their changed vocational aspirations, and their greater sympathy for the classroom teacher;
>
> the understanding and easy rapport that developed between tutor and tutee . . .;
>
> the new pride evident in the tutors as they grew in their new role of "teacher" . . .;
>
> the endless variety of complex and simple materials they devised . . .;
>
> the new confidence that displayed itself in finding ways to communicate with the tutee in an individual relationship;
>
> the successful participation of subprofessional community people (parents who served as paraprofessionals), and the enthusiasm and support they engendered from other parents.[18]

NCRY worked on making the YTY program adaptable to many different settings: schools, community agencies, after-school programs, and employment programs. A series of manuals and a film were developed to help other program operators. Innovative teaching strategies developed by the tutors were exhibited in these materials. With Gerald Weinstein at the Center for Humanistic Education at the University of Massachusetts at Amherst and others, the staff developed training protocols that stressed the affective dimension of the program while offering great clarity about roles, structure, and processes for establishing successful YTY programs. Funding from the U.S. Department of Labor enabled them to train Neighborhood Youth Corps program staff, school personnel, and other youth agency personnel across the county.

The dissemination of YTY was characteristic of NCRY's work throughout its period of operation. First, its focus was on what youth could do. In abstracting from successful models, the NCRY staff reproduced the work of the young tutors and used it as a model. The biggest challenge was to convince adults that youth could do the job themselves with adult support. That is why it was important to stress the inventiveness, effectiveness, and resourcefulness of the young tutors. The NCRY strategy for dissemination often involved having the youthful participants demonstrate what they could do before audiences interested in adopting the program.

Second, there was a stress on practice. NCRY staff worked closely with the tutors, teachers, and paraprofessionals to learn of their problems and successes and to communicate these to others. The principles derived from practice were reviewed by researchers and others with academic backgrounds who compared the practices identified by NCRY as successful with larger patterns of successful practice and helped to select those which had the most promise.

Third, there was an emphasis on the processes as opposed to outcomes. NCRY staff stressed the enthusiasm, level of participation, and creative output of the students. Youth Participation represented a basic value in itself and did not have to be justified by students' academic achievements, although NCRY's leaders recognized the importance of such gains.

Fourth, NCRY emphasized the adaptability of the model to many settings, age groups, and funding sources. More than 300,000 Youth Tutoring Youth manuals were purchased by program operators throughout the country.

YTY became the flagship program for NCRY. The program proved durable and successful. Part of its success doubtless came because YTY was relatively simple and inexpensive to implement. It could be overseen by adults in many different roles—parents, teachers, youth agency personnel—and still succeed.

THE DAY CARE YOUTH HELPER DEMONSTRATION

Day Care Youth Helper (DCYH) was designed "to provide young people of high school and junior high school age the chance to work with preschool children through field experiences in day care centers, coupled with a seminar for the planning of early childhood learning activities and the introduction of child development concepts."

The goals of the DCYH program were to provide teenagers with experiences of genuine responsibility which would enable them to gain personal rewards and to learn about child development. A secondary goal was to help interested young people to learn about the vocation of child care.

NCRY staff purposely selected schools each with a different ethnic population to stress the potential of DCYH for being effective with youth from different cultures. Training and materials were developed to incorporate the approaches to child care characteristic of the dominant culture in each school as well as principles common to all cultures. Initial pilots were conducted in San Antonio, Hartford, and in Hartsdale, a New York City suburb. Once again, outstanding resource people, including experts such as those at the Yale Child Study Center, served as consultants in the development of the program. A rich set of supportive materials was developed including films designed to trigger discussion.

DCYH included several requirements for each implementation site. The child case workers were expected to provide meaningful roles for the youth helpers that would enable them to work directly with the children. The DCYH program had to have a reflective seminar and to include formal study of child development. Schools were urged to give school credit. Thus, DCYH had to be linked to the curriculum in a way that the school's academic leadership found acceptable. In practice, academic credit was earned in courses in home economics, social studies, or even language arts.

DCYH was never as widely adopted as YTY, in part because it was more difficult to implement. The requirement that NCRY have a formal linkage to child care centers sometimes presented problems, especially because NCRY's staff insisted that the quality of care in the centers meet their criteria. Schools found that the time required by DCYH competed with other programs. At times, child care staff resisted giving meaningful roles to the young helpers. The reflective seminar and child care classes required levels of skill and knowledge that many regular teachers found difficult to attain. The DCYH sites were nevertheless successful. But, unlike YTY, DCYH needed ongoing support from NCRY staff to assure high-quality implementation. The intensive demands of the program lessened the agency's resolve to concentrate its limited resources on dissemination and inspiration, and Board members resisted being closely tied to one demonstration over many years.

Dissemination of Youth Participation

Before she opened the doors of NCRY, Mary Kohler had collected information about promising programs. She sent people she trusted to visit these projects in order to learn more about them and to validate claims. With her legal background, she insisted that "case studies" be prepared about the best programs. These descriptions combined materials from observations, articles, evaluations, and interviews and were offered to individuals or organizations that requested information about NCRY's work or related matters. The performance of this clearinghouse function gradually became the center of NCRY's activity.[19]

In 1975, the newsletter *Resources for Youth* (RFY) was launched. Each edition described several programs and offered practical tips for implementing Youth Participation. *Resources for Youth* quickly became a popular quarterly publication with a circulation that grew to 30,000, all by request.

As demand increased, NCRY's staff became more concerned with defining a standard for quality in Youth Participation. The first effort at a more stringent definition was the development of a booklet called *Youth Into Adult*,[20] which described program models and identified several common threads among them. This was followed by the already cited publication, *New Roles for Youth in the School and the Community*. In 1975, NCRY published Bruce Dollar's study, *Youth Participation: A Concept Paper*, a detailed and thorough description of the concept. Also reaching a wide audience was a series of films prepared by film makers Brad and Penny Wright.

NCRY's staff conducted many training activities. At times they worked with entire school systems. In Minneapolis, for example, they held a conference for hundreds of people at all levels within the system. They organized and conducted a national conference for the U.S. Department of Labor as part of its YEDPA (Youth Employment Demonstration Project Act) demonstration. Modest efforts were more common. For example, "idea exchanges" fostered dialogue about

Youth Participation and demonstrated model programs featuring young people and professionals who were involved in strong programs located near the conference sites. Careful preparatory work involved all administrative levels of the participating systems to assure that there would be support for new practitioners. Further, whenever possible, NCRY engaged qualified local practitioners in offering follow-up assistance.

Well before "networking" became the buzzword it is today, NCRY worked to build a national community of practitioners and researchers involved in Youth Participation. Serving as a switchboard, NCRY helped researchers find appropriate projects to study and helped practitioners find people who were doing similar projects. Mailings, films, and conferences helped to remind people that, while they might be alone in their own community, they were linked through NCRY to persons with similar philosophies and interests. The one limitation imposed on this sharing of practices was concern for quality. Fearing that Youth Participation might be discredited by poor practice and overpopularity, NCRY placed great importance on validating projects by having skilled consultants observe and rate them according to criteria NCRY had established.

NCRY addressed a wide range of audiences. While the primary focus of the promotional effort was government and the professional community, Kohler often gained access to elite audiences through her wide range of personal contacts.

Why NCRY Was Effective

In a review of NCRY's work, certain characteristics stand out. First, the agency's commitment to Youth Participation was rooted in a careful study of the needs of young people and their communities. Young people really do want to contribute, as the many program examples demonstrate.

Second, following Ralph Tyler's warning not to diffuse NCRY's effectiveness by adopting too wide a range of activities, NCRY's leaders concentrated on their mission single-mindedly. Mary Kohler's resolute commitment to NCRY's unique mission was demonstrated when a close friend and a formidably wealthy individual, recognizing her power to convince others, asked her to promote projects that were central to his personal philosophy. Kohler thought about his proposal at length; had she complied, it would have meant a secure funding base for NCRY. Further, her friend's philosophy could have been related to Youth Participation. But in the end she decided not to accede. She helped the willing donor to find another program, which he funded grandly, and NCRY went on doing what Kohler felt ought to be done.

Third, NCRY saw itself as an "ad hoc" organization, designed to accomplish one task—wide dissemination of the idea of youth involvement—and then go out of business. The Board had no interest in devoting its energies and resources to building an organization. While this lack of concern for organizational matters may at times have created difficulties, it meant that NCRY's work always had an outward rather than an inward focus.

Fourth, NCRY's leadership remained constant during its short life. Dominated by Ralph Tyler and Mary Kohler, the agency stayed on its singular track.

The Legacy of NCRY

Many themes of NCRY's work continue to be woven into youth efforts throughout the country. A good example of its continuing relevance is the Clinton administration's extensive agenda for American youth, which achieved early successes with the passage of two major legislative initiatives: The National and Community Service Trust Act of 1993 and the School-to-Work Opportunities Act of 1994. These initiatives are similar in that they require the involvement of youth outside of school in activities that are designed both to develop youth and to contribute positively to the community. Both tacitly acknowledge the limitations of current modes of schooling as preparation for adulthood and offer a more active process to complement schooling (School-to-Work Transition) or to supplement it (Community Service).

One concern about the implementation of these two acts is that their similar philosophical bases are not reflected in how they will be executed. They will be implemented by separate units of government at state and federal levels. By the time they reach local communities, their similarities will matter little if at all. Thus, these separate acts perpetuate a tendency to treat the development of young people in a fragmented way that fosters separate constituencies, duplicates unnecessarily the development of organizational capacity, and leads to a diffuse impact on communities. In contrast, NCRY's single broad framework, as represented in Youth Participation, suggests today, as it did twenty years ago, the importance of a unified approach to youth development in both conception and implementation.

Today, some of the most promising efforts to achieve the objectives of Youth Participation are those that concentrate on building community consensus about the needs of youth, followed by coordinated activities that include young people. For example, the Washington based Center for Youth Development and Policy Research has in recent years been a strong voice for bringing a youth development perspective to all policy and programming affecting youth. The Center collaborates with communities nationwide to plan and implement "youth development initiatives" based explicitly on strategies aimed at moving away from categorical programming and toward meeting youth needs and promoting youth participation. At the same time, the Center works at the national and state levels to advance a unified approach. Special attention has been given to building alliances with those in the employment, career preparation, and service learning fields.

Youth development initiatives are concentrated in economically impoverished neighborhoods. There is clearly a need, however, to engage young people and adults of all social classes. A serious obstacle to addressing this need is that not only are material resources dwindling but so is the essential resource of local and national leadership committed to improvement of communities along dimensions that go beyond the economic. Today, national polls reveal widely held concerns about young people's school performance, substance abuse, and attitudes toward work and society. In response to these concerns, the experience of NCRY can be used to refocus attention upon the positive contributions that youth can make to improving their communities and the essential role of adults in supporting them. Adults, both education professionals and lay people, must use their power, resources, and skills to facilitate the efforts of youth to make meaningful contributions to their communities.

Notes

1. National Commission on Resources for Youth, *New Roles for Youth in the School and the Community* (New York: Citation Press, 1974), p. vii.

2. Their analysis is similar to that of several studies of that period. See, for example, James Coleman et al., *Youth: Transition to Adulthood*, Report of the Panel on Youth, President's Science Advisory Committee (Chicago: University of Chicago Press, 1974).

3. "In a recent study of 1,500 households, researchers were startled to find that parents and children spent a quarter of their time together watching television, and that each family member related most directly to the set, but rarely to one another." *New York Times*, 16 February 1993, p. C6.

4. "(The) out-of-school informal teaching is rarely, if ever, paid for with public funds, but it certainly represents a significant portion of the total *social* cost—the actual cost—of education. . . . As the contributions made by significant informal learning experiences are greatly reduced, the total *social* cost of education is correspondingly reduced.

But this also means a serious reduction in educational opportunities at a time when the need for education by children and youth is greater than ever before." Ralph W. Tyler, "Wasting Time and Resources in Schools and Colleges," in Ralph W. Tyler, *Perspectives on American Education, The Patten Lectures* (Chicago: Science Research Associates, 1976), p. 16.

5. "About 40 percent of adolescents' waking hours are discretionary—not committed to other activities (such as eating, school, homework, chores, or working for pay). . . . Many young adolescents spend virtually all of this discretionary time without companionship or supervision from responsible adults." Carnegie Corporation, *A Matter of Time, Risk, and Opportunity in the Non-School Hours* (New York: Carnegie Corporation of New York, 1984), p. 28.

6. "The data from our observations in more than 1,000 classrooms support the popular image of a teacher standing or sitting in front of a class imparting knowledge to a group of students." John I. Goodlad, *A Place Called School: Prospects for the Future* (New York: McGraw-Hill, 1984), p. 105.

7. See Theodore R. Sizer, *Horace's Compromise: The Dilemma of the American High School* (Boston: Houghton Mifflin, 1984), and Deborah Meier, *The Power of Their Ideas: Lessons for America from a Small School in Harlem* (Boston: Beacon Press, 1995).

8. The Foxfire project is still alive, vital, and widely imitated. For information, write Foxfire, P.O. Box 541, Mountain City, GA 30562. Phone, 706-746-5828.

9. See Mary Conway Kohler, *Young People Learning to Care: Making a Difference through Youth Participation* (New York: Seabury Press, 1983).

10. Bruce Dollar, *Youth Participation: A Concept Paper* (New York: National Commission on Resources for Youth, 1975), p. 6.

11. See John Dewey, *Experience and Education* (New York: Macmillan, 1938).

12. National Commission on Resources for Youth, *New Roles for Youth in the School and the Community*, pp. 233-234.

13. These examples are abstracted from Dollar, *Youth Participation: A Concept Paper*.

14. Alan Gartner, Mary Conway Kohler, and Frank Riessman, *Children Teach Children: Learning by Teaching* (New York: Harper & Row, 1971), p. 9. See also, V. L. Allen, ed., *Children as Teachers* (New York: Academic Press, 1976).

15. In developing the YTY model, the NCRY staff drew on the insights of Richard Cloward, Frank Riessman, and Herbert Thelen, who had conducted studies of pilot programs in New York and Detroit.

16. National Commission on Resources for Youth, *Youth Tutoring Youth—It Worked*, Report on an In-School Youth Corps Demonstration Project (Washington, D.C.: Manpower Administration, U.S. Department of Labor, January, 1968), p. 20.

17. National Commission on Resources for Youth, *Final Report, In-School Neighborhood Youth Corps Project* (Washington, D.C.: Manpower Administration, U.S. Department of Labor, 1969), p. 40.

18. Gartner, Kohler, and Riessman, *Children Teach Children*, pp. 31-32.

19. Unfortunately, the NCRY materials and case studies are no longer available through established channels. Readers who want more information may write the author at 387 E. Fourth St., Brooklyn, NY 11218.

20. Mildred McClosky and Peter Kleinbard, *Youth Into Adult* (New York: National Commission on Resources for Youth, 1974).

CHAPTER II

An International Perspective on Service-Learning

DONALD J. EBERLY

Just as in the United States, increasing numbers of young men and women in other countries are utilizing their knowledge and skills to serve others and are learning from their service experiences. However, the rationale behind overseas programs of national youth service and their modes of operation are often quite different from those in the United States. This chapter examines selected models that illustrate the varied approaches to national youth service, and offers some observations on them that may be relevant to the further development of service-learning.

Overseas, national youth service programs are evaluated to a lesser extent than in the United States. Quantitative data on such factors as the value of services rendered and the degree of career growth while in youth service are not available, as they are for some service programs in the United States. Still, most of the programs described in this chapter are at least fifteen years old and have an established track record.

In this chapter, "National Service" refers to programs of full-time service by young people, "service-learning" to the integration of community service with educational growth, and "national youth service" to the whole field embraced by National Service and service-learning. The expression "service-learning" is little used overseas. As a generic descriptor, "study service" is more apt to be employed. More common still is the name of the program itself, such as Germany's *Zivildienst* (Civilian Service) and Costa Rica's *Trabajo Comunal Universitario* (University Community Service).

Even in the United States, students of service-learning are continually discussing how it should be defined and the criteria for establishing programs. This is a healthy situation and probably will continue as

Donald J. Eberly founded the National Service Secretariat in 1966. The Secretariat is now located in Minneapolis. Now retired from the Secretariat and living in New Zealand, he continues his study of national youth service programs in various countries.

long as service-learning does. Part of the debate centers on the extent to which service-learning should focus on the service to be performed as opposed to the growth and education of the youthful participant.

One thing is very clear. Young people in National Service learn a lot whether or not there is an organized educational program that provides opportunities for participants to reflect upon their experiences. Just as experiential education existed before John Dewey arrived on the scene, so did service-learning exist before William R. Ramsay and colleagues at the Southern Regional Education Board coined the phrase in the late 1960s. A study by the Stanford Research Institute found that the frequent comment of returned Peace Corps volunteers, "I learned more than I contributed," was in fact the norm. The study by what is now SRI International discovered that Peace Corps volunteers felt they learned about 50 percent more than they contributed during their two years of service.

It is also clear that the profile of learning varies a great deal, even within programs and similar experiences. One volunteer serving in a nursing home may conclude that nursing homes should be shut down and patients sent to relatives. A second may conclude that government funds should be used to improve services. A third may conclude that euthanasia is defensible. From a public policy standpoint, the individual conclusions reached are less important than the fact that they were formed as the result of intense personal experiences—and some reflection, too—and not as a result of some economic or political theory. With these points in mind, it may be useful to examine selected national youth service programs around the world to illustrate various modes of service-learning.

The divisions in this chapter are not as sharp as the subheadings may imply. Still, there tend to be fairly common forms of service-learning by geographical groups.

In Europe: An Alternative to Military Service

Most European countries have conscription for military service and most of them require conscientious objectors to perform a period of civilian service. Many of them are in the process of liberalizing their policies in the direction of giving conscripts a choice of either military or civilian service. None of them, however, has advanced as far as Germany in its liberalization. We shall examine the German situation closely, as its policy may be the forerunner of youth policies in countries with conscription.

Germany was the aggressor nation in both World Wars and nothing was more important to Germany than a strong military force. When Adolf Hitler came to power in the 1930s, he captured both the educational system and various youth programs and transformed them into instruments of his plans for the conquest of Europe. The West German constitution, written after World War II, declared that "no one shall be forced to do war service with arms against his conscience." When conscription was restored in 1956, that clause assured the right of young men to apply for conscientious objector status. Those who convinced a tribunal they were genuine conscientious objectors were required to perform alternative civilian service, usually in a program known as *Zivildienst.*

For years, only a few thousand young men were in *Zivildienst* at any one time and it was little noticed. In the 1970s and most notably in 1984, measures were taken that made it easier for young men to qualify as conscientious objectors. The result was that Germany now has a *de facto* national service wherein young men can choose between spending twelve months in the military or fifteen months in *Zivildienst.* Upwards of 130,000 young men are now in *Zivildienst* or in one of the two smaller national service programs, Civil Defense and Development Aid.

Today, Germany has virtually no need for military conscription because the threat from Russia has vanished and Germany's military recruitment pool has increased substantially from the merger of East and West Germany. However, there is substantial pressure to maintain *Zivildienst* because it has become a major supplier of social services, especially to elderly citizens. One answer may be the abolishment of conscription accompanied by a kind of *Zivildienst* that is voluntary, that is open to women as well as men, and that receives strong governmental support. The outcome of this dilemma deserves close attention by students of national youth service.

In Africa and Asia: A Force for Nation Building

Many African and Asian countries are quite young, having achieved independence only in the last one or two generations. Moreover, thanks to the insensitivity of colonialists, many of these new countries include peoples of very different cultural and language backgrounds. If such nations are to maintain their identity and cohesiveness, it is necessary for their citizens—and especially their leaders—to acquire a solid understanding of their diversity. A number of these new African and Asian countries have established, or have under serious consideration, a form of national youth service intended to do just that. Nigeria's National Youth Service Corps is an excellent example. The civil war of the late 1960s only served to highlight the deep divisions that had existed ever since Nigeria was created artificially by the European powers meeting in Berlin over one hundred years ago. In an attempt to overcome the causes of distrust, a national service corps was favored by many segments of the population. The national service law was enacted in 1973; it requires all university graduates to serve for one year in a part of the country other than where they grew up. For the most part they serve in a capacity consistent with their education. Major fields of endeavor are public health, agriculture, education, and economic development. The federal government underwrites the stipends of Corps members. During a two-week period part way through the service year, all Corps members serve in teams on labor-intensive projects, usually in rural areas. There they work with villagers on such projects as road construction and school building. At the end of the service year, Corps members gather at a number of sites around the country for a week of reflection and formulation of ideas to improve the program.

Judged both by results and by surveys of participants' attitudes, Nigeria's National Youth Service Corps is meeting its objectives. It has promoted the movement of skilled labor around the country. A number of Corps members have taken up employment far from home as a direct result of their national service experience. More than 80 percent of Corps members say it has contributed to national unity.

The program is strictly administered. Nigerian university registrars send call-up letters to those who have just graduated. Those graduating from overseas universities are required to report to Corps headquarters upon their return to Nigeria. Those completing a year of service receive a certificate of national service, without which no employer may legally hire them.

Botswana has a program with moderate opportunities for reflection. *Tirelo Setshaba* (National Service) was begun in 1980 to give a maturing experience to secondary school leavers before going on to university or employment, to provide educated manpower to help carry out development programs in rural areas, and to encourage greater understanding among people from various parts of the country. The typical participant in *Tirelo Setshaba* serves a year in a remote village living with a local family and keeping a daily journal to describe activities and observations. The journal enhances the educational quality of the experience and serves as a basis of discussion with *Tirelo Setshaba* staff members who visit several times a year. The participants serve in such varied fields as education, public health, land surveys, wildlife management, and local cooperatives.

According to surveys, *Tirelo Setshaba* does indeed have a positive impact on nation building. Participants often return to the villages where they served to celebrate holidays and to attend weddings and funerals.

Indonesia's people come from many parts of Asia and the Pacific. Its youth service programs grew out of its war of independence in the late 1940s. Educated soldiers taught school when they were not fighting. The soldiers saw the difference in lifestyles and standards of living between villages and cities. They saw potential danger in the sharp contrast between the urban rich and the rural poor. So they wanted future leaders to become acquainted with life in the villages just as they had done as guerrillas. But instead of guns, they wanted them to carry books and pencils and work on projects like literacy, public health, clean water supplies, and agriculture.

Upon attainment of independence in 1950, these soldiers—now veterans attending university—petitioned the government to require university students to serve for a time as teachers. This initiative led to Indonesia's first youth service program, one which encouraged university students to volunteer for service as teachers in secondary schools and teacher training colleges.

The programs have evolved over the years according to need. By 1963, the secondary institutions were producing enough primary school teachers, so Indonesia shifted gears. The government called on university juniors to work in the countryside for six months together with professors in the appropriate field—whether engineering or agriculture or literacy—and integrate study with service. Now they are exploring the promotion of entrepreneurs at the village level. The continuing theme is to place the university students in a village for a period of time, where they are expected to do something useful and to acquire an understanding of village life.

Although evaluation of the Indonesian study-service program has been limited, it is clear that the students make a distinct contribution to village life and that they come to appreciate life in the village. A student who recently completed service in KKN, as it is named, said, "Before KKN I was proud, now I feel smaller [more humble]." The level of government funding for KKN has fallen in recent years. The result is that it is much stronger at some universities than others.

Service-Learning in Central America

Mexico made a bold advance with service-learning in 1937 when it began requiring medical students to serve for six months in areas lacking medical services. The students sent weekly reports describing the general conditions as well as the state of sanitation and disease rates. The program, known as *Servicio Social*, made such an impact that the federal government doubled expenditures on public health.

In 1947, *Servicio Social* became mandatory for all students in higher education. However, no federal funding was provided, as it had been for the medical students, so the implementation was left up to the universities. As might be expected, the results were mixed. It is strongest in the medical field; in other areas the strength of *Servicio Social* varies with the university and the faculty.

A high degree of integration between service and learning is found in Costa Rica's *Trabajo Comunal Universitario* (TCU). The typical TCU project finds two dozen students and a couple of professors putting their academic learning to practice on a village project. The projects encompass such areas as public health, teacher training, technical assistance to small farmers and manufacturers, and educational programs that help preserve traditional values.

The groundwork for the project is laid jointly by the University of Costa Rica's Social Action Office and the faculties to be involved in it. All projects are interdisciplinary and involve frequent discussions among faculty and students of the educational implications of the service experience.

An example of a TCU project can be found at the Museum of San Ramon. The multidisciplinary teams that served at this historical and anthropological museum conducted research on traditional values, designed museum exhibitions, developed visitor guides, catalogued museum collections, and solicited donations for the museum. Thus, students exercised and extended their knowledge and skills in areas such as history, science, art, librarianship, and business.

The Special Cases of Canada and the United Kingdom

As a direct result of the separatist movement in Quebec, Canada established a national service program in 1977. It was called *Katimavik*—an Inuit word meaning meeting place—and had several unique features. The twelve-person teams of young people were deliberately made up to reflect the Canadian population: eight spoke English and four French; six were men and six were women; team members came from all parts of Canada. Each team carried on service projects in three locations—one in the east, one in the west, and one in the heartland—and at each of the three locations team members lived separately for a two-week period with local residents. The total service period was nine months.

Not only did these young people work together during the day, they also kept house together. At any one time two members were on duty at the *Katimavik* house and they were responsible for cleaning house, shopping, and cooking. They even had a *Katimavik* cookbook.

But while the Canadians referred to it as national service, service took a back seat to the experience of living together and traveling around the country. Where American Peace Corps volunteers are always keen to talk about their service activities and the Indonesian students like to describe their village projects, the young people in *Katimavik* were more apt to comment on the quality of the cooking that one of the housemates had prepared, or whether the group leader would last out the year. *Katimavik* was well-received by the Canadian public but was not well enough entrenched to survive the change in governments in the mid-1980s. Nonetheless, the *Katimavik* experience has influenced the design of the New York City Volunteer Corps and other programs of national service.

The United Kingdom is making significant strides toward the general adoption of service-learning in schools. Under the generic title of Community Links with GCSE (General Certificate of Secondary Education), Community Service Volunteers has produced a pioneering set of guidebooks that will facilitate the incorporation of service-learning in the curriculum. These guidebooks point out in detail how the individual teacher can integrate student community service with the curriculum. Here are two projects recommended in the guidebook for science students:

Look around your local area for evidence of pollution; take photographs of this evidence. Analyze the type of pollution and its effect upon the environment and suggest ways in which it could be alleviated. Present your findings and solutions to your local council Environmental Health Officer, and those responsible for the pollution.

From your knowledge of dietary requirements, plan a three-day menu for either a preschool child or an active teenager. Discuss your plans with a dietician or a health visitor and modify your menus if necessary. Carry out a survey to find if the children or young people in your area are eating a similar diet to that which you have devised. Make recommendations based on your findings.

Global Service

Of the several approaches to national youth service, global service has the greatest growth potential. We have seen large-scale domestic activities that can be characterized as National Service and service-learning. As yet, global service has operated on a small scale. Still there have been significant efforts, and they are worth reviewing.

Right after World War I, Pierre Ceresole of Switzerland established *Service Civile International* (SCI). Volunteers from several nations—often university students on summer vacation—went to the war-torn countries to help with relief and rehabilitation efforts. SCI continues to operate service projects and to promote international cooperation and understanding on a small scale.

Several well-known overseas service programs were launched around 1960. The British Voluntary Service Overseas, the American Peace Corps, and the Canadian University Overseas sent mostly young adult volunteers to the developing nations of Africa, Asia, and Latin America for periods of one or two years. The largest and most successful efforts were in the field of education. Well-educated foreigners often taught at the high school level and enabled more students to pursue secondary education. The placement of overseas volunteers as "community development" workers was usually less successful as it required a deeper understanding of the local culture and village politics than what the volunteers acquired in their brief training periods. These programs continue today on a modest level and have been joined by similar programs, mostly but not exclusively from European countries.

When the United Nations Volunteers (UNV) was launched in 1971, some observers thought it heralded the kind of multilateral effort that would join large numbers of young people from countries all over the globe in common service efforts. Such was not the case. UNV has grown at the rate of about one hundred volunteers a year and remains a little-noticed program of minor impact. Also, UNV enrolls primarily middle-aged bureaucrats who work in administrative capacities in other countries. Thus, UNV provides the opportunity for international cooperation and understanding but its small scale and the age of its participants militate against its becoming a truly international youth service.

In 1992, the National Service Secretariat sponsored the first Global Conference on National Youth Service and established National Service Fellowships. These Fellowships have permitted national service officials from the Americas and southern Africa to visit national service officials and projects in other countries. A second and larger global conference was held in Nigeria in 1994. Agreement was reached at that conference to establish an International Association on National Youth Service.

Comparisons with the United States

It is useful to compare national youth service in the United States with foreign models because of the implications those models contain for American policymakers. Conscription in the United States ended in 1973. Few people want it to return but the lesson of history is that we cannot rule out that possibility and therefore should be prepared for it. If the draft does return in peacetime or in a period of limited military engagements such as those in which we have been involved since 1950, it is likely that both young women and men will be called to serve and that they will be given some kind of choice as to whether they perform military or civilian service. The civilian service may or may not be limited to persons who can prove that their consciences forbid them to engage in war. We will probably get something like Germany's *Zivildienst*, with hundreds of thousands of young Americans choosing the civilian option.

For a long time Americans have viewed their country as a "melting pot." We still view it as a continually changing but basically stable society. In the first half of this century, Americans, wherever they came from, de-emphasized their ethnic origins by Americanizing their names, neglecting their customs, and adopting American ones. In recent decades, many Americans have rediscovered and placed great emphasis on their ethnic origins. It may not be long before the United States will be looking for ways to restore the "melting pot," to get our youngsters to understand people from different ethnic groups and life in different parts of the country. And we will not be satisfied with teaching such things in the classroom or via the information superhighway. We may turn to countries like Nigeria and Botswana for advice on how to design and execute such programs. And if more and more children grow up with little home life because parents are seldom there, we may turn to Canada to see how to make up for the absence of a constructive home life for children.

Perhaps the most important thing to learn from Costa Rica is the involvement of professors. In examining university service-learning programs in the United States in the late 1960s, I found professors to be a major block to the advance of service-learning. In the 1960s, it was difficult to find university professors willing to assist students in making the connection between service and the curriculum. It appeared that those most willing to take on service-learning were those who had been in the Peace Corps or had had some other kind of national youth service experience. A service-learning initiative can be launched with such persons.

Educational institutions must also make adequate provision for service-learning operations, as is done in Costa Rica. If service-learning becomes a schoolwide policy, administrators and teachers must understand that responsibilities for service-learning are integral parts of their contracts and not something they are expected to do without remuneration.

Prospects for National Youth Service

Over the next decade or two, service-learning could become as well established in schools and colleges as history and mathematics. Federal government support, the opening of service-learning resource centers, the appointment of service-learning coordinators by schools and colleges, and the inclusion of service-learning in the curricula of teacher training colleges all point in that direction. These developments have great potential for improving our educational offerings and for filling a huge gap in our national youth policy, but such outcomes are not automatic.

One danger lies in the possible erosion of the experiential nature of service-learning. Teachers may be enthusiastic as they launch service-learning programs. Then, when students return from the experience with learning outcomes different from those expected by the teachers, the teachers may revert to "canned" experiences, where little service is performed and the outcomes are predictable. Teachers, service supervisors, and students alike must understand the importance of the hyphen in service-learning, so that service informs learning and learning informs service.

A second danger is the budgetary one, as experienced by Mexico, Indonesia, and Canada. In the United States, the money now flowing from the Corporation for National Service may not continue. Schools and colleges must build support for service-learning into their regular budgets.

In the long term, however, the prospects for national youth service are bright. It has too many good things going for it to disappear forever. I have been a student of national youth service since 1950 and have reached the following conclusions about National Service programs that are well run:

National Service participants accomplish important tasks not otherwise being performed, and they do so in a cost-beneficial manner.

Participants in National Service increase their self-confidence and their awareness of the needs of others.

National Service promotes mutual understanding in a plural society. Thus it often appeals to newly independent nations as a way to promote a sense of nationhood among its citizens.

National Service is a vital form of experiential education. Participants learn from experience with or without a deliberate educational component. With preparation in advance and periods of reflection during the service, their learning increases.

Advanced education and training is a fitting reward for those who have contributed a period of National Service. And National Service is a fitting way for those who benefit from higher education—often undertaken in whole or in part at government expense—to give something back to society.

National Service can be a unifying force among those who serve. With the exception of the parent-child relationship, there is probably nothing that binds people together more strongly than working together in a common cause.

National Service can fortify democracy because it is based on reality, not demagogy.

National Service can be a rite of passage from adolescence to adulthood. For too long, the main rite of passage has been found in war and violence. National Service can become—in William James's seminal phrase—the moral equivalent of war.

The experience gained in National Service can enhance one's employability. Research shows that for many participants, a period in National Service gives them good work habits, selected skills, and a chance to explore careers and jobs of interest to them.

After serving in other countries, National Service participants return with increased understanding of their own and of other countries.

National Service programs are much more likely to survive and be successful where there is governmental support, both moral and financial.

Annotated Bibliography

Centre for Research on Youth and the National Youth Leadership Council. *Youth in the 1990s* (Halifax, NS.: Dalhousie University, 1986). Authors from Canada, Germany, Great Britain, the United States, and Venezuela examine various aspects of National Service.

Dickson, Mora. *A Chance to Serve* (London: Dobson Books, 1976). Describes the trailblazing work of the author's husband, Alec Dickson, who founded Great Britain's Voluntary Service Overseas in 1958 and Community Service Volunteers in 1962.

Eaton, Joseph W., and Chen, Michael. *Influencing the Youth Culture* (Beverly Hills, Calif.: Sage Publications, 1971). Focuses on youth participation and acculturation in Israel.

Eberly, Donald J. *National Service: A Promise to Keep* (Rochester, N.Y.: John Alden Books, 1988). Contains an autobiographical account of the evolution of National Service and service-learning in the U.S.A. from 1946 to 1988.

Eberly, Donald J., and Sherraden, Michael, eds. *The Moral Equivalent of War? A Study of Non-Military Service in Nine Nations* (Westport, Conn.: Greenwood Press, 1990). Describes and compares National Service programs in Canada, China, Costa Rica, Germany, Indonesia, Israel, Mexico, Nigeria, and the United States.

Enegwea, Gregory K. et al. *NYSC Yearbook 1991* (Lagos: National Youth Service Corps, 1991). Includes history, statistics, and procedures for operation of the National Youth Service Corps of Nigeria.

Hardjasoemantri, Dr. Koesnadi. *Study-service as a Subsystem in Indonesian Higher Education* (Jakarta: PN BALAI PUSTAKA, 1982). Focuses on community service by university students as part of the educational process and as a contribution to rural villages.

Kwafo-Akoto, Kate; Moahi, Kgomotso H.; and Monageng, Syella B. *Report of the National Conference on Tirelo Setshaba, 19-23 November 1991: Strategies for Future Implementation* (Gaborone, Botswana: Tirelo Setshaba, Private Bag 116, 1991). Reviews the progress and setbacks of Tirelo Setshaba in its first ten years and considers future options.

Rosenstock-Huessy, Eugen. *Planetary Service* (Norwich, Vermont: Argo Books, 1978). Originally published as *Dienst auf dem Planeten* (Stuttgart: W. Kohlhammer, 1965), this book makes a case for a truly international civilian youth service. The author argued for a work service corps in Germany as early as 1912 and took refuge in the United States in 1933.

Special Senate Committee on Youth. *YOUTH: A Plan of Action* (Ottawa, 1986). The Committee, chaired by Senator Jacques Hébert, recommends a Young Canadians' Community Service Program open to all Canadians aged 17-24 as a major part of a comprehensive youth policy.

CHAPTER III

Service Learning: A Theoretical Model

BARRY G. SHECKLEY AND MORRIS T. KEETON

Service learning occurs in many forms and in many settings. Second-graders entertain patients at a nursing home.[1] High school students design and produce anti-drug messages for radio, TV, and newspapers as part of a writing course.[2] College students volunteer in a homeless shelter or soup kitchen to fulfill requirements of a political science curriculum.[3] All these and many similar types of projects are termed "service learning." As it has been used, the term "service learning" can be loosely defined as an educational activity, program, or curriculum that seeks to promote students' learning through experiences associated with volunteerism or community service.

Service learning receives wide support as an educational activity that enhances student learning. For example, the National Commission on Youth,[4] endorsed service learning as a way to assist youth in the transition to adulthood. In a 1987 report sponsored by the Carnegie Foundation, service learning was advocated as a way to resolve the much debated "crisis in education."[5] This growing support for service learning culminated with President Clinton's signing of the National and Community Service Trust Act of 1993 that provided funding for programs encouraging community service by students in schools and colleges.

The practice of service learning, however, does not match the strength of the endorsement provided by national reports and federal legislation. In 1989, Rutter and Newmann reported that only 27 percent of all high schools nationally were offering some form of community service.[6] Similarly, Markus, Howard, and King indicated in 1993 that service learning centers are currently active on 10 to 20 percent of college campuses in the United States.[7] While these figures suggest that service learning does have a strong support base, they also indicate that it is *not* actively employed by a large plurality of high schools and colleges throughout the United States.

Barry G. Sheckley is Professor and Head of the Section on Adult and Vocational Education at the University of Connecticut. Morris T. Keeton is Senior Scholar and Co-Director of the Institute for Research on Adults in Higher Education at the University College, University of Maryland.

Theory and Research

According to Conrad and Hedin, educators may be reluctant to adopt service learning programs because there is not sufficient research demonstrating that they result in any higher scores on tests of academic achievement than do traditional courses.[8] Similarly, there is not a clear theory that describes the process by which service enhances learning. Overall, the literature on service learning is heavily weighted toward anecdotal presentations of program outcomes and detailed prescriptions for program design. Neither comprehensive theoretical formulations that explicate the dynamics underlying service learning nor methodologically sound disciplined inquiries that document its educational benefits are common in the literature.

When evaluative research has been conducted on service learning programs, it generally indicates that service learning promotes the social, psychological, and intellectual development of students. "Researchers consistently report a heightened sense of personal and social responsibility, more positive attitudes toward adults, more active exploration of careers, enhanced self-esteem, growth in moral and ego development, more complex patterns of thought, and greater mastery of skills and content that are directly related to the experiences of the participants [in service learning programs]."[9]

Markus, Howard, and King, for example, demonstrated that 37 students randomly assigned to service learning sections of a course on "Contemporary Political Issues" at the University of Michigan were significantly *more likely* than 52 students randomly assigned to traditional discussion sections to report that they had performed up to their potential in the course, had learned to apply principles from the course to new situations, and had developed a greater awareness of societal problems.[10] On a nine-point scale (A+ = 9) students in the service learning sections also received higher grades (mean = 7.5) than students in the traditional sections (mean = 6.4). Of note in this research were the medium to large "effect sizes" attributed to the service learning program.[11] For example, the service learning program accounted for about 20 to 30 percent of the between-group variance on educational outcomes like: "I learned to apply principles from this course to new situations"; "I reconsidered many of my former attitudes"; "I developed a greater sense of personal responsibility." Unfortunately, research that provides such specific evidence for the positive learning outcomes of service learning is not widespread.

When researchers write about the theoretical underpinnings of service learning,[12] they usually cite experiential learning theory (ELT) as it has evolved from the writings of John Dewey in the 1930s to the more recent formulations by David Kolb in the 1980s.[13] As depicted by the Experiential Learning Cycle shown in figure 1, learners *grasp* information via concrete experiences and abstract concepts. They then *transform* (make personally meaningful) this information using reflective observation and active experimentation. Students in service learning situations encounter concrete experiences (e.g., work in a homeless shelter) which they reflectively observe (e.g., what are the main features of the homeless life-style?) and form abstract conceptualizations about the experience (e.g., how factors like poverty are related to people being "homeless"). To complete the learning cycle, individuals then experiment actively with the concepts (e.g., how can I help most effectively?). In a service learning setting, this cycle is repeated continually.

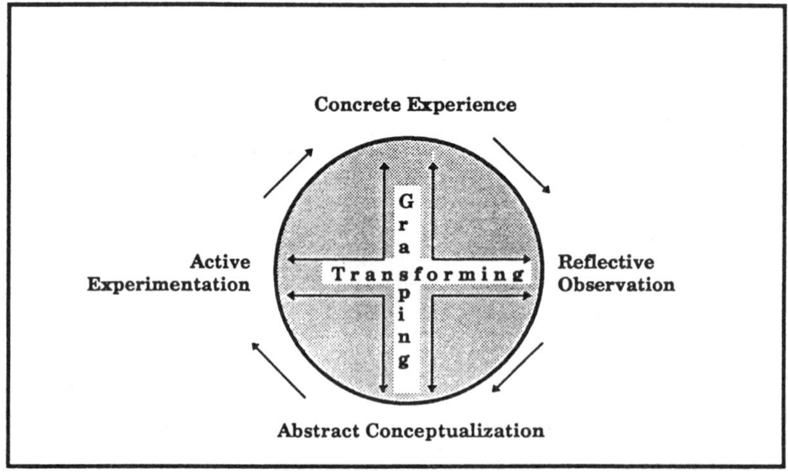

FIGURE 1
Experiential Learning Cycle

Recent analyses of ways in which experience enhances learning,[14] however, indicate that experiential learning theory—and the related proposition that experience in volunteer settings enhances learning—is not readily accepted throughout the educational community. In fact, experiential and service learning are routinely criticized. In the following section we describe the most common critiques and suggest ways in which the statements of experiential learning theory need to be clarified or amended to take appropriate account of these criticisms. In so doing, we will highlight themes and issues that need to be incorporated explicitly into a theoretical model of service learning.

Criticisms of Experiential Learning Theory

In one line of critique, Hopkins argues that "Kolb attempts to account for experiential learning without a coherent theory of experience, such as might have been found in phenomenology, which he virtually ignores."[15] To address this point, we propose that: (a) learners who "experience" a situation *construct* their experience via a dynamic interplay between the representations of immediate experience that enter episodic memory and the expectations and images for the experience that are stored in semantic memory;[16] and (b) the outcome of this interplay determines in part the nature of the learning from the experience.

In one of the most frequently cited criticisms of experiential learning theory, Jarvis argues that not every experience results in learning as the experiential learning cycle suggests.[17] Specifically, Jarvis writes that an experience may lead to: (a) nonlearning (i.e., the person has an experience but does not reflect upon it); (b) nonreflective learning (i.e., a powerful experience like touching a hot stove will result in direct, nonreflective learning); or (c) reflective learning (i.e., learning that results from reflection on experience). Likewise, Merriam and Clark propose that individuals learn from experience only when that experience, is attended to, is reflected on, and has personal impact.[18] To address these criticisms, we propose that a core process involving a *conduit effect*,[19] which we explain later, be recognized in the analysis of the experiential learning cycle to describe learners' tendencies to process information with minimal reflection.[20]

In his critique, Mezirow argues that *active* reflection is essential for individuals to learn from experience.[21] He contends that if, as ELT suggests, an individual simply observes passively or experiments without reflection, no learning will occur. As an alternative to Kolb's postulation, Mezirow argues that individuals must engage in reflective judgment (as opposed to reflective observation) and/or reflective action (as opposed to active experimentation) if they are to learn from experience. Following this analysis by Mezirow as well as the widespread emphasis on the importance of reflection in experiential learning,[22] we suggest that an *accordion effect*, a process involving *reflective judgment* and *reflective action*, represents a core experiential learning process.

Like related adult learning models, the experiential learning model is criticized by Clark and Wilson for having an exclusive emphasis on human agency without offering a full consideration of the social and cultural context within which learning occurs.[23] Additionally, many current discussions of adult learning theory typically omit any reference to

Kolb's formulations as a theory of learning, instead referring to the experiential learning framework only as a model of learning styles.[24] Finally, Sheckley, Allen, and Keeton suggest that the smooth flowing cycle depicted in figure 1 is only an approximation of the tumultuous recursive path that experiential learning follows.[25] In consideration of these final three points we propose that: (a) the influence of culture on experiential learning, a *cultural effect*, should be delineated explicitly in statements of experiential learning theory; (b) since Kolb's work extends beyond a discussion of learning style preferences to provide a broad treatment of experiential learning, this broad perspective should be included in theoretical formulations of experiential learning; and (c) as we have already noted, experiential learning proceeds via tumultuous, recursive cycles.

If the practice of service learning is to expand within schools and colleges, we believe that the theoretical links between service learning and experiential learning theory must be extended and clarified in order to provide advocates of service learning with a framework that can be used to guide further research and to improve practice. For this reason, throughout this chapter we address each of the major criticisms of experiential learning theory and, in so doing, explicate a core set of service learning processes. By describing these core processes we attempt to outline the key elements that contribute to the effectiveness of service learning.

Experiential and Service Learning

Do individuals experience reality directly or do they filter their experiences through a perceptual screen composed of cultural norms, individual values, and personal expectations? Can meaning be "discovered" only through direct, experiential contact, or is meaning "constructed" by the individual? Can individuals learn from experience without expert guidance, or do learners need a teacher or guide to assist them? Educators and philosophers have long grappled with issues such as these but still have not arrived at a conclusive answer to the question: How do individuals learn from a service learning experience?

In addressing this question we propose that the superior learning outcomes exhibited by learners in a service learning program, in comparison to those of students in a lecture-discussion classroom, are due to several fundamental dynamics of the experiential learning process that ultimately lead to a greater *depth of processing* of concepts during a service learning experience.[26] However, these dynamics, which depict learners as sociocultural and seemingly chaotic information-processing systems,[27] are not commonly explicated in discussions of service learning.

SERVICE LEARNING

The belief that service learning experiences are unfettered by cognitive and perceptual filters is called "naive realism" by epistemologists. As depicted in figure 2, individuals shape ("construct") their service learning experiences through an ongoing interplay between *attention* to pertinent stimuli, *assessment* of the context within which the experience occurs, *storage* of perceptions about the experience, and *retrieval* of expectations based on prior experiences.[28]

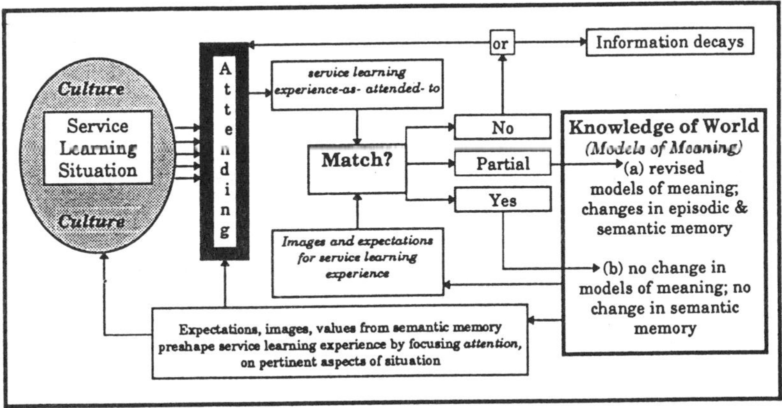

FIGURE 2

Simplified view of how individuals construct a service learning experience

Since all humans have a limited capacity to attend to all the stimuli in a setting, individuals overlay on a service learning situation a cognitive-affective template of images[29] or expectations[30] that focuses attention on *pertinent* aspects of the situation. In this way learners preshape a service learning situation *before* they even begin to attend to a set of stimuli within the situation.[31] (We will discuss the sociocultural, contextual nature of this process in a following section of this chapter.) In effect, this cognitive-affective template sets up a "search strategy" that influences the images, information, and stimuli to which individuals will pay attention—as in the case of hungry children riding in a car who, despite distractions set up by parents, readily spot a fast-food restaurant in the distance.

As a result of this focused attention, a set of filtered, pertinent information about the service learning experience (i.e., service learning *experience-as-attended-to*) enters into episodic memory. This information will remain temporarily in episodic memory only as long as the individual is paying attention (*attending*) to it—as when we look up a telephone number and remember it only long enough to initiate a call. If information is not attended to, it decays and eventually disappears from episodic memory.

The temporary information about service learning *experience-as-attended-to* can be transformed into durable *knowledge-about-the-world* via an interactive process in which learners "test" the compatibility between information about the service learning *experience-as-attended-to* held in episodic memory and models of meaning stored in semantic memory.[32] This compatibility test can yield a full or partial match (confirmation) or mismatch (disconfirmation) of these expectations. The outcome of the matching process influences the nature of the learning that occurs from the service learning experience.

Case 1: Confirmation. As a testament to the strength of the process by which learners preshape experience, Read found that 60 percent of adult learning projects involve a match or confirmation.[33] In other words, as learners interact with the world, their experiences rather conveniently tend to match the expectations they have for these experiences. Service learners, for example, may find that an assignment to work in a homeless shelter confirms (fully or partially) their general expectations that the occupants in the shelter were strongly influenced to use the shelter by the forces of "poverty" and "unemployment." Even if they have to refine slightly their preconceived notions of "poverty" and "unemployment" to resolve a partial "match," overall these learners "construct" the service learning experience so that the viability of their expectations, values, and models of meaning is maintained.

As Thorndyke notes, positive confirmation of an expectation for service learning experience is a valuable learning outcome.[34] When a match occurs, the learner encounters another instance in which expected properties of a concept were confirmed and adds this instance to the models of meaning in semantic memory. With each confirmation the concept becomes more robust and its expected properties become more clearly refined. In many cases, matching of expectations is a desired learning outcome because confirmations maintain a coherent, unified, expectation-confirming and knowledge-consistent view of the world.[35]

Case 2: Disconfirmation. In a minority of cases (about 40 percent) learners find that their expectations are disconfirmed.[36] Service learners working in a homeless center, for example, may find that in some instances occupants exercise a degree of choice and "decide" to live in the shelter. Faced with this disconfirmation of their expectations, the service learners have two choices: (a) cease attending to this disconfirming evidence and maintain the model of meaning they use to construct the situation as in Case 2-a below; or (b) accept the evidence and change the model of meaning used to construct the experience as in Case 2-b that follows.

Case 2-a: No change. Those learners who take the first choice, like an unsuccessful military commander who refuses to change a battle strategy that is leading to defeat, deny that the disconfirmation exists and doggedly attest that their expectations for and constructions of the service learning experience still hold true. In this example of a homeless shelter, service learners would selectively filter the disconfirming evidence in a way that allows them to hold steadfastly to their expectations and to conclude that, despite evidence to the contrary, the occupants actually had no "choice" but to live in the shelter.

Case 2-b: Change. Service learners faced with disconfirmation can revise the models of meaning and expectations that they use to construct their service learning experience and thereby modify the very cognitive/affective representations that they use to structure and make meaning of and preshape their world. Service learners faced with disconfirmation of their expectations could change their thinking about shelter occupants as helpless victims to consider them as adults who, within some explicit limits, exercise a degree of control over their lives.

Disconfirmation and learning. Interestingly, adults report that they "learned more" from experiences in which their expectations were disconfirmed than from experiences where expectations were confirmed, even though the disconfirming learning projects were more frustrating, anxiety producing, and stressful.[37] Apparently when an expectation is confirmed, the instance is seen by the learner as a reinforcement of prior learning and, for this reason, is viewed as a case in which relatively "little learning" occurred. When disconfirmation surprises learners, however, they tend to rethink, reconceptualize, and even transform the ways in which they view the world. In these instances they see themselves as "learning a great deal" from the experience. Mezirow, for example, describes how a "disorienting dilemma" often initiates a transformative learning process that leads to a profound change in the meaning perspective by which a learner makes sense of the world.[38]

We believe that the process by which individuals learn in a service learning setting involves ongoing, dynamic, and recursive interactions between: (a) learners' expectations for the experience, and (b) the confirmations and disconfirmations of the expectations that they encounter. We will begin our description of this dynamic process with a discussion of the *conduit effect*.

THE CONDUIT EFFECT

When, as in Case 1 above, learners construct service learning experiences so that their expectations for the experience are confirmed, a "cognitive conduit" is formed.[39] Perceptions that conform to the model of meaning used to preshape the service learning experience are processed automatically along this conduit path as shown in figure 3. Following Bargh, this automatic processing may be *preconscious* (i.e., does not require conscious awareness), *postconscious* (i.e., priming of attention as the result of a prior conscious experience), or *goal-dependent* (i.e., the presence of a goal will elicit a specific set of responses that are not used when the goal is absent).[40]

Individuals usually process information via the "conduit effect" because it frees cognitive resources for other, more pressing matters. For example, Sternberg describes how individuals make cognitive tasks automatic because these automatic tasks can be performed with very little cognitive effort.[41] Think, for example, about how little cognitive effort experienced drivers put into the task of deciding the route to use when driving home from work and of monitoring the progress of the car en route. Similarly, in their research on contingent decision behavior, Payne, Bettman, and Johnson found that, all else being equal, people used a tried and true decision rule because it required the least effort to reach a desired result.[42] Bandura describes the advantages of the conduit effect: "If one had to think about the details of every skilled activity before carrying it out in recurrent situations, it would consume most of one's attentional and cognitive resources."[43]

As outlined in figure 3, the conduit effect operates via a convergent, minimally reflective path joining a learner's expectations for a service learning experience and the attributes of the experience to which the learner pays attention. From prior experiences learners develop, and store in semantic memory, durable models of meaning and expectations for situations.[44] When learners move into new situations, they will be particularly sensitive to those specific attributes of the situation that are compatible with their values and the images and expectations that are stored in semantic memory.

The conduit effect is strongly influenced by semantic memory.[45] When the conduit effect operates, predictions, expectations, and images flow from the well-formed, robust, durable models of meaning

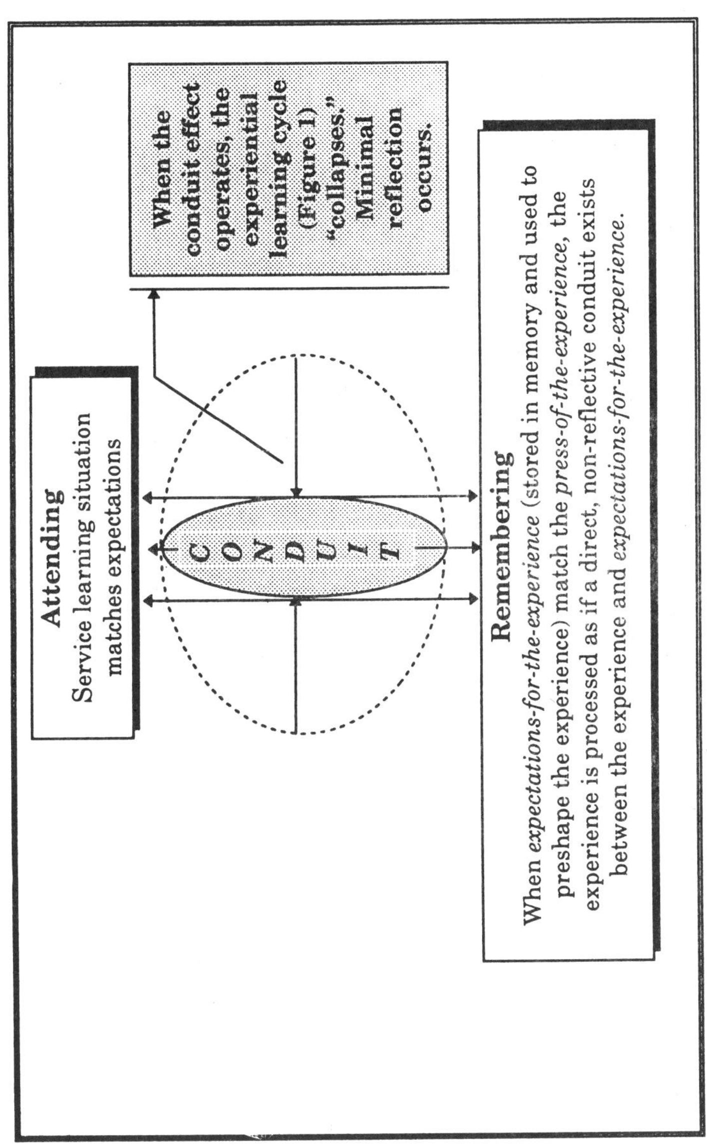

FIGURE 3
The Conduit Effect

stored in semantic memory to preshape and impose these predictions and expectations on the service learning experience. The conduit effect operates in a manner similar to what Immanuel Kant referred to as *determinate judgment*, a process in which an individual applies a preexisting concept to an experience.[46] In instances (such as Case 1 above) where determinate judgment prevails and models of meaning from semantic memory can be imposed on the service learning experience with minimal discrepancy, the conduit effect operates smoothly and little or no reflection on the service learning experience is required. In effect, use of what Kolb refers to as the transforming processes (i.e., reflective observation and active experimentation) diminishes when the conduit effect is in operation.[47]

As discussed previously (Case 1 above), through use of the conduit effect the concepts learners use to make sense of their service learning experiences become more robust if confirmed. With each confirmation via the conduit effect, learning occurs in that the expected properties of a rule, model, or abstraction are reinforced. In many cases, use of the conduit effect results in desired learning outcomes because confirmations maintain a coherent, unified, expectation-confirming and knowledge-consistent view of the world. The overall importance of the conduit effect in the life of a learner is underscored in cases such as Alzheimer's disease when memory decays and automatized information processing via use of the conduit effect no longer occurs.

In some cases, the conduit effect may actually impede new learning. For example, in a study of how managers learned a new job, Morrison and Brantner found that individuals with prior experience in a related job had a more difficult time learning their new job than those managers who had no related experience.[48] According to the study, individuals with related experience tried to fit unsuccessfully the skills they used in their old job (via the conduit effect process) to the situations they encountered in their new job.

Fortunately or unfortunately (depending on one's perspective), the conduit effect cannot be used to process accurately all situations learners encounter. Since most learners do not live in a world that always conforms to their models of meaning, learning activities also involve a process that enables learners to make reconciliations when experiences do not conform to their expectations. We call this process the *accordion effect*.

THE ACCORDION EFFECT

A service learning experience can also enhance learning by virtue of "surprises" that do not fit within the existing models of meaning, expectations, images, values, or constructions learners use to make meaning of their worlds. As in Case 2 above, these surprises result when (a) departures from expectations, images, values, rules, models of meaning are noticed; (b) information is missing, is in an unexpected format, or has extreme values; (c) there is little prior knowledge related to the experience; or (d) the situation is more complex than ones encountered previously.[49]

When mismatches occur between service learning experience as attended to and expectations for the service learning experience, these "surprises" are processed via an interaction between the equivocal, temporary information stored in episodic memory and the unequivocal images, expectations, and rule-based symbols stored in semantic memory.[50] To resolve the discrepancies learners must invent, infer, create, or devise a way to make sense of the discrepancy.[51] As in Case 2-b above, such surprises can lead to a transformation of the knowledge-of-the-world stored in semantic memory. In order to make sense of these surprises, learners sometimes must abandon, refine, alter, or transform the durable knowledge-of-the-world that they have stored in semantic memory.[52]

When, as in Case 2 above, surprises disrupt the automatized conduit effect then the learning cycle, like an accordion, expands outward as shown in figure 4. (To be true to our metaphor we should refer to the *conduit effect* as a "collapsed accordion" and the *accordion effect* as a "stretched accordion." For ease of discussion, however, we will use separate metaphors [that is, conduit and accordion] to describe experiential learning processes.) The difference between the accordion effect and the conduit effect is analogous to the difference between determinate and reflective judgment. As in Case 2-a, when determinate judgments prevail, the conduit effect dampens the accordion effect and learners use mental models that are already available in semantic memory to make sense of a service learning experience.[53] In contrast, during the reflective, accordion effect process, as in Case 2-b, pre-existing mental models are no longer validated by experiential input. In this instance learners must reflect imaginatively on a service learning event in an attempt to devise a durable way to represent and store the information about the event in semantic memory.

When the accordion effect operates, as in Case 2-b above, the context of the service learning experience, and the accompanying events that affect the learner's order of attention, exert more influence on the learner's construction of the service learning experience than do the expectations and models of meaning that are stored in semantic memory.

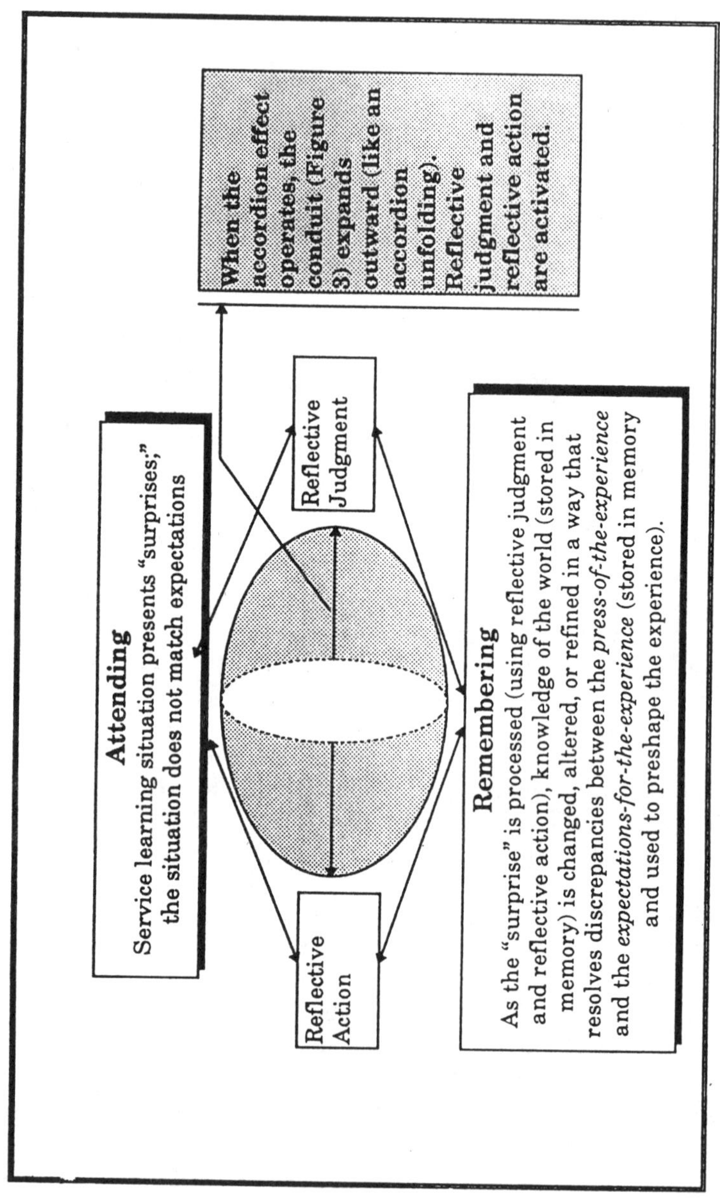

FIGURE 4
The Accordion Effect

In contrast to the conduit effect (Case 1, Case 2-a), the accordion effect can be characterized as an immediate-experience-based process that is used to process and make sense of information about the service learning experience represented in episodic memory. The more prevalent the accordion effect, the more important are contextual factors in guiding the interaction between episodic and semantic memory. When the conduit effect operates (Case 1), the learner imposes a meaning on the service learning experience that is validated by the experience. In contrast (Case 2-b), when the accordion effect operates, a reverse situation occurs in which the actual experience does not validate the expectations for the service learning experience. In this way the experience itself influences strongly the model of meaning the learner develops to make sense of the service learning experience.

Ideally, as in Case 2-b, learners will allow the automatized conduit process to give way to the more reflective accordion process when they encounter surprises. In actuality, however, as in Case 2-a, learners tend to use the conduit effect more often than the accordion effect.[54] Specifically, attempts to use the more reflective accordion processes tend to be less than successful when (a) the situation is stressful; (b) learners have little prior knowledge in the area; (c) learners have limited training in recognizing alternatives within the experience; (d) learners are functioning at lower levels of cognitive or ego development (e.g., dualistic thinkers); or (e) learners cannot accurately assess and evaluate contextual factors that influence the service learning situation.[55]

Before we discuss how the conduit and accordion effects interact to promote learning within a service learning setting, we will elaborate more fully upon the contextual factors which impact learning. We term these influences broadly the *cultural effect*.

THE CULTURAL EFFECT

As noted earlier, one of the major criticisms of theories of experiential and service learning is the overemphasis on the central role of individual psychological processes to the exclusion of the powerful ways in which society and culture influence service learning.[56] In recognition of this critique, our position is that service learning is not only an individual act but also a sociocultural event. As human beings come to understand the meaning of their service learning experiences, they cannot escape the pervasive influence of their culture. As argued by Valsiner and Leung, "all environments of human beings are cultural, since cultural norms and meanings regulate persons' transactions with every aspect of the physical environment."[57]

Just as the metabolic processes of a fish cannot be understood apart from the aquatic context in which they occur, so too service learning cannot be understood apart from the cultural context in which it occurs. First, culture sets the parameters for the learning process (especially the conduit effect) because, as Bruner argues, culture shapes human life and the human mind. "It does this by imposing the patterns inherent in the culture's symbolic systems—its language and discourse modes, the forms of logical and narrative explication, and the patterns of mutual dependent communal life."[58] Second, because all individuals are embedded within a culture that shapes the ways in which they view the world, the service learning process, cannot be comprehended apart from the culture in which the individual resides.[59] Third, the classic research of the linguists Edward Sapir and Benjamin Whorf has shown that, through language, culture mediates the images and models of meaning that individuals use to make sense of an experience.[60] Finally, by setting norms and taboos, culture also mediates the service learning experiences in which an individual within a culture is "permitted" to engage.

The framework for understanding and analyzing culture developed by Hofstede can be used to contrast the service learning experiences in a homeless shelter of two individuals from different cultural backgrounds.[61] According to Hofstede, culture is the collective mental programming of the people in an environment. Learner A, with values that reflect one segment of U.S. culture, might believe that (a) less powerful members of our society have the right to full services from all government agencies, (b) individuals should act as agents on their own behalf, (c) individuals should display characteristics like assertiveness and autonomy, and (d) a certain amount of ambiguity in policies and rules is necessary for individuals to exercise their individual freedom. This cultural value set could strongly influence Learner A (via a culturally structured conduit effect) to perceive (construct) homeless clients as individuals who should take full advantage of the social services available to them and pull themselves up by their own bootstraps.

In contrast, Learner B may enter the service learning experience with a very different set of cultural beliefs: (a) not everyone in society deserves equal access to power and privilege; (b) an individual's value is reflected by the collective status of his family within a community; (c) caring for others in the family and community is more important than assertively acquiring property and wealth; (d) a society must follow specific, unambiguous rules to ensure that a social order exists. Learner B would likely understand the service learning experience not in terms of government programs or individual efforts but in terms of homeless clients' need to reestablish familial relationships within their community.

Even though the service learning experiences for Learner A and Learner B in the homeless setting may appear to be identical, the way in which each learner constructs the experience differs. These differences can be attributed to the unique ways in which their cultural background has influenced their service learning experiences via (a) the sociocultural models of meaning stored in their semantic memory; (b) the conduit effect they use to make meaning from their service learning experiences; and (c) their willingness to process discordant information using the reflective accordion effect.

Service Learning in Action

As indicated by the research of Markus, Howard, and King cited earlier, learners who participate in a service learning experience, more so than their classroom-based counterparts, will change the attitudes, images, and beliefs that they use to make sense of the events related to their service learning experience.[62] We believe that this outcome is related to the recursive and developmental learning processes that promote greater *depth of processing* of concepts within a service learning setting.[63] Depth of processing, according to Tulving, involves an interaction between the durable information in semantic memory and the information from immediate experience held in episodic memory.[64] From such interaction the durable models of meaning in semantic memory are elaborated with new information from immediate experience. Concurrently, the information from immediate experience in episodic memory becomes more durable because it possesses a more robust memory trace and a stronger link with semantic memory.

When, as in Case 2 above, the learner first attends to information about a person "choosing" to live in the homeless shelter, this information is represented temporarily in episodic memory. If, as in Case 2-a, the information is not continually attended to, it will decay and disappear. In this case, the learner will not have changed in any way his or her model of meaning used to make sense of the service learning experience. If, however, the information is reflected upon, acted upon, connected with related information in semantic memory (i.e., if it is more deeply processed), as in Case 2-b, the information will acquire a more durable memory trace. With a more durable memory trace, this model of meaning, *people-choosing-to-live-in-the-homeless-shelter*, will be used as a search strategy to preshape future interactions within this service learning setting. As subsequent experiences within the homeless shelter validate continually this model of meaning (and it is continually reflected upon, acted upon, and connected with related models of meaning within semantic memory), this memory trace will develop greater complexity.

This example of depth of processing highlights the degree to which service learning is a developmental process that proceeds along the hierarchical levels of semantic memory.[65] At the first level, depth of processing results in information from a service learning experience being encoded into durable models of meaning that enable a learner to "recognize" an event, as when a learner in the homeless shelter says: "That is clearly an example of discrimination, but don't ask me why." At the second level, this model of meaning evolves to contain rules about the event, as when this learner now says: "That is a case of discrimination under the law because it involves a person being denied equal opportunity to get that job because she may choose to have a child." Expansion of the model of meaning continues to a third level where this learner now develops an optimal model to describe and predict the event: "If the employment agencies continue to refer young women only to jobs that don't require travel, then these women will not have an equal opportunity to compete eventually for higher paying management jobs if they so choose." The complexity of the model of meaning continues to develop to a fourth level where this learner now develops abstractions that can be used to compare, distinguish, and synthesize forms of discrimination (e.g., age, racial, ethnic) into an integrated model that the learner can use to describe and predict fair and equitable practices within a workplace.

Notice here that by virtue of their continued experiential involvement in the service learning setting, as students "learn" they concurrently develop more complex, more highly integrated, and more refined models of meaning that they use to make sense of their experiences in the world. Unlike their counterparts in lecture-discussion classrooms, service learners achieve a greater depth of processing of information because of the experiential learning process that occurs in service learning. With each recursive interaction of the conduit, accordion, and cultural effects within a service learning setting, learners develop more inclusive, differentiated, permeable, and integrative meaning perspectives.[66] In so doing they move toward higher levels of reflective judgment[67] and higher orders of consciousness.[68]

Moreover, this example highlights the degree to which service and experiential learning is an interactive, recursive process. At any one point in time all the processes addressed in this chapter (attending, conduit effect, accordion effect, cultural effect, retrieval and storage of information in episodic and semantic memory) are interacting. In a service learning setting, semantic memory preshapes experience and initiates the automatized conduit effect. Feedback from the service learning setting may then provide a "surprise" which indicates that the model of meaning used to construct the service learning experience (via the conduit effect) does not adequately explain this situation. Memory responds to the surprise and calls the accordion effect into play to reflect upon the service learning experience and perhaps to initiate a change in the models of meaning that are used to make sense of the experience. The learner's cultural background mediates the entire process through language, norms, and taboos. Surprises abound. The conduit effect gives way to the accordion effect. Memory then stabilizes (automatizes) the accordion effect into a higher-order conduit effect that persists until the next service learning experience brings along a surprise that does not fit the refined models of meaning within semantic memory. In a service learning setting, because the meaning-making process (learning) is dynamic, recursive, and never static, learners engage concepts and experiences with a greater depth of processing than their counterparts in lecture-discussion classrooms.

According to the theoretical framework that we have outlined in this chapter, service learning immerses learners in a highly effective learning environment that promotes depth of processing of the concepts and experiences they encounter.[68] Predictably, learners will enter a service learning setting with a degree of naïveté about the nuances, subtleties, and complexities of the situation. Their first attempt at understanding the service learning experience will involve full use of the somewhat incomplete and inaccurate models of meaning, expectations, and images stored in their semantic memory (as outlined in Case 1 above). The conduit effect will be in full operation as they try to make the service learning experience conform to their expectations. In most cases, the automatized conduit effect will work—to a certain degree. As it does, the individual will learn more instances in which the images, values, expectations, concepts that they use to understand the world can accurately predict and be used to understand experiences.

Within the service experience learners will also encounter "surprises" that disconfirm their expectations (as outlined in Case 2 above). To learn from these surprises, learners may need assistance from instructors to loosen the grip the conduit effect has on preshaping service learning experience so that the learners can use the more reflective accordion effect (as in Case 2-b). As they reflectively judge or reflectively act upon the experience (via the accordion effect), learners may develop new representations of the service experience that will be stored in their semantic memory. In this way the models of meaning and related images, expectations, values, rules, principles, and concepts learners use to make sense of the world will be changed or transformed. As pointed out earlier, with each recursive interchange between the conduit and accordion effects within the service learning setting, a learner's understanding of the world will become developmentally more complex and his or her level of intellectual functioning will move toward a higher level of reflective judgment and a higher order of consciousness. For example, learners working in a homeless shelter may change their view of "poverty" from a simplistic notion (e.g., lack of money) to a developmentally more complex understanding of the historical, structural, political, and sociological factors associated with poverty. We view this developmental outcome of the service learning experience as its most important contribution to the education of individual learners.

In closing, we would like to emphasize the important and central role reflective seminars play in maximizing the educational benefits of the service learning experience. As outlined in our theoretical model, the experiential learning process is strongly influenced (and sometimes constrained) by two factors: (a) the expectations, images, values, and models of meaning developed from prior experiences that learners hold in semantic memory; and (b) the values, norms, and beliefs that learners have assimilated from their cultural experiences. If students are placed within a service learning setting without the assistance of a reflective seminar, we believe that iterations of conduit effect will prevail. The influence of images, expectations, and cultural values that exist in semantic memory will govern the process by which the learner makes meaning of the service learning experience. In this scenario, learners will assimilate additional instances in which the expectations they use to make meaning of the world provide accurate representations of the experiences they actually encounter. With the supportive and structured guidance of a reflective seminar that accompanies a service learning experience, however, learners will more readily engage in the reflective processes associated with the accordion effect and thereby evolve more developmentally complex understandings of their experiences.

To spur the reflective process, instructors facilitating the seminar can use the theoretical model outlined in this chapter as a guide.

Specifically, during the first meetings of the seminar learners would have opportunities to discuss and describe their constructions of their service learning experiences. If our model is correct, these descriptions will represent outcomes of the conduit effect (i.e., the expectations, images, rules, principles, values, and models of meaning that learners are bringing to the service learning setting). As the semester moves along, the instructor could set up discussions, debates, and readings that challenge the viewpoints expressed by learners and encourage them to judge the service learning experience reflectively using a different set of perspectives. The instructor could also set up an accordion effect by encouraging students to "try out" different actions within the service learning setting and then assess the outcomes of these actions.

Similarly, we encourage researchers to assess the accuracy of this theoretical model by mapping out the ways in which the service learning process is influenced by affective and emotional forces,[70] transference between learners and instructors,[71] developmental experiences,[72] different cultures,[73] and interventions designed to promote reflection.[74] Researchers could also assist by evaluating the degree to which the complexity of the attitudes, beliefs, concepts, and abstractions learners use to understand a service learning setting changed over the course of the experience. Finally, researchers could help to expand the model by identifying which of the many components of the service learning experience were the most influential in promoting development and learning.

If both practitioners and researchers use the theoretical model presented in this chapter as a starting point, we all, working together, can improve the practice of service learning by advancing the theoretical underpinnings of the experiential learning process.

The authors acknowledge the assistance of Eileen Eckert who conducted a comprehensive review of research pertaining to service learning.

Notes

1. Thomas Woehrle, "Growing Up Responsible," *Educational Leadership* 51 (November 1993): 40-43.

2. Jeffrey Roth and Jo M. Hendrickson, "Schools and Youth Organizations: Empowering Adolescents to Confront High-risk Behavior," *Phi Delta Kappan* 72, no. 8 (1991): 619-622.

3. Gregory B. Markus, Jeffrey P. Howard, and D. C. King, "Integrating Community Service and Classroom Instruction Enhances Learning: Results from an Experiment," *Educational Evaluation and Policy Analysis* 15, no. 4 (1993): 410-419.

4. National Commission on Youth, *The Transition of Youth to Adulthood: A Bridge Too Long* (Boulder, Colo.: Westview, 1980).

5. Ernest L. Boyer, *College* (New York: Harper and Row, 1987).

6. Robert A. Rutter and Fred M. Newmann, "The Potential of Community Service to Enhance Civic Responsibility," *Social Education* 53 (October 1989): 371-374.

7. Markus, Howard, and King, "Integrating Community Service and Classroom Instruction Enhances Learning."

8. Daniel Conrad and Diane Hedin, "School-based Community Service: What We Know from Research and Theory," *Phi Delta Kappan* 72, no. 10 (1991): 743-751.

9. Ibid., p. 747.

10. Markus, Howard, and King, "Integrating Community Service and Classroom Instruction Enhances Learning."

11. Jacob Cohen, "A Power Primer," *Psychological Bulletin* 112, no. 1 (1992): 155-159.

12. J. R. Porter and L. B. Schwartz, "Experiential Service-based Learning: An Integrated HIV/AIDS Education Model for College Campuses," *Teaching Sociology* 21 (1993): 405-415.

13. David A. Kolb, *Experiential Learning: Experience as the Source of Learning and Development* (Englewood Cliffs, N.J.: Prentice-Hall, 1984).

14. See, for example, Barry G. Sheckley and Susan Warner-Weil, "Using Experience to Enhance Learning: Perspectives and Questions," in *Prelude to a Global Conversation*, edited by Morris T. Keeton (Chicago: Council for Adult and Experiential Learning, 1984), pp. 1-16.

15. Richard Hopkins, "David Kolb's Experiential Learning Machine," *Journal of Phenomenological Psychology* 24, no. 1 (1993): 46.

16. Throughout our discussion we use Tulving's distinction between *semantic memory* (that is, memory that is symbolic, automatic, inferential, durable, conceptual, sociocultural "thinking") and *episodic memory* (that is, memory that is oriented to the present, maintained by attention, noninferential, nondurable, self-referenced "sensing"). See Endel Tulving, *Elements of Episodic Memory* (New York: Oxford University Press, 1983), and idem, "What Kind of a Hypothesis Is the Distinction between Episodic and Semantic Memory?" *Journal of Experimental Psychology: Learning, Memory, and Cognition* 12, no. 2 (1986): 307-311.

17. Peter Jarvis, *Paradoxes of Learning: On Becoming an Individual in Society* (San Francisco: Jossey-Bass, 1992).

18. Sharon B. Merriam and M. Carolyn Clark, *Lifelines: Patterns of Work, Love, and Learning in Adulthood* (San Francisco: Jossey-Bass, 1991).

19. Michael Vincenti, "Automaticity in Experiential Learning Theory: The Conduit between Experience and Conceptualization," Unpublished manuscript, Department of Adult and Vocational Education, University of Connecticut, 1995.

20. Arthur D. Fisk, Monk D. Lee, and Wendy A. Rogers, "Recombination of Automatic Processing Components: The Effects of Transfer, Reversal, and Conflict Situations," *Human Factors* 33, no. 3 (1991): 267-280.

21. Jack Mezirow, *Transformative Dimensions of Adult Learning* (San Francisco: Jossey-Bass, 1991).

22. See, for example, Evelyn M. Boyd and Ann W. Fales, "Reflective Learning: Key to Learning from Experience," *Journal of Humanistic Psychology* 23, no. 2 (1983): 99-117, and Robin Usher, "Adult Students and Their Experience: Developing a Resource for Learning," *Studies in the Education of Adults* 18 (1985): 24-34.

23. M. Carolyn Clark and Arthur L. Wilson, "Context and Rationality in Mezirow's Theory of Transformational Learning," *Adult Education Quarterly* 41, no. 2 (1991): 75-91.

24. See, for example, Sharon B. Merriam and Rosemary S. Caffarella, *Learning in Adulthood* (San Francisco: Jossey-Bass, 1991).

25. Barry G. Sheckley, George Allen, and Morris T. Keeton, "Adult Learning as Recursive Process," *Journal of Cooperative Education* 28, no. 2 (1993): 56-68.

26. Constance Walde, "Developing a Foundation for Learning: Qualitative Depth of Processing," Dissertation proposal, Department of Adult and Vocational Education, University of Connecticut, 1995.

27. Jeremy Campbell, *Grammatical Man: Information, Entropy, and Life* (New York: Simon and Schuster, 1982); James Gleick, *Chaos: The Making of a New Science* (New York: Penguin Books, 1987).

28. Alan Allport, "Visual Attention," in *Foundations of Cognitive Science*, edited by Michael I. Posner (Cambridge, Mass.: MIT Press, 1993), pp. 630-682; Donald A. Norman, "Toward a Theory of Memory and Attention," *Psychological Review* 75, no. 6 (1968): 522-536.

29. Terence R. Mitchell and Lee Roy Beach, " '. . . Do I Love Thee? Let Me Count . . .': Toward an Understanding of Intuitive and Automatic Decision Making," *Organizational Behavior and Human Decision Processes* 47 (1990): 1-20.

30. George A. Kelly, *The Psychology of Personal Constructs*, 2 vols. (New York: Norton, 1955).

31. Allport, "Visual Attention"; Norman, "Toward a Theory of Memory and Attention."

32. Mitchell and Beach, "'Do I Love Thee?'"; Tulving, *Elements of Episodic Memory*; idem, "What Kind of a Hypothesis Is the Distinction between Episodic and Semantic Memory?"

33. Holly E. Read, "A Recursive Model of Adult Experiential Learning," Doctoral dissertation, University of Connecticut, 1994.

34. Perry W. Thorndyke, "Applications of Schema Theory in Cognitive Research," in *Tutorials in Learning and Memory: Essays in Memory of Gordon Bower*, edited by John R. Anderson and Stephen M. Rosslyn (New York: Freeman and Co., 1984).

35. John W. Alba and Lynn Hasher, "Is Memory Schematic?" *Psychological Bulletin* 93 (1983): 203-231.

36. Read, "A Recursive Model of Adult Experiential Learning."

37. Ibid.

38. Mezirow, *Transformative Dimensions of Adult Education*.

39. Vincenti, "Automaticity in Experiential Learning Theory."

40. John A. Bargh, "The Ecology of Automaticity: Toward Establishing the Conditions Needed to Produce Automatic Processing Effects," *American Journal of Psychology* 105, no. 2 (1992): 181-199.

41. Robert J. Sternberg, *The Triarchic Mind* (New York: Viking Penguin, 1988).

42. John W. Payne, James R. Bettman, and Eric J. Johnson, *The Adaptive Decision Maker* (Victoria, Australia: Cambridge University Press, 1993).

43. Albert Bandura, "Conclusion: Reflections on Nonability Determinants of Competence," in *Competence Considered*, edited by Robert J. Sternberg and John Kolligian, Jr. (New Haven: Yale University Press, 1990), p. 348.

44. Tulving, *Elements of Episodic Memory*; idem, "What Kind of a Hypothesis Is the Distinction between Episodic and Semantic Memory?"

45. Bargh, "The Ecology of Automaticity."

46. Immanuel Kant, *Critique of Pure Reason*, trans. J. M. D. Meiklejohn (London: George Bell, 1897).

47. Kolb, *Experiential Learning*.

48. Robert F. Morrison and Thomas M. Brantner, "What Enhances or Inhibits Learning a New Job: A Basic Career Issue," *Journal of Applied Psychology* 77, no. 6 (1992): 926-940.

49. Payne, Bettman, and Johnson, *The Adaptive Decision Maker.*

50. John R. Anderson, *The Architecture of Cognition* (Cambridge, Mass.: Harvard University Press, 1963); Tulving, "What Kind of a Hypothesis Is the Distinction between Episodic and Semantic Memory?"

51. Payne, Bettman, and Johnson, *The Adaptive Decision Maker.*

52. Brian Gaines, "Between Neuron, Culture, and Logic: Explicating the Cognitive Nexus," *International Journal of Expert Systems* 7, no. 1 (1994): 21-51; Mezirow, *Transformative Dimensions of Adult Learning.*

53. Kant, *The Critique of Pure Reason*; Mark Johnson, *The Body in the Mind: The Bodily Basis of Meaning, Imagination, and Reason* (Chicago: University of Chicago Press, 1987).

54. Read, "A Recursive Model of Adult Experiential Learning."

55. Payne, Bettman, and Johnson, *The Adaptive Decision Maker*; Nancy L. Travers, "To Learn or Not to Learn: Dynamics within Experiential Learning," Unpublished manuscript, Department of Adult and Vocational Education, University of Connecticut, 1995.

56. Clark and Wilson, "Context and Rationality in Mezirow's Theory of Transformational Learning."

57. Joan Valsiner and Man-Chi Leung, "From Intelligence to Knowledge Construction: A Socio-genetic Process Approach," in *Mind in Context*, edited by Robert J. Sternberg and Richard K. Wagner (Cambridge: Cambridge University Press, 1994), p. 210.

58. Jerome Bruner, "Folk Psychology as an Instrument of Culture," in Jerome Bruner, *Acts of Meaning* (Cambridge, Mass.: Harvard University Press, 1990), p. 34.

59. Pierre Erny, *The Child and His Environment in Black Africa: An Essay on Traditional Education* (Nairobi: Oxford University Press, 1981).

60. Nancy Bonvillain, *Language, Culture, and Communication: The Meaning of Messages* (Englewood Cliffs, N.J.: Prentice-Hall, 1993).

61. Geert Hofstede, "Motivation, Leadership and Organization: Do American Theories Apply Abroad?" *Organizational Dynamics* 9 (Summer 1980): 42-63.

62. Markus, Howard, and King, "Integrating Community Service and Classroom Instruction Enhances Learning."

63. Walde, "Developing a Foundation for Learning."

64. Tulving, *Elements of Episodic Memory.*

65. Gaines, "Between Neuron, Culture, and Logic."

66. Mezirow, *Transformative Dimensions of Adult Learning.*

67. Patricia M. King and Karen S. Kitchener, *Developing Reflective Judgment* (San Francisco: Jossey-Bass, 1994).

68. Robert Kegan, *In Over Our Heads: The Mental Demands of Life.* (Cambridge, Mass.: Harvard University Press, 1994).

69. Walde, "Developing a Foundation for Learning."

70. See, for example, Travers, "To Learn or Not to Learn."

71. See, for example, Martha Summerville, "The Relational Effect: A Core Learning Experiential Process," Dissertation proposal, Department of Adult and Vocational Education, University of Connecticut, 1995.

72. See the following dissertation proposals in the Department of Adult and Vocational Education, University of Connecticut: Jeanne Christie, "Women's Leadership Development: The Effect of the Experiential Learning Process, Support Systems, and Gender Issues in a War Zone" (1995); Kathleen A. Guglielmi, "The Development of

Cognitive Complexity: The Effect of Perceived Level of Support within a Formal Learning Culture" (1995). See also, Barbara Hanna, "Dynamics of Transformative Learning," Unpublished manuscript, Department of Adult and Vocational Education, University of Connecticut, 1995.

73. See the following dissertation proposals in the Department of Adult and Vocational Education, University of Connecticut: Sandra Inga, "The Construction of Knowledge Related to Infant Caretaking among the Tiv of Nigeria: A Culturally Relevant Learning Model" (1995); Moctar Kone, "Adult Learning for Environmental Protection and Management in Mali" (1995); and Marianne LeGrow, "Effects of Prior Critical Events on Reflective Judgment Development in Sojourner Adaptation" (1995).

74. See the following dissertation proposals in the Department of Adult and Vocational Education, University of Connecticut: Henrietta Pranger, "The Development of Cognitive Complexity in Collegiate and Extracollegiate Settings" (1995); and Karen Sladyk, "Factors that Influence Clinical Reasoning in Occupational Therapy Students" (1994).

CHAPTER IV

Research and Evaluation in Service Learning: What Do We Need to Know?

RICHARD P. LIPKA

While the names of the schools, teachers, and students change, the script remains the same. Across the land professional educators committed to learner-centered approaches to curriculum development are assisting young people to engage in a variety of service learning projects as part of their ongoing education.[1] It has been stated that service learning not only provides opportunities to apply skills and concepts learned in school. It also affords students opportunities to gain knowledge about the politics and procedures of democratic living.[2] Further, it is suggested that involvement in these types of projects leads to adult behaviors favoring participation and leadership in formal and informal community organizations.[3]

The problem with this assumption lies not in the nobility of its purpose, but in its validity. In reality, there is relatively little research available to inform us about whether there is a connection between service learning experiences and adult life, particularly in terms of persistent, long-range effects on behavior, attitudes, and predispositions. Researchers tend to focus on economic measures alone, to define long term in time increments which are really short term, to employ limited techniques for data gathering, and to emphasize service learning experiences in post-secondary education. Most important, these studies are unconnected, lacking a broad conceptual framework which explicates the theory, practice, and current status of research on long-term effects of service learning.

Left with ambiguous and disconnected conclusions about the relationships between service learning experiences and adult life, educators must resort to assumption, estimation, and intuition. Claims about long-term effects, whether positive or negative, are relatively free from criticism or challenge. If school programs are to be planned or changed with an eye to future consequences for learners based

---

Richard P. Lipka is Professor of Education in the Department of Special Services and Leadership Studies, Pittsburg State University, Pittsburg, Kansas.

upon reasonable empirical evidence, research into long-term effects is needed. In this chapter I propose ways to achieve greater clarity in this area of research. Given the public nature of service learning, care must be taken during the life of a project to make data-based decisions that maintain fidelity to its expressed purposes. Examining the steps and procedures in gathering data is the purpose of this chapter.

Initiating the Process of Research and Evaluation

Educators interested in working with service learning projects must be open to and comfortable with the processes of evaluation and research. There is a need for an empirically oriented knowledge base that approaches in scope and size the rhetoric devoted to service learning. Through research the service learning community will be afforded generalizable knowledge concerning theoretical models and the functional relationships found in the implementation of service learning.[1] Through evaluation educators involved with service learning have the potential for improving their projects during the ongoing phase as well as for identifying consequences of actions taken to forward the goals of the project.[5]

A partnership should be formed between the educators responsible for the project and social scientists who can deal with the technical aspects of conducting research and evaluation. Educators involved in the project bear ultimate responsibility for judgments of value concerning the realization of the goals of the projects. Their effectiveness largely depends upon the quality and quantity of the information they have available to them. For this reason social scientists must be asked to bring their expertise to bear upon this question, "To what degree are the goals and objectives of the project being achieved?" This major question embraces such issues as how and when to collect usable data. These issues will be addressed later in this chapter.

The time to include the researcher and/or evaluator is at the inception of the service learning project to insure that the project assessment will be proactive rather than reactive. From the beginning the researcher/evaluator should be able to identify individuals or groups who, by attitude or skill, have the potential to be supporters of, or detractors from the project, and to present this information in ways that will have utility for the individuals developing and/or administering the project. Another advantage of early involvement is the increased potential for the collection of systematic, continuous data which are useful for both formative and summative judgments.

Suggestions about wording of objectives, activities, and procedures may go a long way in securing usable data. Additionally, the researcher/evaluator may be the personification of a conscience. In a real sense he or she is a detached party who can ask "Why?" "What if?" and "How come?" during the development and implementation of the project.

How Should the Evaluation/Research be Conducted?

Many research designs are available[6] and numerous frameworks for planning evaluations exist in the literature.[7] Riecken suggests that in selecting the appropriate tools, techniques, or individuals to conduct the inquiry, focus should be placed upon questions such as the following:[8]

Will the bulk of the inquiry depend as much as possible upon data collected directly from the participants?

Will the inquiry aim for systematic coverage of all the objectives of the project?

Will the inquirer be an active participant from the inception of the project?

Will the instruments and techniques employed in the inquiry be of known reliability and capable of producing quantifiable results?

Will steps be taken to secure an adequate and representative sample of participants from both the project and comparison group?

Will all steps be taken to insure accurate assessment of change during and after the course of the project?

Will all steps be taken to insure an accurate description of the context, events, and experiences of the project group?

Will there be a detailed justification for the exclusion of any of the aforementioned questions?

OBJECTIVES

For our purposes, service learning projects are activities in which young people, under the auspices of the school, are actively engaged in efforts to improve community life. School personnel will help youth select a variety of objectives from among the following:

To develop and apply participation skills such as planning and cooperation which are a part of effective citizenship.

To become aware of community problems and needs.

To develop a sense of self-worth through personal contributions to community life.

To develop a sense of personal responsibility for the quality of life.

To gain insight into other people's lives through interactions with citizens from various walks of life and of different ages and diverse backgrounds.

To develop predispositions toward active community participation and service which will carry over into adult life.

In order to promote these learnings, properly organized service learning projects are built around two elements. First, they involve direct experience through actual improvement projects in the community. Second, they involve reflective thought about the meaning of those experiences through discussions, journal writing, and other in-school activities. This blend of theory and practice, thought, and action provides the necessary ingredient to bring together the cognitive and affective dimensions which result in authentic learning. Without reflection, activities may become a random series of trial and error attempts. Without direct experience, reflection is merely a hypothetical act lacking a test in reality.

From the standpoint of curriculum organization, service learning projects are most closely related to the learner-centered curricular approach presently known as "contemporary issues." In this approach, students are engaged in the study of units organized around compelling problems in society. These may include topics like "How Technology Affects Our Lives," "Conservation of Natural Resources," "World Peace," or "Living in Our Community." Such units give students an opportunity to study problems and consider how they might be resolved. The identification of community needs and development of service projects may also strengthen and enliven the more commonly used subject-centered approach. Students who undertake a project related to environmental problems may apply information learned in science courses. Students conducting a citizen survey use mathematics skills in tabulating and presenting their findings. Those who prepare a school-community newsletter use language arts skills of interviewing, recording, and writing. Service projects may also be used to strengthen the learner-centered curricular approach known as the "emerging needs approach" which addresses personal-social growth, and in which students demonstrate improvement in their sense of self-worth, human relations skills, and sensitivity to the needs and problems of others. In other words, the perception that service learning projects grow only out of units in the social studies program is a limited one. Service projects may also emerge from other subject areas, from interdisciplinary efforts, or from attempts to promote personal-social growth of learners. Likewise, they may be carried out under a special schoolwide program designed specifically for this purpose. In short, service learning projects not only have a legitimate place in the school program, but they may be initiated from virtually any aspect of it. As such, the projects themselves may be of many and varied types. Some characteristics which may be observed in service learning projects are:

- Projects should arise from real community needs. Students themselves may identify possible projects, but in other cases projects may be initiated by teachers, administrators, counselors, or by citizens or representatives of local agencies.
- Participation in projects should be on a voluntary basis, but in some cases classes or small groups may be assigned a project, as when the project is a part of a course. Where projects involve individual activities, participants should meet in discussion groups to reflect on their experiences.
- Projects may involve activities ranging from a simple level (e.g., cleaning up at a local park) to a complex level (e.g., designing and conducting a citizen survey or organizing a peer counseling program). School officials must monitor projects, however, to be certain that they represent legitimate service learning rather than cheap labor.
- While to date most reported projects are carried out at the high school level, there is no reason why elementary and middle level students may not be involved. In fact, they often are.[9] With its influence on self-worth, social growth, skill use, and citizenship, service learning is of benefit to any age group.
- Projects may be of varying duration, ranging from a few days to two or more years. They should, however, involve sufficient time to allow in-depth planning, implementation, and reflection.

The pioneer work of Tyler should be most helpful in developing the objectives for service learning projects.[10] According to Tyler, the first step is to establish broad goals or objectives. While these objectives should reflect the project at hand, they should be tested for conceptual clarity by using criteria appropriate for community service projects. Olsen has suggested two types of criteria that can be used for this purpose:

Criteria in Terms of Educational Values

Can the project be related to the present living experiences of boys and girls?

Does the activity contribute to the development of needed skills, habits, ideals, outlooks, and abilities?

Does the activity promote critical thinking?

Is the experience consistent with the maturity level of the children?

Does it provide for differences in abilities and interests?

May students share in planning and evaluating the program?

Does the activity lead to a desire to participate actively in community life, rather than to withdraw from it?

Does the project stimulate awareness of our need to improve human relations?

Does the activity cultivate a disposition to act for the general welfare?

Does it permit the student to assume realistic citizenship?

Criteria in Terms of Curriculum Development

Does the experience acquaint the pupils with the resources of their community?

Does the study show the relationships between the several aspects, processes, and problems of community life?

Does it provide contact with persons who are seen as human beings with needs, desires, ideals?

Does it offer opportunity to analyze conflicts as well as cooperation between individuals and groups in the community?

Does the project relate to a basic process, problems, or trend rather than to superficial aspects?

Does the activity make vivid and real the basic trends and tensions of life today?

Does the experience involve firsthand participation in community living?

Does the experience include constructive personal contribution to human welfare?

Can the project actually improve the quality of living?

Is the activity within the power of the students to complete with a minimum of adult dominance?[11]

The second step is to distill the broad objectives into more specific language so that they may be classified and used in the selection or development of measurement devices.[12] This would mean clustering the objectives under such rubrics as knowledge, skills, and attitudes. Undertaking these analyses provides even further guidelines for the "what," "when," and "who" questions related to the measurement process.

MEASURES

In the "measures" dimension, the key issue is that of short-term and long-term outcomes. Under the rubric of short-term, consideration should be given to ongoing as well as summative measures. The utilization of ongoing measures with fidelity to the goals of the project offers the potential for refinement or redirection of efforts—no small feat given the economic costs and feeling tone of many service projects. Short-term summative measures may be necessary for a variety of purposes. Judgments about student participants may be needed in order to conform to the grading formats and time lines utilized in the school. Short-term summative data may also be necessary to justify a project's inclusion in future school budgets or to address the "accountability" movement being tied to federal dollars or as the underpinning of a proposal for a grant from a private foundation to finance continued operation.

In making decisions about specific measures, it is necessary to refocus on the fact that service learning projects originate in learner-centered approaches to curriculum development. As such, the potential exists for a wider range of learner responses than that associated with traditional classroom instruction. According to Hamilton, in addition to cognitive learning we should maintain expectations for ethical and emotional reactions as well as physical activity and social engagement.[13]

This diversity of expected outcomes reveals the limitations of paper and pencil measures and the need for "triangulation of measurement."[14] Using multiple measures requires construction of decision matrices to facilitate the selection and/or development of specific measures. For example,

1. For each paper and pencil measure equal consideration should be given to observations and interviews.
2. For each unstructured interview equal attention should be given to structured interviews.
3. For each obtrusive observation equal consideration should be given to unobtrusive observation. For example, data on students could include daily school attendance, daily tardiness rate, number of high school graduates, participation rates in organizations like scouting and YMCA, number and nature of books borrowed from libraries, and percentage of graduates remaining in the community who become involved in adult service organizations.

Using project goals and objectives in conjunction with rational decision making can lead to measures that support the contention of Webb et al.:

> The most persuasive evidence comes through a triangulation of measurement practices. If a proposition can survive the onslaught of a series of imperfect

measures, with all their irrelevant error, confidence is increased by minimizing error in each instrument and by a reasonable belief in the different and divergent effects of the sources of error.[15]

Long-term measures, on the other hand, address the issue of transfer from school experience to life experience or, simply put, the long-term effects of schooling. At present, "long-term effects" has had a limited definition in the research and evaluations conducted on service learning. In most cases, such works have actually involved relatively short-term follow-up studies ranging from a few weeks to a few months and on rare occasions a few years after completion of a project.[16]

Studying Relationships between Adult Characteristics and Project Goals

From a methodological perspective, the study of the relationships between adult characteristics (e.g., knowledge, skill, attitudes) and project goals might generally be done in one of four ways. The first involves longitudinal studies of students who have completed particular kinds of service learning programs. One might, for example, follow the participants in a service learning project from graduation through adulthood, periodically recording their experiences and attitudes.[17] This method has obvious advantages because the researcher can be reasonably certain about the nature of the service learning program being studied, since complete and accurate descriptions of it should be available. Similarly, by having continuous access during the longitudinal study to participants who had completed the service learning program, the researcher can be reasonably certain about the characteristics of those participants. In addition, statistical analyses of data may be used to provide control for subsequent events (in the family or in occupations) that could have influenced participants' original attitudes. The method may suffer, however, if subjects drop out of the study or if they become aware of its purposes. Finally, this method will not expedite timely decision making or inform debate since years must pass before data are available.[18]

A second method involves the analysis of recollections of adults who have particular characteristics. For example, the researcher/evaluator would identify adults whose lives are characterized by the patterns proposed in the goals of service learning and ask these persons to recall school experiences which they think may have influenced their present lives (hoping, of course, that they mention service learning projects). This method offers the advantage of sample certainty since only those persons who actually demonstrate the desired characteristics would be included. In addition, this method may offer the opportunity to gather data nonreactively since participants need not know why they were chosen or that the researcher is focusing on particular program characteristics. On the other hand, the method is open to serious question inasmuch as it hinges upon subjects' recall, which is highly tenuous as a data source.[19] In the end, the researcher/evaluator would have to verify recollections by examining the projects remembered, an overwhelming task especially if subjects are graduates of multiple schools.

A third method involves analysis of characteristics of adults who are known to have participated in a particular kind of program. In this case, participants in a service learning program are studied at some time after the completion of the program to ascertain whether their present lives reflect the project's stated goals.[20] If program reconstruction is done carefully, this method offers the advantage of providing a strong degree of certainty about the program and those who participated in it, and of avoiding response bias. This method differs from the first study suggested above in that it is a cross-sectional technique, is applied once rather than periodically, and may investigate a program for which no follow-up investigation was originally planned. The third method, however, may be disadvantaged by the lack of control for intervening influential experiences. On the other hand, it may be applied as time and circumstances warrant, that is, when there is a need to offer data to expedite decisions about the desirability of certain types of programs, particularly if long-term longitudinal data are not available.

The fourth method is in reality a hybrid of the first three methods plus the utilization of cohort analyses. The three elements of this methodology are fidelity of implementation, simulated longitudinal study, and cohort sequential design.

Fidelity of implementation. When conducting research on long-term effects it is essential that the program under study be carefully reconstructed so that objectives, activities, and participants can be clearly and accurately described. Lacking such reconstruction, connections between the program and effects must remain as unclear as they would in an experimental study without adequate control. Further, the reconstruction is necessary to identify both the intended effects and the population which serves as the subjects in the study. Beyond this, the reconstructive phase also serves the purpose of verifying how the program was implemented and that it was a legitimate example of the planned variation under study.

The fidelity of implementation phase should consist of at least the following activities:

1. acquisition and perusal of various documents, including school board records, newspaper and magazine accounts of projects, state department of public instruction records, descriptions of projects contained in professional literature, evaluation documents submitted to accrediting agencies, records maintained by the local government and public library, curriculum records maintained by the school;
2. interviews with administrators, teachers, town officials, and former students;
3. securing responses to questionnaire items in which subjects are asked to indicate whether they actually participated in the project(s) under study.

Simulated longitudinal study. Time- and age-related responses could be included to aid in reconstructing or simulating a longitudinal study. Interview schedules and questionnaire items would be constructed so as to indicate whether the experiences mentioned by interviewees reflect the entire period of adulthood or an early segment or recent part of their adult life. Answers to questions related to a specific time (e.g., after five years, ten years) would contribute information on such issues as: "After many years following engagement in the service learning project is there maximum involvement in formal community organizations?"

Cohort sequential design. Where longitudinal sequences can be constructed and program consistency verified, school records and other demographic databases will be used to construct a cohort sequential design,[21] a design which addresses the issue of generational effects as a source of error impairing the internal validity (meaning) of cross-sectional studies and the external validity (generalizability) of longitudinal studies.

For example, it should be possible to collect data on students born in 1980 who entered a service learning project at age 10 and left at 14 years of age, and compare these data to students who were born in 1984 and also entered the project at age 10 and left at age 14. By constructing many such sequences, including some with more disparate dates of birth, it would be possible to ascertain the enduring effect of service learning projects over many years in almost any phase of life. Further, it would be possible to determine if any one generation has benefited more than others from service learning projects by examining involvement rates and outcomes.

Equally valid in this discussion of long-term effects are the steps in the triangulation of measurement mentioned earlier in the discussion of short-term measurement. However, the commitment to long-term effects introduces at least one additional step into the triangulation process—sample integrity. Population today is highly mobile, even in rural environments. If research into long-term effects of service learning is to have an adequate database, it is necessary to have current addresses of participants. Schools are ordinarily not among those notified when alumni addresses change. However, schools with active alumni organizations can be contacted to learn how they maintain contact with graduates.

USING OTHER POPULATIONS IN RESEARCH ON SERVICE LEARNING

Support exists in the literature for the utilization of experimental and quasi-experimental designs for evaluation of and research on service learning projects.[22] As Hamilton points out, "The main point to be made here is that simply measuring some sort of change among program participants provides us an inadequate basis for inferring that the change resulted from participation in the program. It is also necessary to compare program participants with nonparticipants using the same measures."[23]

These "nonparticipants" constitute a comparison group rather than a control group. They constitute a comparison group because they will have had a known but different intervention from that provided in the service learning program of record. Care must be taken to provide a complete documentation and description of the comparison program to facilitate the answering of such questions as whether the young people in this group have attitudes, motivations, and interests similar to the project students. Obviously, questions of age, race, gender, and socioeconomic status of the comparison group will be included.

For an even richer interpretation of the findings, it is suggested that educators involved in the delivery of a service learning program serve as a database. In the short term, data on teacher practices and attitudes may contribute to the refinement of the program; in the long term, the data may suggest teaching strategies, skills, and attitudes that could be incorporated into preservice and in-service teacher education programs. Data should also be collected from community members affected by the project to identify potential attitudinal and economic support for such projects at a future date. Letters of feasibility and support from consumers continue to play a large role in institutionalizing projects and obtaining outside funding.

In summary, a complete and rich database can and should exist in service learning education. From this database, knowledge can be generated to judge the effectiveness of individual projects and to influence the conduct and training of educators. The generation of this knowledge requires practitioners and social scientists to make systematic and deliberate plans at the inception of a project to ascertain the short- and long-term effects of their money, work, and emotional investment. To paraphrase an old saying, any service learning project worth doing is worth evaluating and researching carefully.

Notes

1. James A. Beane, Conrad F. Toepfer, Sr., and Samuel J. Alessi, Jr., *Curriculum Planning and Development* (Boston: Allyn and Bacon, 1986).

2. Richard P. Lipka, James A. Beane, and B. E. O'Connell, *Community Service Projects: Citizenship in Action* (Bloomington, Ind.: Phi Delta Kappa Educational Foundation, 1985).

3. James A. Beane, Joan Turner, David Jones, and Richard P. Lipka, "Long-term Effects of Community Service Programs," *Curriculum Inquiry* 11 (1981): 143-155.

4. Blaine Worthen and James R. Sanders, *Educational Evaluation: Alternative Approaches and Practical Guidelines* (New York: Longman, 1987).

5. Ibid. See also, Henry W. Riecken, *The Volunteer Work Camp: A Psychological Evaluation* (Cambridge, Mass.: Addison-Wesley, 1952).

6. Donald T. Campbell and Julian C. Stanley, *Experimental and Quasi-experimental Designs for Research* (Chicago: Rand McNally, 1963).

7. See, for example, Lee J. Cronbach, "Course Improvement through Evaluation," *Teachers College Record* 64 (1963): 672-683; Robert E. Stake, "The Countenance of Educational Evaluation," *Teachers College Record* 68 (1967): 532-540; Malcolm M. Provus, "Evaluation of Ongoing Programs in the Public School System," in *Educational Evaluation: New Roles, New Means*, edited by Ralph W. Tyler, Sixty-eighth Yearbook of the National Society for the Study of Education, Part 2 (Chicago: University of Chicago Press, 1969), pp. 242-283.

8. Riecken, *The Volunteer Work Camp.*

9. Joan G. Schine and Diane Harrington, *Youth Participation for Early Adolescents: Learning and Serving in the Community* (Bloomington, Ind.: Phi Delta Kappa Educational Foundation, 1982); Margaret F. Kelliher, "Community Service Learning: One School's Story," *Equity and Excellence in Education* 26, no. 2 (1993): 12-14; Carol W. Kinsley, "Community Service Learning as Pedagogy," *Equity and Excellence in Education* 26, no. 2 (1993): 53-59; Susan Seigel and Virginia Rockwood, "Democratic Education, Student Empowerment, and Community Service: Theory and Practice," *Equity and Excellence in Education* 26, no. 2 (1993): 66-70.

10. Ralph W. Tyler, "General Statement on Evaluation," *Journal of Educational Research* 35 (1942): 492-501.

11. Edward G. Olsen, editor and chief author, *School and Community* (New York: Prentice-Hall, 1954), p. 123.

12. See Eugene R. Smith and Ralph W. Tyler, *Appraising and Recording Student Progress* (New York: Harper, 1942).

13. Stephen S. Hamilton, "Experiential Learning Programs for Youth," *American Journal of Education* 88 (1980): 179-215.

14. Eugene J. Webb, Donald T. Campbell, R. D. Schwartz, and Lee Sechrest, *Unobtrusive Measures: Nonreactive Research in the Social Sciences* (Chicago: Rand McNally, 1966).

15. Ibid., p. 3.

16. Lipka, Beane, and O'Connell, *Community Service Projects.*

17. See, for example, Jerald B. Bachman, Patrick M. O'Malley, and J. Johnson, "Blueprint for a Longitudinal Study of Adolescent Boys," in *Youth in Transition*, vol. VI (Ann Arbor, Mich.: Institute for Social Research, 1978).

18. Paul B. Baltes and L. R. Goulet, "Exploration of Developmental Variables by Manipulation and Simulation of Age Differences in Behavior," *Human Development* 14 (1971): 149-170.

19. Marian R. Yarrow, John D. Campbell, and Roger V. Barton, "Recollections of Childhood: A Study of the Retrospective Method," *Monographs of the Society for Research in Child Development* 35, no. 5 (1970): 1-83.

20. Beane, Turner, Jones, and Lipka, "Long-term Effects of Community Service Programs"; Lipka, Beane, and O'Connell, *Community Service Projects.*

21. K. Warner Schaie, "A General Model for the Study of Developmental Problems," *Psychological Bulletin* 64 (1965): 92-107; L. R. Goulet, "Longitudinal and Time-lag Designs in Educational Research: An Alternative Sampling Model," *Review of Educational Research* 45 (1975): 505-523.

22. See, for example, Riecken, *The Volunteer Work Camp*; Campbell and Stanley, *Experimental and Quasi-experimental Designs for Research*; Hamilton, "Experiential Learning Programs for Youth."

23. Hamilton, "Experiential Learning Programs for Youth," p. 197.

CHAPTER V

Service Learning in Curriculum Reform

GENE R. CARTER

We are living through a period when our entire conception of human knowledge—what we know, what we believe, and how we apply those beliefs in the classroom—is being challenged. Daily our schools face the challenge of new realities. The classroom environment is no longer protected from the impact of the outside world. Our vision of the kinds of schools we want often collides with the daily tasks of surviving in the schools we have inherited. No aspect of school reform can escape the impact of this period of widespread change. We are challenged to rethink our most basic assumptions about the changing school curriculum.

As educators seek to transform current practice into something more appropriate and effective for the twenty-first century, they must contend with conflicting community opinions, declining resources, and families in crisis. As we face the new millennium, knowledge continues to explode and the decisions we must make about what is important for children to learn become more complex. These decisions will be made and remade in the years ahead; curriculum content will be constantly reconsidered and altered to encompass new knowledge. But in this rapidly changing environment, the obligation to equip children with the tools and skills they will need to live in a society of diversity, to make responsible and informed decisions, and to work collaboratively is a constant. The classroom will need to become more closely connected to the outside world. Service learning, as well as other types of action learning, can make that connection and can link the community to the curriculum in ways that bring new meaning to what is learned in school.

As communities have become increasingly concerned about the alienation of their young people, service learning has gained momentum. With the realization that curriculum has not changed significantly since John Dewey called for school reform, there are those who

Gene R. Carter is Executive Director of the Association for Supervision and Curriculum Development, Alexandria, Virginia.

see the components of service learning—citizenship, caring, community building, and active pedagogies—as major agents for school reform and for re-engaging youth.

Service learning offers a philosophical challenge to traditional ways of thinking about education. By integrating efforts to understand and address the community's needs into the curriculum, we can create a focal point for showing students the connection between school and the real world. As James Beane reminds us, the curriculum must make "sense as a whole; and its parts, whatever they are, are unified and connected by that sense of the whole."[1] Service learning programs challenge participants to make connections between service experiences and academic learning. As students perform a service activity that applies curriculum concepts, they can see how the learning in separate disciplines is in fact interrelated, and how that learning applies to their own lives.

National Standards

There is growing advocacy for a national voice in the curriculum to provide coherence and a standard of accountability. Proponents claim such a system would better serve our national interest and meet our economic needs. In the national debate, curriculum is seen as one mechanism for improving student performance, measured against national goals and standards of achievement. But our vision must extend beyond the development of national standards to include an articulated and acceptable concept of the type of system and schools that will help all children attain high outcomes. "This vision must reflect the values, understandings, and conditions of each state or locality and serve as the basis for policy design."[2]

Standards are not simply directives from the top. They must be translated at the state level into curriculum frameworks. It is these frameworks that put national standards into action. Service learning supports and enriches these frameworks by providing opportunities for students to apply the concepts contained in the frameworks.

Many education leaders see national standards as a profound shift in the governance of public education. Changes in curriculum call into question what is worth knowing and how knowledge should be organized. Today's developing standards reach beyond what students should know to what they should be able to do. Service learning enables the student to make sense of the concepts in the curriculum by applying them in real life situations. When the educational program encourages the students to take the academic enterprise of the classroom into the community, it provides students with an effective means of reinforcing their learning.

Whether standards and assessment processes are developed at national, state, or local levels, their effectiveness will depend on the degree to which classroom teachers are able to use the standards to improve student learning. The teacher who uses service learning to reinforce the teaching of abstract concepts can turn the standards into significant tools for teaching and learning. Service learning can thus help drive the transformation of teaching. This is already evident in some classrooms, especially in those states where the State Framework includes a requirement for service projects. As innovative programs are introduced, information about them is disseminated, often by the originating teacher or by the local or state education agency.

Many of the current reform initiatives, including the setting of standards, aspire to very ambitious achievement for students. These results are not likely to be achieved with textbook-bound or recitation-style teaching. Experiential learning, as exemplified in service learning, can be an aid in making the abstract concrete for students struggling to understand complex concepts.

From Delivering Knowledge to Facilitating Learning

Today, we must transform schools from teaching centers to learning organizations that support active learning. For a change of this magnitude to occur, we must shift our thinking about education. In practice, we must shift from a mode of delivering knowledge to a mode of facilitating learning. New roles for teachers must be forged.

In the 1990s, children in our schools are racially, ethnically, and linguistically more diverse than a decade ago; and this trend will continue into the future. Moreover, by the year 2000, a quarter of the nation's children are expected to be living in poverty, compared with about 20 percent in 1990. Additionally, the United States Department of Education estimates that the proportion of at-risk students will range from 20 to 40 percent. Since the nation's future is tied to the use of these children's talents, educators and the public must pay attention to their needs. Clearly, children coming into today's schools are different; and we need new ideas to help them succeed. Moreover, the concern over educational equity, the increased pressure for accountability, and the emphasis on the need for national standards give teachers mixed messages regarding the extent of their influence and autonomy.

Through curriculum inquiry, practitioners discover a coherent set of questions around which to construct a curriculum crafted by both the individual and collective actions of teachers. Concomitantly, service learning, as a teaching methodology, has the potential to revitalize our classrooms and provide the kind of learning and experiences students need to lead a successful and fulfilling life. Teachers who integrate service learning into the curriculum assume the new role of "coach," helping students to make informed decisions and to use their knowledge in solving problems. As students become less dependent on teachers to provide answers, they learn from their own experiences. They work with professionals and community members to jointly determine needs, courses of action, and ways to measure successes. Service learning encourages collaborative effort; students learn to understand problems in more complex ways, and work on alternative solutions. The evidence shows that service learning benefits students academically, socially, and psychologically.

Public schools have traditionally been called on to perform the most heroic of tasks: the shaping of the next generation of Americans. Similarly, teachers are being asked, as never before, to diagnose the needs of students and provide appropriate learning activities to ensure success. At a time when these demands have become more insistent, and when schools are often criticized for having limited relevance and worth to students, service learning awakens new visions of learning. It presents a vision where people are accountable to one another and work together to shape the common good. By moving beyond traditional teaching and by using the community as a classroom, teachers can provide experiences in the community that reinforce what the students have learned in school. The integration of service learning, then, does not detract from the existing curriculum. In fact, the curriculum is enhanced by service learning.

Professional Development for Service Learning

As we approach the twenty-first century, the current cohort of teachers will play a major role in reshaping and improving our schools. We must commit ourselves to providing the best education and training possible for prospective classroom teachers. Teachers in public schools must be prepared to look beyond the backdrop of societal and economic conditions and focus on what we know we can do to improve curriculum and instruction. School reform has little chance to succeed unless there are reforms in the preparation of teachers. The very best curriculum can become high-quality instruction only if those who teach it are well-qualified and trained, and if they have the time and resources to prepare carefully and to do the necessary followup.

An emerging consensus holds that the kind of experiences typically provided in teacher education programs and programs for professional development for teachers have not gone far enough in preparing teachers for the challenges and opportunities that exist in schools today. The fate of public schools will depend, in large part, on our ability to prepare teachers to deal with the complex problems of our nation's schools.

Colleges and universities play a critical role in preparing teachers to reform schools. Teacher education programs in those institutions must aim to prepare teachers who possess the basic skills of a well-educated person, have substantial knowledge of subject matter, and know how to promote student learning. Such programs must include work with innovative practices that have strong theoretical foundations as well as with well-established methodologies.

The core ideas of service learning as a methodology of teaching are based on the concept of direct experience as an aid to learning, in contrast with learning acquired through reading, listening to lectures, or, in an increasingly technological environment, the ubiquitous electronic media. From time to time, the notion surfaces that technology, and especially, in some circumstances, the computer, will threaten the teacher's role. Far from being replaced, teachers will become more powerful, more effective, and more needed than ever before. Programs of teacher education will need to offer training in accessing information and in techniques for teaching students to use and manage our dramatically expanding information base.

Teachers will become a resource for students in finding and using information, in applying technologies to assess the value of that information, and in strategies for using that information to solve problems. At the same time, they will play a critical role in guiding students in finding a balance between the impersonal world of the media and the world of human interaction. Service learning can be an antidote to the increasingly isolated world of simulation and virtual reality children experience in front of the television and at their computer workstations.[3]

Schools of education may choose to prepare students for leadership roles in service learning by providing opportunities for the students themselves to participate in service learning experiences. Service learning programs enable students to learn by participating in real life situations where they are providing service to the community, to the school, or to individuals. These experiences can be a source for identifying problems to be studied in the academic program or can serve to reinforce and give additional meaning to concepts already encountered in their studies. Recognizing the potential of service learning for motivating students and for developing democratic values, teacher training institutions should include providing tomorrow's teachers with the special skills necessary for leaders in experiential learning.

Initiating a service learning program requires that teachers and others who will be participating in it are adequately prepared for the responsibilities such work entails. For example, they will need to become well acquainted with the community served by the school. They will need to know how to locate opportunities for service in the community. They must know how to establish and maintain collaborative relationships with agencies that are potential service sites for students. They will need to become skillful and creative in determining how the service learning program can be integrated with the instructional program of the school. Most important, they will need to be able to facilitate the process through which students regularly reflect seriously on their experiences in a service role—a critical feature of any well-run service learning program. The benefits that students can derive from participating in service learning do not occur automatically. They are most likely to occur when a well-planned program is under the guidance of sensitive teachers who are well prepared to provide the necessary leadership.

Ongoing Professional Development for Service Learning

Professional development continues far beyond the teacher training program. High-quality, career-long professional development is important not only for teachers, but also for administrators, curriculum specialists, and all others concerned with the implementation of reforms in schooling. This is especially true when new developments on the educational scene place demands upon school personnel whose previous training and experience have not prepared them for new responsibilities. Although service learning programs are increasingly found in schools across the country, as is clearly demonstrated in this volume, in many schools service learning is still a new idea.

While a service learning program may begin with the involvement of only one or two teachers in a school, the fact that the program exists in that school should reflect a schoolwide commitment to the underlying purposes and philosophy of service learning. One of the purposes of professional development in such a school would be to develop that shared commitment, so that the program is viewed positively and is supported even by staff members who are not directly involved.

Teachers who are most directly involved in service learning can be expected to encounter unanticipated problems and situations with which they would welcome assistance. In addition to the support they should be able to find in a strong local professional development program, they can look to outside sources. One such source is SELNET, the Service/Experiential Learning Network established in 1994 under the sponsorship of the Association for Supervision and Curriculum Development. This Network identifies its mission as "to help other educators identify persons and resources for implementing a service learning/experiential learning model as a part of the school reform movement. . . ." Its agenda includes offering opportunities for professional growth, and providing "resources and connections for innovative school districts desiring a 21st Century vision for schooling." SELNET held its first annual Curriculum Workshop in June, 1996.

Conveying Values through Service Learning

Historically, America's public schools have had the dual role of making students "smart" and "good." Traditionally, families, communities, schools, and religious institutions worked in concert to teach and mutually reinforce shared ethical values. During recent decades, however, each of these institutions has become less effective in transmitting those values. The media remind us daily about the country's crisis of character. People from all walks of life are concerned about values and character in children and, indeed, of the broader society as well. What should educators do when they recognize the magnitude of the values problem but also understand that "moralizing" by itself is of little consequence?

While it is generally accepted that the primary responsibility for the teaching of values lies in the home, we must acknowledge that the school has a major role in transmitting to the next generation the values that are at the core of a democratic society. There are problems for schools in determining how to respond to the growing pressure to teach values. Although the question of "whose values" should be taught is frequently used in a manner that pits one faction of the community against another, there is abundant evidence that in community after community people of all races, creeds, and socioeconomic groups have broad agreement on a significant set of core values. The Public Agenda Foundation report entitled *First Things First: What Americans Expect from the Public Schools*, found that 95 percent of Americans say schools should teach honesty and the importance of telling the truth. Ninety-three percent of respondents said schools should teach "students to solve problems without violence."[4] Other items near the top of the public's "values to teach" list reiterate a concern for equality, fairness and "getting along." The common core of shared values is generally believed to include, as well, responsibility, caring, civic participation, respect for self and others, and other attributes of constructive citizenship. Schools in particular will acknowledge the values of academic integrity, civility, and self-discipline.

Young people spend much of their lives in schools. In schools they will learn, either by chance or design, moral lessons about how people behave. Our schools must provide opportunities for students to discover what is most worth knowing, as they prepare not only to be good citizens, but also good workers and good private individuals. As education leaders we can be powerful catalysts for changing what is actually done inside our schools. There is no way of teaching subjects without teaching values. There is no such thing as value-neutral schools or value-free education. Schools teach values every day by design or default. "Do as I say, not as I do" does not work. Quality teaching, combined with an ethic of caring and respect for students as learners, is a strong combination of behaviors that creates a positive moral climate in the classroom. The school that includes service learning as an integral part of the educational experience sends students a clear message: As a community, one of the values to which we subscribe is that of service to others and of constructive participation in the society. A well-designed service learning program provides not only the opportunity to serve, but through consistent structured reflection encourages the participants to explore the meaning and moral implications of their service.

As we close out the turbulent twentieth century and prepare our schools for the new millennium, schools need to look at themselves through a moral lens and consider how everything that goes on in schools affects the values and character of students—if we care about the future of our society and our children. Integrating the historical legacy and values of the civil society into every aspect of the curriculum provides a context and framework for children to understand the importance of service learning in the community. It helps them develop an ethic of service, and the character and habits of good community participation needed to ensure preparation for responsible citizenship. Service learning can improve learning and instill an ethic of service and citizenship in our youth. By engaging youth in learning activities, service learning provides an education in good citizenship.

Conclusion

Most educators now understand that in today's world, in the words of Albert Einstein, "problems cannot be solved by the same level of thinking that created them." That is why to compete in the global economy of the twenty-first century we must raise education standards, teach more appropriate curriculum, and restructure how we deliver instruction in our schools.

During the last decade educators learned, sometimes painfully, that trying to "fix" parts of education systems did not have an enduring impact on learner achievement. Rapid advances in information and communications technologies, as well as critical social and economic issues, challenge comfortable characterizations about the purpose, process, and place of education.

New learning theories, new technologies, economic imperatives, motivational and social issues call for programmatic, methodological, and technological innovations if we are to implement the education reform agenda. Curriculum revision is at the heart of education reform; the new curriculum must be rigorous, focused, and trimmed to the essentials with clear and attainable goals. Moving toward a coherent curriculum offers possibilities of utility and connectedness among everyday activities in schools and educational experiences for students that make more sense in terms of education's larger purposes.

Across the country, many programs have been created that address serious community needs. Service learning is a growing movement for social change that complements and reinforces the work of school curricula. Because service learning provides a way for students to apply knowledge and skills, it should not be seen as an add-on. Instead, it should be closely coordinated with the curriculum. Combining service and learning is a powerful tool for enhancing education, revitalizing communities and teaching the importance of community participation as well as an appreciation of democratic values. Students who serve learn skills in communication, problem solving, and leadership. Schools that adopt service learning as an integral part of curriculum are redefining their roles in communities. Service learning offers a philosophical challenge to traditional ways of thinking about education, and is one way to help students understand that their lives today are a part of the continuum that leads directly to the future.

Notes

1. James Beane, *Toward a Coherent Curriculum* (Alexandria, Va.: Association for Supervision and Curriculum Development, 1995).

2. Jennifer O'Day, "System Reform and Goals 2000," in *National Issues in Education: Goals 2000 and School-to-Work*, edited by John F. Jennings (Bloomington, Ind.: Phi Delta Kappa International and Washington, D.C.: Institute for Educational Leadership, 1995).

3. Jeremy Rifkin, "Preparing the Next Generation for the Civil Society," *Education Week*, 31 January 1996, pp. 44, 33.

4. Jean Johnson and John Immerwahr, *First Things First: What Americans Expect from the Public Schools* (New York: Public Agenda Foundation, 1994).

CHAPTER VI

Service Learning in the Comer School Development Program

NORRIS M. HAYNES AND JAMES P. COMER

The value of a good education lies in the extent to which it prepares students for life as productive members of their communities and the wider society. Schools in many ways are microcosms of the society. Therefore, the adult members of the school community—parents and staff—must support the total development of all children, preparing each child to be a productive, contributing member of society.

The need for understanding, tolerance, fairness, and respect in American society has never been greater. Service to others, particularly those who are in need and less fortunate, and service to the larger society through unselfish acts of caring and kindness are defining characteristics of a great and compassionate nation. But because of the increasing pluralism in our society, uncertainty about the future, and skepticism surrounding services to the poor and the most needy, there sometimes seems to be a retreat by many from the altruism and compassion which have helped to make this nation great. Many educators believe that service learning in schools can nurture these qualities and should be an important and integrated component of students' educational experience to prepare them for life and for service in the larger community.

Schools are complex communities where important lessons about life are taught and learned every day just as in the larger society. Children and adults with diverse individual and cultural backgrounds are brought together in learning communities where a healthy respect for the dignity of others must be at the center of the educational enterprise.

A school's program is most effective when derived through a conscientious effort to address and satisfy each child's needs, with sensitivity to the past and present social and personal experiences of students.

Norris Haynes is Associate Professor at the Yale University Child Study Center and Director of Research and Evaluation in the School Development Program. James Comer is the Maurice Falk Professor of Child Psychiatry in the Yale University Child Study Center and Associate Dean of the Yale University School of Medicine.

Efforts to know and understand children and their families undergird the most effective educational interventions in schools, including the Comer School Development Program, which we briefly describe in this chapter.

In our most successful schools, children too are taught to become more aware of the idiosyncrasies and needs of others, and to respond with caring and sensitivity. Just as in the larger society, in schools the past and present life experiences of all students and adults are interconnected and interrelated in powerful ways that play themselves out in a dynamic process of reciprocal influence and impact. Students must learn that their actions and behaviors have significant impact on others, just as their lives are influenced by the actions of adults.

It is for this reason that the organization, climate, curriculum, instructional methodologies, and assessment strategies in our schools and classrooms must engage our children in ways that stimulate their interest in becoming fully participating and productive citizens of their communities. In schools we are preparing children for life, and life in the larger society requires the capacity to live and work well with others. Schools today must assume a major role in inculcating positive prosocial values.

In a compelling and provocative address to the National Association of Independent Schools, the late Ernest L. Boyer, then president of the Carnegie Foundation for the Advancement of Teaching, spoke of the social and moral imperative of education to prepare young people for life and service as members of their communities. He said, "A basic feature of the social and moral imperative of education is to help students see the connectedness of all things—social, personal, religious—to the past, to the natural, and to the eternal."[1]

This "social and moral imperative" is essential to the development of character. It teaches responsibility, caring, altruism, and a respect for the dignity and basic human rights of others, while caring for and respecting oneself. Thus, education extends beyond the learning of academic subject matter and the development of good habits of mind. It is also concerned with the cultivation of good habits of heart and work.

Schools as Service and Learning Communities: The Comer School Development Program

Boyer's observation reflected the thinking behind the early work of the second author of this chapter when he began his work in two New

Haven public schools in 1968. In developing the Comer School Development Program, his intention was to help establish school contexts in which children learned the essential values of life while having their developmental needs met by caring adults.

He tells the story of a fourth grader who had just transferred to a school that had been using our School Development Program. When another student accidentally stepped on this youngster's foot his fists immediately went up to challenge the innocent offender to fight. Other students quickly gathered around and chided his readiness to fight: "Hey, man, we don't do that in this school." His fists fell and he hung his head with embarrassment, recognizing that he was in a different school environment where problems were talked through and not fought out. There was no other recorded incident of this youngster being so eager to fight.

The lesson in this story is that caring, responsibility, and respect are positive values that are contagious and can quickly spread. If properly taught in an environment where adults practice them, these values can become entrenched principles that guide behavior among students.

The Comer School Development Program seeks to create positive school environments in which adults and children coexist in challenging and mutually respectful learning communities where good citizenship is encouraged, supported, and rewarded. This is accomplished through the nine elements of the program: three guiding principles (decision making by consensus, collaborative working relationships, a no-fault approach to problem solving); three operations (staff development, development of a comprehensive school plan, continuing assessment and modification of programs and strategies); and three components that provide the infrastructure for the community (the School Planning and Management Team, the Student-Staff Support Team, and the Parent Program).

THE THREE COMPONENTS

The School Planning and Management Team (SPMT) includes parent, student, and staff representatives. It is the planning and governance structure of the school. This team develops a comprehensive plan for the school and orchestrates all school activities, including staff development, assessment, and modification. The team is responsible for monitoring the academic and social climate of the school. In a real sense, this team parallels governance structures in the larger democratic society, where the voices of the people are heard through their representatives. The presence of students on the team at some middle and high schools provides a unique and important opportunity for students to practice democracy and collaboration, as well as to be involved in meaningful dialogue with adults around critical issues that affect their daily lives. The presence of parents on this team reinforces the notion and spirit of collaboration and partnership that we espouse as a society in addressing issues that affect us all, and especially the lives of our children. We seek to bridge the communications gap that often exists between service provider and service consumer.

The Student-Staff Support Team is basically a service group of child development and human relations professionals in the school who address the global climate of the school, as well as individual student, parent, or staff needs. As noted earlier, children and adults bring unique personalities and experiences, as well as diverse needs to the school. As a service community, schools must be able to respond not only to the intellectual and academic challenges that staff, students, and parents face, but also to the psycho-emotional concerns that are often inseparably connected to intellectual and academic issues. In schools in the Comer School Development Program, this service component is crucial to promoting a healthy academic and psychosocial climate. In many schools this team addresses conflicts among and between students and parents and staff. It provides consultation to staff and counseling for students and families, identifies and develops proactive interventions such as problem solving and conflict resolution skills for students, and assists with the planning of staff development on important and sensitive issues including racial and cultural sensitivity and diversity. This resource has made a tremendous difference in the quality of life for students, parents, and staff in schools across the country.

The Parent Program involves parents in every aspect of the life in the schools in the Comer School Development Program. With parental input at every level, schools truly become caring service and learning communities because parents bring their perspectives as primary caretakers of children and as knowledgeable residents of the larger community in which the school is located. In a recent visit to a Comer School, the first author of this chapter observed and talked with a dozen parents and grandparents as they along with staff and students prepared Thanksgiving boxes for delivery to neighborhood homeless shelters and soup kitchens. During a previous visit to this school, the author observed about the same number of parents and grandparents actively assisting with daily tasks in the school. They feel welcome and appreciated. The school for them is a part of the community, a place where their ideas count, their voices heard, and their support accepted. Service to the school or to the community beyond the school is integral to the "life style" of the school.

THE THREE GUIDING PRINCIPLES

Every community needs principles that guide how members of that community live and work together. In Comer School Development Program schools, the principles of "no-fault," "consensus," and "no paralysis" define the human interactions that take place. "No-fault" means that members of the community do not blame others when problems arise; they are solution-oriented rather than blame-inclined. "Consensus" means that solutions are arrived at with open and respectful discussions, in which each person's ideas are valued. Solutions are identified, prioritized, and tried sequentially, based on agreed-upon procedures. The "no paralysis" principle describes a win-win situation for everyone, with no one—the principal, the staff, or the parents—feeling or being paralyzed. These guiding principles help to create the essential elements of the service climate in schools.

Essential Elements of the Service Climate

The climate of a school is the sum total of the physical conditions, psychosocial dynamics, and human interactions in that school. There are a number of key elements in the climate of any school in which service learning is an important component of the program. These elements are:

- *Sensitivity:* The extent to which a school's staff, students, and parents show awareness of, willingness to consider, and readiness to respond to the special needs of members of the school community.
- *Caring:* The active demonstration of concern and compassion by members of the school community for one another through acts of thoughtfulness and kindness.
- *Trust:* A prevailing sense of interdependence, bonding and confidence in one another among members of the school community.
- *Respect:* A pervasive atmosphere of mutual positive regard among members of the school community.
- *High Expectations:* The maintenance of high performance standards for and among all members of the school community.

- *Dedication:* The individual and collective commitment to service to the school and larger community beyond the normal call of duty.
- *Collaborative Leadership:* The participatory and shared decision making in the school, in which everyone's voice and ideas are heard and valued.

Taken together, these seven elements constitute the psychosocial and human conditions that nurture students' desire to be of service to others in school and in the larger community outside of school. A service orientation is reflected in the manner in which the members of the school community treat one another, and in the spirit of unity and common purpose that they share.

These attributes of school climate, though essential, are not enough. There must also be programs and activities that occur within the school to connect students in a meaningful way to the outside world.

Service Learning Activities

Service learning activities in schools may be internally or externally focused. Both internally and externally focused activities are deliberately connected to students' cognitive and psychosocial developments through well-planned and specific learning opportunities, coupled with reflection.

Internally focused activities. There are many in-school opportunities for service learning. Some of these include work on a school newspaper, serving as classroom monitors or student crossing guards, raising and lowering the school flag, mentoring younger students, and beautifying the school compound by planting flowers in the spring. It is easier with some of these activities than with others to make the connection to cognitive development. For example, work on the school newspaper requires thinking, writing, and organizational skills, as well as good verbal and social interaction skills. Reflecting on one's work and receiving the benefit of feedback from peers and from one's teacher are important developmental aspects of this activity. The raising and lowering of the flag requires little cognitive engagement and little or no reflection or feedback. However, both activities offer recognition for doing something for others and for the school, and both activities are good preparation for service in the larger community.

More altruistic service opportunities can be identified, particularly in schools in poor inner-city and rural communities where large numbers of children come to school undernourished, unkempt, and physically and psychologically abused. Many schools have established procedures through which students can anonymously contribute items of food and clothing to their needier peers. Peer counseling and buddy programs in which students provide social, psychological, and emotional support contribute to an ethos of service. These activities allow students the opportunity to be of service to others while also developing important human relations skills.

Externally focused activities. Externally focused service learning should be an important and integrated part of students' education. Some may question the academic and social benefits to students of spending time outside the classroom and the school. Kielsmeier, however, sees it differently:

> Service learning is not "feel-good," make-work activity to keep young people busy. Carefully planned and well-structured, service learning is a rigorous teaching/learning methodology with the capacity to teach academic information, life skills, and values while allowing students to see themselves as useful energized citizens. Service learning as a learning strategy is directly in keeping with current research on cognition and learning.[2]

Benefits of service learning activities. Spiritual, social, and academic benefits accrue to students from participating in well-designed service learning experiences that include serious and concentrated reflection. Not only are students' characters enhanced but so too are their minds. Their cognitive and intellectual capacities are nourished and nurtured.

The policies and programs in the school reinforce the positive prosocial values that are modeled by the adults and are evident in the seven essential elements of the service climate. Service learning becomes an integral part of the school's ethos. Referring to service learning, Theodore Sizer, chairman of the Coalition of Essential Schools, writes: "This is more than a program; it's part of a culture . . . a way of doing business so that something happens to young people, who then act in a certain way when we're not looking."[3] Students internalize the positive values they learn as a result of their exposure to and participation in service learning activities. Doing good becomes an integrated part of their psyches.

Within the Comer School Development Program, the school's comprehensive plan, which is developed, implemented, and monitored by the School Planning and Management Team, is the vehicle used to translate service goals into constructive service activities.

Service training and preparation in schools occur in many ways. However, these ways may be subsumed within two categories: (1) through active participation in civic and humanitarian activities in the community; (2) through in-school lessons tied to short-term field experiences in preparation for the workplace. The first set of experiences is designed to develop and promote attributes of altruism, civic responsibility, and good citizenship among students while the latter set of experiences is designed to promote career consciousness, work productivity, and economic and financial responsibility and independence.

Although the second set of activities, geared toward career awareness and workplace productivity, are important, authentic service learning refers principally to the first set of experiences in which students learn the value of humanitarian service to others and to the community. These kinds of experiences and their benefits to the community and to students themselves are described elsewhere in this volume.

Many school districts and schools in the School Development Program now incorporate these kinds of service learning opportunities in their comprehensive plans. In one school's comprehensive plan the service goal was to promote good citizenship among students by involving them in meaningful community work linked to their academic work in school. This goal was accomplished by engaging students in a recycling project linked to their study of science, and by arranging for students to spend time in residential facilities for senior citizens where they read to the elderly and engaged in recreational activities with them as part of a social science and human development experience.

Examples of Service Learning in Sarasota County

As a result of the implementation of the Comer School Development Program in Sarasota County some service learning programs have been introduced. Three examples are given here.

PEER MEDIATION TO REDUCE SCHOOL AND COMMUNITY VIOLENCE

The McIntosh Middle School Peer Mediation Project was established to reduce violence in two Sarasota County public schools through the use of peer counseling and mediation. Initial participants in the program included 250 seventh grade students (75 of whom formed the cadre of "peer mediators"), 25 fourth grade students, and 2 trainer/coordinators. The goals of the program are (1) to reduce by at least 10 percent the number of conflicts that lead to violence in the two schools; (2) to assist in meeting the school improvement goal of service learning and character education through improved student communication and conflict resolution skills; (3) to provide conflict resolution/peer mediation training for 66 percent (250) current seventh grade students at McIntosh Middle School; (4) to utilize trained student mediators to coordinate training of 25 selected fourth graders at Fruitville Elementary School, McIntosh's largest feeder school (these students will also plan a curriculum to work in small groups at Fruitville and with the McIntosh population of educable and trainable mentally handicapped students where the goal is to teach communication and conflict resolution skills, and to promote social acceptance of this high-risk population); and (5) through collaboration with the Twelfth Judicial Circuit Court and the Sarasota Bar Association, to offer training opportunities to other schools and community youth programs such as Girls, Inc., and local scout troops as requested.

As a result of these efforts, discipline referrals at McIntosh Middle School were reduced by 14 percent, from 224 incidents in 1993-94 to 192 incidents in 1994-95. In 1995-96, the McIntosh Middle School Peer Mediation Project was refunded to train students in more feeder elementary schools.

The Sarasota High School/Alta Vista School Learn and Serve Project was designed as an intervention vehicle to reduce violent acts and behavior referrals. The project collaborated with Drug Awareness and Resistance Education (DARE) program from the Sarasota City Police Department, and with court mediators from the Twelfth Judicial Circuit Court. Representatives from these agencies, along with school personnel and students, functioned as the core in the planning and implementation of the program. The program was integrated into the Peer Counselor program at the high school and the "skills for growing" curriculum and classroom guidance instruction at the elementary school. The purpose was to develop effective emotional management and self-control in order to control aggressive verbal and/or physical behavior. The goals of the program were directly related to reducing student confrontations at school and on the school bus. The resulting referral rate directly related to identified aggressive behavior.

One of the outcomes of this program was that fifty students from Sarasota learned and utilized peer counseling and peer mediation skills as revealed by observations of facilitators. The mediation was considered successful if there were no repeat incidents involving the same students. Elementary students trained in peer counseling and peer mediation showed a higher self-concept, less aggressive behavior, and, as measured by teacher observation and a pre/post check list completed by teachers, fewer suspensions and teacher referrals.

YOUTH SERVICE LEARNING COUNCIL GRANT, 1995-96

The Sarasota school administration believes that service learning not only assists in improving academic learning, attendance, and graduation rates, but that it also addresses vital community needs and promotes civic responsibility. With this in mind and a history of successful community service learning projects, a Sarasota Learn and Serve Mini Grant program was established. Schools are eligible to apply for funding to implement school-based community service learning projects. Applications are reviewed, evaluated, and selected by a Youth Service Council, with monitoring of the projects done by an adult advisor and the school district's grants manager. The Youth Service Council includes one student selected from each high school and middle school (ten students in all) and two adult advisors (one from high school and one from middle school). The students were trained to serve on the Council. They implemented their own service project (Special Olympics).

Twenty mini grants were awarded to students, teachers, and/or administrators. The accepted proposals included tutoring, recycling, collection drives, Special Olympics, community histories, new student buddies, environmental projects, neighborhood beautification, work with the elderly, and programs for prevention of peer violence. The Youth Service Learning Council Grant was refunded for the 1996-97 school year.

The evidence shows that the service orientation in the Sarasota school district has had a positive impact. Significant changes in the attitudes and behaviors of students, especially in their interactions with one another and with adults, have been noted. Children have become more respectful and caring. They have become more self-confident and feel increasingly a part of a caring, learning community.

In Conclusion

The school is a microcosm of society. Students and the adults in the school community must practice socially responsible behaviors. Service to others must be an essential component of the school's program to develop and nurture the whole child, including prosocial values and wholesome attitudes toward others in school and in society at large.

Service learning occurs most effectively in schools where certain basic conditions exist. These conditions include:

1. governance structures that allow for the meaningful and constructive input of all members of the school community in making decisions about service programs and that coordinate all service activities in the school;

2. service and support structures that capitalize on the knowledge and skills of members of the school community in identifying, developing, and providing needed services to the school community, particularly students and families;

3. a climate that is caring, supportive, and responsive to individual needs;

4. a clearly articulated plan for engaging students in internal and external service learning activities that contribute to their academic and psychosocial growth and development.

Notes

1. Ernest L. Boyer, "The Educated Heart: The Social and Moral Imperative of Education," Paper presented at the Annual Conference of the National Association of Independent Schools, New York City, 1981, p. 3.

2. Jim Kielsmeier, "Foreword," in Susan J. Poulsen, *Learning Is the Thing: Insights Emerging from a National Conference on Service-Learning, School Reform, and Higher Education* (Roseville, Minn.: National Youth Leadership Council, 1994).

3. Theodore Sizer, *Horace's School: Redesigning the American High School* (New York: Houghton Mifflin, 1992).

CHAPTER VII

Service Learning in the Classroom: Practical Issues

WINIFRED PARDO

By integrating site-based experiences into the curriculum, service learning makes it possible for schools to enrich their students' learning and at the same time to benefit the community. But inevitably questions arise, roadblocks are perceived, timidity reigns.

Many schools, both public and private and elementary through high school, have raised questions, then moved on to success. The Shoreham-Wading River Middle School in exurban Long Island is a case in point. Its experience may help to illuminate practical considerations for others contemplating service learning.

The Shoreham-Wading River Middle School (recently renamed for Albert Prodell, the retiring president of the Board of Education) is a school of 550 students in grades 6, 7, and 8. Located seventy miles east of New York City in a predominantly white, middle-class community, the school was one of the pioneers in the middle school movement and has received national attention for its innovative programs, among them service learning.

The idea of involving students in work in the community as part of their regular school curriculum was initiated in 1973 by an eighth grade English/social studies teacher and the school's principal. Since that time the program has expanded to include the entire school community, with students serving in many community agencies.

In 1973, there were few models for school-initiated community service and, therefore, for Shoreham-Wading River, not a few fears. Would service learning be perceived as taking time from the school day already crowded with all the things children needed to know? Would it not detract from academic "content" and other skills? Teachers and administrators were already on overload. How could they face additional responsibilities? Yet, if they instituted after-school community service as an alternative to school-day service learning, who

Winifred Pardo was the first coordinator of the service learning program at the Shoreham-Wading River (New York) Middle School. She is now retired.

would organize and supervise it? And would not many students who would benefit the most be unable to participate?

Other questions surfaced. What could students do in the area of service and was curriculum material available? Where could they go and how would they get there? Were there projects that could be done in the school building itself? Next came the questions of how to get support from co-workers and the district administration. What about time to devote to such a program, to securing funding, transportation, supplies?

Beyond the school organization itself, questions inevitably arose concerning parent approval and the possibility that parents would feel that field work would detract from students' learning. And what about community agencies? Would they want to be bothered with volunteers, especially those in late elementary or middle school grades? These questions and reservations were dealt with, often with far more ease than might have been expected. This school and others have successfully implemented service learning. In some cases, programs have been in operation for a great many years.

Beginning a Service Learning Program

At Shoreham-Wading River we began with four basic assumptions, the first one recognizing that children at all ages, at all grade levels, and at all levels of ability are capable of service learning to different degrees and at different levels of sophistication. We also assumed that the vital contribution that service learning makes to a young person's development and to the life of the larger community is worth whatever is required to establish a service learning program. Our third assumption was that service learning can and should be incorporated as part of the regular school day and that its site-based work should be integrally connected with academic core subjects as well as with the arts, music, and physical education. Even if the service component were to be scheduled after school hours, the program would remain under the sponsorship and supervision of school personnel. Our fourth assumption was validated by subsequent experience: the possibilities for meaningful service and for firsthand learning experience were extensive. Once we began to reach beyond the school itself we were well-received by community agencies. For many years now, Shoreham-Wading River has had a waiting list of agencies desiring student help.

A fundamental lesson we learned was the importance of realistic and thorough planning. We avoided the common mistakes of "biting off more than you can chew" and being careless about details. The establishment of credibility with school officials, with agency personnel and clientele, and with students and parents finally "sold" the program. To be specific, this meant:

1. When arranging for students to work at a work site, definite days, times, and dates for beginning and ending the project were established. The students were there without fail, and were prepared.

2. Definite times were scheduled for students to have orientation to the site and its population; for evaluation and discussion of how things were going, including problems and possible strategies; for preparation for activities by having ideas and materials available.

3. School personnel supervised students in the field so that agency personnel did not feel "put upon" for programming and supervising. In instances where this was impossible, frequent visits were made and parent volunteers were utilized.

4. Careful attention was paid to paper work: schedules, who was doing what and when, thank-you letters, acknowledgments.

5. Public relations were crucial. The benefits of service learning were communicated in district publications and local newspapers, and presentations were made to the Board of Education and to agency boards. Student presentations, photo displays, written comments by teachers, students, agency personnel, and parents were assembled.

If at the beginning we had struggled to set up elaborate committees representing many constituencies and to establish procedures requiring several levels of approval, we might have encountered difficulties. Instead, as the five steps described above were accomplished by small groups of students and teachers, the quality and benefits of the program became apparent and we felt confident in expanding and in welcoming other teachers aboard with projects of their own. We made sure that new projects adhered to the high standards set by the initial program.

Any school staff contemplating service learning must decide whether the program should be districtwide or confined to one building. Our experience at Shoreham-Wading River, as noted above, suggests the wisdom of beginning small. An individual teacher or a team of teachers at a single grade level may begin the process, first securing the blessing of the administration and promises of support from parents and the Board of Education. The teachers have an existing group of students, class time for orientation and preparation, and access to materials. Schedules are adjusted to allow for double periods or some other suitable block of time during which students can move into the community. Teachers need to be allowed the time and flexibility to implement the program. Some schools have implemented service learning throughout a school at the encouragement, or even mandate, of the administration. In these cases, the expectation was that adequate support, such as block scheduling, teacher time for preparation, the services of support staff, supplies, curriculum materials, and transportation would be provided. Excitement and creativity could reign as each class or team developed its own service learning experience. When service learning was specifically mandated by the administration, the challenge was to inspire enthusiasm and creativity among potentially reluctant faculty.

In districts where the administration and the Board of Education elect to institute service learning districtwide, the challenge is to encourage "ownership" among teachers and building administrators so that energy and creativity are forthcoming. Of crucial importance is the involvement of those affected at all levels in the planning process, as well as effective communication with the community. A districtwide commitment to service learning has the obvious advantage of assuring the financial and logistic support needed. It has the potential for providing valuable experiences for large numbers of students and their partners in community agencies. There is, however, also the potential for small "glitches" to be magnified by their high visibility, with the consequent possibility of eroding support.

A first step for teachers initiating service learning is identification of possible sites for work in the community, and of the classroom components which might round out the program. Students from intermediate grades and above may be involved at this stage in brainstorming for possible service themes or projects and for identifying field sites. Once approvals are granted, students may select agencies, or decide on what course of action to pursue on problems of concern to the community.

At Shoreham-Wading River and elsewhere the actual planning and implementation of any given component of service learning are the province of an individual teacher or coordinator, or perhaps a small group of staff. While considering the possibilities, teachers and others may visit schools that have established programs where they may observe students at work in their field sites. Studying materials and ideas gathered from agencies such as the National Helpers Network, planners draw upon the experience of pioneers in service learning programs. They consult with teachers and others who are active in successful programs.

Initial contacts may be made with many possible sites for service learning experiences such as adult homes, day care centers, special education classes, Head Start classes, animal shelters, museums, outdoor education programs. Because agency staffs have frequently been disappointed by earlier experiences with volunteers who proved less than dependable, they must be assured that the students will not disappoint them.

One lesson learned at Shoreham-Wading River is that any project should allow for continuity. While the "one-shot" community service project, such as singing Christmas carols at a nursing home, is commendable, no continuing relationships are established, the residents remain remote, and the children are sometimes frightened or repulsed. When the caroling is done at a site where students have been visiting weekly and are able to relate to persons in the audience, it becomes a positive experience. Similarly, a Thanksgiving food drive where the food goes to a community kitchen in which students have been helping serve meals is far more satisfying and educative than assembling food packages for the "generic" poor.

The ideal is for students to work closely with particular individuals and a specific population. It is the depth of relationships formed that best serves the student and the person being served. This suggests a minimum of eight or ten visits or perhaps a full semester. Only then can a student become skilled at what works effectively with a given age group. Only then can a classroom teacher build rich classroom experiences around the field experiences. And only then will the student and his or her teacher get past the stereotypes and fears of working with the elderly or the handicapped or overactive preschoolers.

Finding Opportunities for Service Learning

In asking "Where might we go? What might we do?", program developers learn to look with new eyes at the community and at school programs. For example, students in intermediate grades may tutor children, while they in turn are taught by high school students. Younger children respond enthusiastically to what older students can offer them in the role of "teacher."

Work with handicapped children can provide a particularly productive service learning experience. Beyond the classes which exist within a school district, there are special schools for mentally and/or physically challenged children. Shoreham-Wading River students work at the Maryhaven School, the North Country Learning Center in Stony Brook, and at the St. Charles Learning Center attached to St. Charles Hospital in Port Jefferson, New York.

Many of the elderly are in special need of relationships with children and, in turn, have much to offer. Increasingly, there are "day care" centers for seniors in need of assistance, as well as the traditional recreation centers for those who are more able. Residential facilities include adult homes, health-related facilities, and nursing homes. Many students visit centers like these on a regular basis. Elsewhere, as in Macomb, Illinois, adolescents can shop for and deliver food to the homebound elderly. And the Grandfriends Club in Commack, New York, pairs students with elderly "buddies."

Some schools forge links with animal shelters, recycling centers, marine refuges, wildlife preserves, and outdoor education sites. In Burns, Oregon, elementary school children replant native flora in the Harney High Desert Interpretive Garden. Also in Oregon, ninth and tenth graders rehabilitate trails and other facilities in the Sunrise Youth Camp under the sponsorship of the Beaverton School District and the Outdoor Education Program of the Washington County Education Service District.

Some service models are ideally suited to urban settings. Gardens sprout from formerly littered lots; walls are transformed by budding artists; city blocks are cleaned up. A group called WAVES, ten- to seventeen-year-olds living on the lower east side of Manhattan, participated in a folk-life research project and developed a "pictionary" about the people and culture of their neighborhood.

Another New York City school, the Community Service Academy (Intermediate School 218) in Washington Heights, has demonstrated creativity in serving the community. One example is a Kiddy Corner in a local welfare office, where the middle school students work with young children as they wait, often for hours, with their parents. Another important service grew in response to a riot which ensued when a local youth was shot by a police officer. The students, realizing that communication between the community and the police was unsatisfactory, helped the officers to learn Spanish, the language of many neighborhood residents.

Public libraries and museums in urban, suburban, or rural settings offer many opportunities for volunteers. An example is the Kohl Children's Museum, in Wilmette, Illinois, where fourteen- to eighteen-year-olds serve as junior volunteers, leading younger visitors in activities at the museum.

Students trained in the Mental Health Players on Long Island plan role playing on important social issues such as drug abuse and teen pregnancy, presenting their plays in schools and community agencies and at conferences. Through agencies such as the Constitutional Rights Foundation (CRF), civic responsibility and service learning go hand-in-hand. City Youth, CRF's Education and Community Action program for middle school students in Los Angeles, is one example of this combination. In Hempstead, New York, high school students developed and presented HIV/AIDs prevention workshops, demonstrating their willingness and ability to deal with a critical problem.

A central purpose of service learning is to build bridges between youth and those of other ages and between the school and its community. In addition to working outside the school, students may invite others into the life and learning of the school itself. When the students host those with whom they have been working regularly, another dimension is added to their relationships. Handicapped children may visit their partners' school for craft activities, music, lunch, games. Three- and four-year-olds may be readily accommodated in a middle school or high school in story hours led by the older students. Adult home residents may visit for a concert or school play. Fourth graders may visit an eighth grade science class or share a nutrition unit with a home economics class.

An intergenerational chorus or a "prom" with one's special senior citizen is rewarding for both generations. Students may teach jewelry making or computer skills, areas in which they are often more skilled than their elders, to parents or senior citizens. The reverse is true when adults join a social studies class, recounting their own experiences from times before the students were born.

An academic classroom is enlivened when a teacher is able to discuss the economic and social issues of migrant farm labor in the context of in-school or field experiences with the farm workers themselves. Service learning consistently offers opportunities for intense engagement, integrating traditional "content" areas and real-life experiences.

Structuring the Service Learning Program

Scheduling. How do Shoreham-Wading River and other districts find time in the school day for service learning? Classroom time is the most easily provided, since the teachers can devote class time in English, social studies, science, art, or other relevant subjects to discussion and preparation for the field experience. Time out of the classroom is another issue, and may depend on whether the school is within walking distance of the site where service is to be done. In a city school, visiting residents of a nursing home on the next block may require only one hour a week (perhaps one class period plus the lunch period). A suburban school may need to allow travel time, which would require a double period. In all instances, student safety is a critical issue. Standard procedures for insurance coverage and for permission from parents and the school district must be observed.

If service learning is a priority for the school, schedules will be devised to insure blocks of time for any given group of students and teachers. Increasingly, school faculties are being organized into teaching teams representing the basic academic subjects and often special areas such as art, physical education, special education, and music as well. The team structure is ideally suited to service learning. At Shoreham-Wading River, each seventh and eighth grade teacher in the academic core has been responsible for two subjects—English and social studies or science and mathematics. Because the English/social studies teachers and their teammates in science/mathematics share students and schedules, it has been possible to rearrange classes, provide double periods for the field experience, and free teachers to participate in the service learning program.

Program patterns. Shoreham-Wading River has successfully utilized a variety of patterns for service learning programs. One pattern is an interdisciplinary program for a class or team. In this model, an entire class or team participates in either in-school or in-field service experiences weekly for a period of six, eight, or ten weeks. Ordinarily, the teachers participate in all field work. Because the school staff includes a service learning coordinator, as well as teacher assistants specifically assigned to the service learning program, the teachers have access to valuable planning and logistical support so that they can implement an extensive interdisciplinary service program.

One such unit, for example, focuses on the elderly. In English classes, the reading assignment for the month is a novel about an elderly person or about a child and her grandparents. Students write letters to partners at the nursing home. (In one school students are learning to use e-mail as they share letters and photos with "their" seniors.) They write articles and supply photos for a local newspaper. They keep journals.

In social studies and library research projects, students investigate characteristics of aging, social and economic issues, and possible social action. The science class focuses on medical problems, handicaps, and preventive health care. Classes in visual arts, ceramics, music, and dance plan activities for the nursing home residents.

A second interdisciplinary service learning unit focuses on early childhood. Here too, the field experiences are the vibrant focus for academic class work. Students learn about birth and child development in the early years of life. They learn to read and often to write books for little children. There are journals, essays, art and music projects to plan and execute. Students learn what little ones can and cannot do at ages two, three, or four, and how to plan activities appropriate for them. Depending on the work sites, students are confronted with societal problems of poverty, health, and the quality of education.

A second pattern incorporates service learning into separate content areas where the service experience may either supplement or complement the curriculum. In a module on early childhood in a course on human development, one group of students may work at a nursery school, another group at a Head Start program, and a third group in the district's preschool class, all during the same time block. Cross-age tutoring is particularly effective as a technique to reinforce content areas. High school science classes conduct science experiments with middle schoolers. Middle school students devise mathematics games and take them to elementary school classrooms. French language students teach beginning French to fourth graders.

Ideally suited to service learning is a full-blown high school course, such as Community Organization or Health Careers, that is offered for credit and lasts one or two semesters. Such an arrangement makes it possible to give total attention to both the content and the techniques involved in service. Rigorous academic work is built around the characteristics and needs of the population served, social, economic, and psychological issues, and group process skills.

Projects develop in specific classes in other ways. An environmental study may lead to recycling; a social studies class may engage in social action on a particular issue; students in a language arts class may write letters to nursing home residents.

Slow readers in intermediate grades can read simple children's books to primary children, or write and bind books for or with them. Science or mathematics students can have fun doing experiments or puzzles, French students brush up on their vocabularies, home economics classes prepare food with children in lower grades.

There are many possibilities for improving skills in the arts through serving the community. Performing groups in music, dance, and theater may visit schools for the handicapped or senior centers, or conversely, invite those audiences into the school. Better still, there may be joint choruses, art taught by students to seniors, or dances shared. Service and learning go hand in hand.

A third pattern may be used when service experiences occur outside the classroom. A club, a homeroom, or an advisory group, for instance, may commit to a community service project. Although this pattern offers less curricular depth than a class-centered service experience, it can be valuable for young people as an opportunity to assume responsibility and to have the experience of caring for their environment or for persons in their community.

When an entire class or teaching team is either unwilling or unable to become involved in service learning, a pull-out program may be a viable alternative. In this type of program small groups of students may be released from one or two classes once a week to participate in a service program under the supervision of a teacher or a teaching assistant, either at community sites or at other areas within the school. In high school programs, it is often possible to arrange for larger blocks of time for more intensive work and for travel to sites away from school.

Preparing for the service experience. Generally, the agency at which students will work assists with orientation, encourages students to lead activities, and makes staff and clientele available each time the students arrive to work. In return, the school provides its own orientation, supervises and evaluates the students, assists them in preparing activities, arranges transportation, and provides insurance for the program. Whatever conditions are agreed upon, clarity and openness are the keys to a successful collaboration. Experience suggests that it is wiser to seek alternative sites than to try to enlist a reluctant partner. Yet, significantly, often an agency that resisted early in the life of the program will become an eager collaborator once it is established.

Students are responsible for planning and executing activities at their field sites. They must therefore become informed about characteristics of the age group and techniques for working with the target population. The school's library is a source for appropriate videos and books. If the project includes work with children, picture books are available in the classroom and a children's librarian may be invited to demonstrate how to read to young children. A speaker from the placement site can be invited to acquaint students with the problems and behaviors they are likely to encounter. Role playing by puppeteers and by organizations like the Mental Health Players on Long Island could also be used for this purpose. A preliminary tour of a site has proved helpful. Students may diagram the site, noting special-purpose areas and the like. They can observe the population, take notes, and keep journals.

Successful programs share some characteristics. The schedule ordinarily includes at least one preparatory period weekly. Class time is dedicated to study, discussion, writing, and reading which provide the framework for the project. The preparatory period allows for evaluation of the previous site visit, and discussion of problems and of activities for subsequent visits. In community service projects scheduled outside the regular school day, these elements are no less important. Regardless of the setting, successful programs provide consistent adult guidance, regularly scheduled times for discussion and preparation, resource materials, supplies, and logistical support.

Funding is a central question and one indicator of the strength of the school's commitment. It must be emphasized that preparation for projects that are an integral part of the curriculum is part of the teacher's normal work load. This is true for administrators as well. Similarly, supplies, books, and audio-visual materials are provided from the regular budget.

Administrative structure. One staff member will have responsibility for administrative functions unique to service learning programs. These include making arrangements for placement, providing assistance to teachers, planning with students, arranging orientation and securing supplies and curriculum material. In some schools a teacher assistant assumes this role; in others a teacher or guidance counselor is assigned to the program. A clerk or secretary may assist.

The Shoreham-Wading River Middle School experience provides an interesting illustration. In 1973, help was sought from a parent volunteer for the fledgling program. The obvious effectiveness of that year's service experience for the small group of students involved was such that the following year a five-hour-a-day teacher assistant position was devoted to coordinating and expanding the program. With increasing requests by teachers to participate, additional teacher assistant time was provided and the coordinator's position became a teaching position. Although the involvement of other teachers in service learning has continued to be voluntary, all teams in the school now participate. This means that each year hundreds of eleven- to fourteen-year-olds serve their community in special ways and that each individual student has several different service experiences during her or his middle school years.

The service learning coordinator participates with other teachers in overseeing students' preparation and work in the field. In a comprehensive program like the one at Shoreham-Wading River, teacher assistants are assigned to work with the teachers and coordinator in transporting students, planning with specific groups, and supervising their work in the field.

Materials and supplies are necessary, but costs are easily contained. Art and craft supplies should be assembled specifically for community projects. A classroom library and curriculum and resource materials for students and teachers can be assembled over time.

This may all sound overwhelming to those contemplating "putting a toe in the water." As indicated earlier, a modest project can serve as a start. The minimum requirements would include administrative approval, a staff person assigned at least on a part-time basis for logistical support, scheduled in-school time for staff and students to meet and prepare for the service learning activities, and some art and curriculum materials.

Funding becomes easier as the program develops a history. The benefits of service learning to students and the community are such that they generate enthusiasm among parents, Board of Education members, and faculty. At Shoreham-Wading River, the budget was increased gradually to allow the addition of teacher assistants, minibuses, better and more sophisticated art materials, videos, and books. The service-learning projects themselves became richer, more diverse and complex as teachers and students learned from each other what to do and how to do it well.

In recent years both private and public funding sources have offered support for service learning. Funders often respond favorably to proposals for intergenerational programs, such as those where high school students tutor elementary school children or where middle school students work with the elderly, or for projects that involve special education classes in the community.

Enriching the Curriculum through Service Learning

Service learning introduces students to career possibilities and preemployment skills, thus helping to counteract charges made in recent years in media and business circles that schools fail to provide students with rudimentary employment skills and that young people are often ill-informed about career choices.

Many benefits are derived from the hands-on nature of community service. When a student works in a setting outside his or her classroom, there is an immediacy about being responsible for "real, live people." If a student misses a visit, it is not merely a homework assignment that will come in a day late; it is an elderly person or a young child who will be disappointed, who will miss the student worker's presence.

This sense of responsibility is further reinforced by the pride and self-fulfillment a student feels when he or she has served effectively in a community endeavor. The student who has fulfilled a commitment responsibly understands the satisfaction of a job well done. A better preparation for success in a future career or in a part-time job is hard to find.

The student learns the importance of deadlines, and the need for attention to detail. The minibus stands at the school door; there is no recourse for one who has not yet checked out a preschooler's story book from the library, neglected to cut out a pattern for the snowman, or forgotten the blunt-nosed scissors.

Students not only acquire precareer skills through service learning, but, in the tradition of John Dewey, they are able to apply the hands-on experience to reach an understanding of the larger forces that shape their lives. Economic and political issues and constraints take on new meaning for the student serving meals to the homeless or lobbying for recycling facilities or affordable day care. So does the need for education and special skills in an increasingly sophisticated technological society. Jobs are not as easy as they might seem. They require skills and education. The challenge of a service experience may give the student the motivation to take his or her own education more seriously. Employers look favorably upon a student's work experience in community service.

The choice of career may be directly influenced by a service experience that offers firsthand knowledge of a field—what it is like, what is needed to get there. Many a student has been motivated by work with the elderly, has tested out ideas of being a teacher or physical therapist, has thought of working in the public interest as a lawyer or an environmentalist.

On the other hand, some students learn that particular careers are not for them. The aspiring veterinarian, after working at the animal shelter, may decide that this is not quite what she had envisioned. The budding teacher of the handicapped may decide to look in other directions. How much better to learn this at age fourteen or sixteen than to discover it during one's junior year at college or to realize, once on the job, that a career decision was a mistake.

Schools today are challenged to strive for goals that go beyond the learning of skills and content associated with specific disciplines. They are expected to attend to affective development and to educate students for responsible citizenship. How better to do this than through service learning?

In service learning students develop skills in dealing with persons of different ages and situations. In a way perhaps unique among in-school experiences, young people are prepared for the demands of adult life. This is as true for boys as for girls. It is true that when service is optional, it is more common for girls than boys to volunteer. However, when boys share the experience, they too learn that the caring functions belong to both sexes.

As a service-learning program progresses, students learn that their efforts are important, and they rise to the occasion. They experience the rewards of patience and perseverance, as did a Shoreham-Wading River youth when, after many frustrating visits, the autistic boy with whom he was paired finally responded to him and to him alone. Others have experienced sadness or loss when senile nursing home residents forgot them, or when a special senior citizen died.

Service learning can generate social concern and may lead to social or political action. Often students continue as volunteers in community agencies outside the school program. Some are led to choose careers in the helping professions. On occasion, whole classes or clubs or other groups become activists on behalf of the environment, moving into nonpartisan political action, advocating for clean-up of toxic waste sites, or lobbying legislators for protection of water supplies. Students working at an animal shelter may organize in support of more humane conditions. Those working in parks may become involved in the complex issues that divide developers and naturalists.

Educating for character and responsible citizenship implies appreciating diversity. Service learning provides bridges between age groups otherwise separated by societal structures. It builds connections between the physically or mentally challenged child and others who are not thus challenged. It provides unique opportunities for students to work among persons of a race, class, or ethnicity different from their own. While educators search for curricula that can help counter stereotypes, understanding and acceptance of difference flow naturally in service learning settings. Friendships form across barriers and stereotypes are overcome.

Concluding Statement

What, then, about the fears and hesitations? Does a school dare to plunge into service learning and will the results warrant the investment of time and energy? Let it be said unequivocally, this is one race worth running.

There are countless opportunities out there, needs crying to be met. There are students of all ages and abilities waiting to be challenged and ready to put their great energy to good use. There is eloquent testimony from schools that have incorporated community service in their curricula. Teachers share the enthusiasm of their students as they see how classroom learning takes on new excitement. Parents listen to their children and soon are asking that younger siblings be placed in classes that offer service learning. More agencies call in for help than can be accommodated.

The power of service learning is illustrated by comments from an eighth grade team at Shoreham-Wading River that does community service weekly for part of the school year at an adult home in a neighboring community. At the end of the year, one of the students voluntarily wrote the Board of Education to describe the impact of the program upon her life. She had participated in service learning during each of her three years at the middle school. Of her experience at the adult home she wrote:

> You wouldn't begin to imagine, unless you were there for yourself, exactly what goes on. We make an incredible difference in their lives and they affect ours so much. While we are visiting them we light up their lives and put meaning into their glum days. When we leave we wonder and worry about them and they are always thinking about us. Sometimes you get so close to the person you work with that it's hard to let go. . . . I still write and visit those friends I have made through Community Service. . . . Without Community Service many of the people we help would have nothing. Sometimes we are the only friends or family they have. I just want to say thanks.

The Recreation Director of the home wrote:

> We feel fortunate to be part of the Community Service Program. Sixty residents out of the 120 who live at our facility do not have any known next of kin. Some feel alone and cut off from the world. The youth bring the world in. These students . . . bring laughter and smiles. The message they bring to our residents is "You matter."

A parent summed up her child's service learning experience: "The project turned out to be more than an assignment. It became a labor of love."

CHAPTER VIII

Service-Learning in Higher Education

ALLEN J. WUTZDORFF AND DWIGHT E. GILES, JR.

The terms "service" and "learning" have long been associated with institutions of higher education. While there is general consensus about the meaning of learning, there is no commonly understood definition of the service component of a college or university. Often the debate about service is centered around faculty and the type of research or community outreach each faculty member does in order to relate the work and life of the campus to broader societal or community concerns. Until recently, student service was viewed as an outcome of higher education, to be put into action after graduating, rather than as something to be incorporated into the curriculum. Even if the college's stated mission included education for citizenship, service experience was not often required. It was assumed that a college curriculum would give students the intellectual tools to become contributing citizens and engaged participants in their communities and professional settings.

Over the past fifteen years, a growing number of educators have been challenging the assumption that a disposition to serve emerges spontaneously as a result of a college education. They have become advocates for service-learning, arguing that service demands a set of skills and an approach to social issues that must be intentionally instilled as a part of the undergraduate experience. As this movement has grown and taken hold, there has been an explosion in the number of campus-based programs designed to provide students with community service opportunities. The variety of ways in which these opportunities have been incorporated into campus life reflects the nature of the institution as well as the degree to which service is seen as an integral part of the formal learning program.

Allen J. Wutzdorff is the Executive Director of Lowcountry AIDS Services in Charleston, South Carolina. He was Executive Director of the National Society for Experiential Education in Raleigh, North Carolina, from 1991 to 1995. Dwight E. Giles, Jr. is Professor of Human and Organizational Development and Director of Internships at Peabody College, Vanderbilt University, Nashville, Tennessee. He is co-principal investigator with Janet Eyler on a national service-learning research project ("Comparing Models of Service-Learning in Higher Education") funded by the Fund for the Improvement of Postsecondary Education.

In this chapter we will address the major factors that have led to the current interest in service-learning in postsecondary education and illustrate some of the issues and tensions service-learning has presented as colleges wrestle with various curricular and co-curricular models. We will examine the relationship between service-learning and other elements within higher education that have either supported or impeded the incorporation of a service component into the curriculum. Service-learning programs differ in the degree of emphasis placed on "service" and "learning," and a number of different approaches exist.[1] Some programs focus on providing service opportunities, without explicit ties to academic courses, while others incorporate service experiences into a coherent multicourse set of offerings where the learning is as important as the service. We will conclude with a discussion of research regarding the impact of service-learning programs.

Traditions in Postsecondary Education that Support Service-Learning

Experiential Education. The term "experiential education" is both a philosophy and a method for teaching. It is a philosophy that asserts that the development of knowledge and the acquisition of skills belong as partners in education, where each transforms the other. In practice, experiential education refers to various pedagogical methods that are used to engage the learner actively in what is being studied. Most typically, experiential education connotes an off-campus program, such as internships or international field studies.

Over the past twenty-five years, internships have become an accepted part of the college experience, although not always granted the same status as classroom-based courses. Internships are often offered as an option, graded on a pass-fail basis, or carry no academic credit. Campuses have established offices of experiential learning which list placements and assist students in finding appropriate internship settings. On the academic side, many institutions have developed mechanisms such as internship seminars to assist students in critically reflecting on their experiences. Thus, with the advent of service-learning, many campuses already had structures and processes in place for engaging students in off-campus learning. Perhaps more significantly, internships helped to create a receptivity to involving students beyond the classroom, particularly in those liberal arts disciplines not traditionally associated with hands-on experience.

A belief in involvement. College catalogues nearly always include assurances that graduates will become active citizens who will contribute to their communities and to society at large. When service-learning is understood to go beyond charity and volunteerism to include meaningful action accompanied by critical reflection about social issues, it finds a warmer reception on the college campus because it builds upon an espoused purpose of higher education: to prepare students to be involved and informed members of society.

Service-Learning Milestones in Postsecondary Education

Service-learning has many traditions in American higher education, but immediate antecedents of the service-learning movement can be identified by specific milestones in the last twenty-five to thirty years. The term "service-learning" first arose in 1964 in connection with community service programs developed by the Oak Ridge Associated Universities in Tennessee. This program was later expanded to fifteen states under the auspices of the Southern Regional Education Board. Its goals were to involve students in internships related to social and economic development: "The term 'service-learning' has been adopted as best describing this combination of the performance of a useful service for society and the disciplined interpretation of that experience for an increase in knowledge and in understanding one's self."[2]

The next milestone occurred in 1972 when the University Year for Action, a federal program, involved students from campuses across the country in serving their communities. A number of campus-based service-learning programs date their origins to this year, including those at the University of Vermont and at Michigan State University as well as the Joint Educational Project at the University of Southern California.

In the early 1970s, the National Center for Service Learning was opened within the federal government. This stimulated service-learning-type programs, although many were not called service-learning then or even later. In 1985, a significant development in the history of service-learning was the formation of Campus Compact: The Project for Public and Community Service (a project of the Education Commission of the States). Campus Compact is a consortium of college and university presidents who support the educational value of service and make a commitment to foster public service on their campuses. While this originally included a very limited number and types of colleges and universities, it expanded and has become a major catalyst for postsecondary service and the development of service-learning programs. In 1989, the

Student Literacy Corps (SLC) was initiated by the U.S. Department of Education. SLC made grants to encourage colleges and universities to become involved in efforts to increase literacy in their local communities. One of the requirements of these grants was that the literacy programs be tied to academic courses so students would receive credit for their tutoring efforts. However, the Student Literacy Corps was discontinued in 1994, and most programs were not able to sustain themselves beyond the two years of funding which had been allowed by the grants.

In 1982, the National Society for Experiential Education (NSEE) established a Special Interest Group in Service-Learning which has now become a significant forum for faculty and program directors and convenes annually at the NSEE national conference. Once a small group, it has grown to a membership of several hundred people from secondary and postsecondary service-learning programs. In 1990, NSEE published a three-volume resource book, *Combining Service and Learning.*[3] The volumes include a bibliography, examples of programs, and a rich set of theoretical and practical perspectives for establishing and strengthening service-learning programs at all educational levels.

Two pieces of federal legislation, the National and Community Service Act, signed by President Bush in 1990, and the National and Community Service Trust Act of 1993, signed by President Clinton, have helped to accelerate and expand service-learning at all educational levels. The 1993 Act established the Corporation for National Service, which funds higher education service-learning programs under its Learn and Serve America grants, as well as the AmeriCorps program, which allows students to receive assistance with college tuition in exchange for a year or two of service to the community.

In 1995, the American Association for Higher Education (AAHE) chose the theme "The Engaged Campus" for its annual conference, reflecting the growing interest shown by educators in establishing or strengthening connections with their surrounding communities. As further testimony to the growth of service-learning, the 1996 AAHE conference included service-learning as a subtheme. Similarly, at the Annual Meetings of the American Educational Research Association the number of sessions devoted to service-learning has increased from zero to around a dozen over the last five years.

Most recently, there have been several indicators of the movement toward curricular integration of service. Some of the larger disciplinary groups, including the American Sociological Association, the American Psychological Association, and the American Political Science Association now regularly feature service-learning at their conferences. In

1994, the *Michigan Journal of Community Service Learning* published its first issue, and *Service-Learning in Higher Education* was published in 1996. This latter volume includes a wide range of program examples as well as discussions of curricular integration and the many administrative and policy issues that emerge when a service-learning program is undertaken on a college campus.[4]

Additionally, the American Sociological Association, Campus Compact, Michigan State University, and Stanford University have published curriculum materials on service-learning and undergraduate education within specific disciplines. The National Society for Experiential Education, in partnership with the University of Vermont, has published an interdisciplinary reader for use in a wide variety of service-learning courses. The intent of this anthology is to stimulate critical reflection on service experiences from spiritual, psychological, socioeconomic, and many other perspectives.

At this writing, service-learning is growing so fast that even those of us who study the field find it hard to track all the emerging developments. The movement is still young and growing and still faces significant challenges. It is also very diverse, with many different approaches appearing under the banner of service-learning. These approaches range from the more traditional volunteer-linked courses to more efforts to effect sweeping social change, such as community partnerships and participatory action research courses. The range of programmatic types reflects a number of factors, including institutional attitudes toward the academic value of service-learning, funding availability, institutional mission and traditions, and structures that are in place which can readily accommodate a service-learning program.

Institutional Structures

One thing can be said with certainty about the institutional structures which house service-learning programs: there is no normative model. As we have worked within the field of service-learning, we have encountered well-integrated service-learning programs run by faculty committees with very little in the way of formal structures or designated offices. We have seen offices for service-learning housed on the Student Service side of the academy but nonetheless strongly linked to academic courses, and we have seen programs housed in the academic sector that require little connection between course content and service experiences. What has been emerging is an exciting array of models uniquely tailored to the culture and traditions of individual institutions.

Whether service-learning is administered by a well-established and visible entity such as the Haas Center for Public Service at Stanford University or by a faculty task force such as that at Alma College in Michigan, the crucial questions are: What is the purpose of this program? Are service and learning goals of equal importance? What are the roles of faculty, students, and members of the community? When these questions are answered, and when the institution is clear on the service and learning outcomes it expects, then the institution can determine what are the most feasible and desirable structures to undergird the program.

For those interested in learning more about existing models for implementing service-learning at all types of postsecondary institutions, a number of published and electronic resources and resource centers are available. A listing of some of these is provided at the end of this chapter.

Impact of Service-Learning

Questions of institutional structure are often accompanied by questions which essentially ask, "Does service-learning make a difference?" Practitioners often assert that service-learning has a positive influence on students, institutions, and communities. For many years, most of the evidence informing such conclusions has been based upon direct experience. This anecdotal evidence has helped the field to grow and develop, but more systematic data are needed in order to answer many questions that have emerged as a result of the rapid proliferation of programs. As service-learning struggles for legitimacy within the academy, serious questions will continue to be raised about its overall impact, particularly as programs compete for ever more scarce resources.

The research data collected thus far have been encouraging and bear out the general perceptions of practitioners, but the picture is far from complete. Nearly all studies have found some type of positive impact on students (who have most often been the subjects in such studies). But the studies have been few and have not addressed the full range of issues needed to achieve an in-depth understanding of service-learning and its effects. One reason for this is that service-learning is a relative newcomer to the college curriculum. Another is that policies at many major research universities, as well as academic journals, place a higher value on basic or "pure" research than on practical applied research. A third stems from the methodological difficulties associated with field research.

In 1991, a foundational step was taken toward a more complete body of service-learning research. The National Society for Experiential Education (NSEE) published *A Research Agenda for Combining Service and Learning in the 1990s*.[5] The agenda, which resulted from a Wingspread Conference of leading researchers and practitioners, sets forth three impact areas for service-learning programs: impact on participants, impact on institutions, and impact on communities. While there was general agreement during the development of this agenda that all areas were important, only one area, impact on students, seems to have been the subject of the small but growing body of research literature in service-learning. This is probably because the effects on individuals are easier to define and measure, and because there are more political pressures to demonstrate learning outcomes for students than other possible outcomes in the three impact areas. An exception to this is evaluation of community impact, which was the focus of a national evaluation of the Student Literacy Corps, and is currently an area of emphasis under the Learn and Serve America grants of the Corporation for National Service. Campus Compact has surveyed participation of its member schools, but no detailed study of the impact of service-learning on institutions of higher education has yet appeared.

IMPACT ON STUDENTS

Most of the studies investigating the impact of service-learning on students have focused on comparisons of sections within a course which incorporate service as a component with those sections that do not. In some cases, comparisons had to rely upon pre-post comparisons within the same course because of the difficulties involved in control-group studies.[6] The first synthesis of research on impact on students focuses on the implications for practitioners designing courses for optimal learning and development.[7]

At this point we can identify three national studies that are underway. One compares learning outcomes across programs and courses.[8] Another is examining how critical reflection affects the learning process in service-learning.[9] The third study is evaluating the Learn and Serve America programs in higher education that are funded by the Corporation for National Service.[10]

In studies conducted at individual institutions, students have been found to develop empathy for the people with whom they work and thus reduce stereotypical views and social distance.[11] Students also enhance their sense of responsibility.[12] In a pilot phase of one of the national studies, Eyler, Root, and Giles found that students classified as "experts" in service-learning had more structurally sophisticated views of social problems and solutions to these problems than "novices" with little or no service-learning experience.[13] Similarly, students seem to develop more complex ways of analyzing problems as a result of service-learning courses.[14] When service-learning projects are of value to community clients and are rooted in the subject matter, students show greater mastery of the conceptual material than when the projects do not have these characteristics.[15]

A number of studies about impact on students have included self-report data. When queried about effects of service-learning, students have reported increases in civic skills, in tolerance, and in a tendency to become involved. Students also report that they learn more in service-learning classes than in regular classes, and are developing a commitment to social justice.[16]

While the research is still in process and the data are not yet conclusive in some areas, such as impact on critical thinking, the findings to date are fairly convergent and suggest a positive and sometimes strong impact on learning, problem solving, and the elements that are often categorized as social responsibility.

Implications for practice are unclear until more is known about the characteristics of the program and the conditions that produce these impacts. Results thus far indicate that service-learning experiences lasting a year or more produce greater impact than shorter experiences.[17] At this point, strong predictors of learning outcomes are the degree of integration of the service with the curriculum and the extent to which the service is perceived by students to be linked to theory and content.[18] At this writing, there are a number of studies in progress including a retrospective study under the direction of Nancy Gansneder at the University of Virginia in Charlottesville and an in-depth qualitative study being conducted by Anne Ruggles Gere and Deborah Minter at the University of Michigan School of Education.

FACULTY INVOLVEMENT

Two studies have looked at faculty involvement. Hammond surveyed faculty involved in service-learning and found that the major motivation for using this approach is that faculty believed that service-learning was good pedagogy.[19] In a case study of faculty who adopted service-learning, Stanton found that faculty identified "institutional support" and "mission" as crucial factors for developing and maintaining the more labor-intensive pedagogy of service-learning.[20]

INSTITUTIONAL IMPACT

To date, there has been no comprehensive study of the impact of service-learning on institutions. However, a number of specifically focused studies provide some snapshots of service-learning at particular kinds of institutions. Studies have been conducted by the Council of Independent Colleges (CIC),[21] Campus Compact,[22] and by the National Service-Learning Research Project, which is funded by the Fund for the Improvement of Postsecondary Education.[23]

The combined findings of these studies indicate a growth in curricular integration of service-learning at large research universities and at private liberal arts colleges. The Campus Compact studies showed growth each year in the number of institutions reporting the presence of service-learning courses, and many of those were incorporated into departments and majors. Further, there was an increase from 1989 to 1995 in the number of schools reporting that credit could be earned for service learning. Such results were supported by the CIC study, which found "substantial progress" in movement toward curricular integration.[24] In a similar vein, the National Service-Learning Research Project found that service experiences were regularly incorporated into a wide variety of courses, mostly within the arts and sciences, and that service was often linked to the theoretical content of the course.[25]

In an investigation of the institutional impact of service-learning conducted at the University of Montana, Ward found that the greatest commitment to service-learning occurred when it was explicitly linked to the mission of the institution.[26] Evidence of this kind of institution-wide commitment can be found at Portland State University in Oregon and the University of California-Monterey Bay; at both institutions service-learning has been incorporated into the mission statement.

A highly visible program at the University of Pennsylvania is often cited as an example of large-scale institutional commitment and impact. The West Philadelphia Improvement Corps (WEPIC) is a central element of the University's participation in the West Philadelphia Partnership, a community-based collaborative that includes community groups and institutions. The WEPIC project sprang from the University's need to establish a more positive relationship with the inner-city neighborhood that is home to the university. A significant feature of WEPIC is its function as a vehicle for engaging the resources of the academy in the interests of the broader community. Equally significant is the university's recognition of that community as a resource for student learning, not simply as a laboratory in which to test students' skills and knowledge, but also as a rich source for increasing their understanding of community, of diversity, and of social change. As a multilayered model of service-learning in higher education, the WEPIC project differs from other campus-based programs. More than three hundred University of Pennsylvania students, as well as faculty and staff volunteers, worked in the West Philadelphia community in the 1995-96 term. One third of the students were involved through the academic curriculum, which offers thirty-six service-learning courses. Penn students have introduced and run a number of innovative programs in the West Philadelphia schools, including evening and weekend programs, and they have introduced service-learning programs across the middle school curriculum, focusing on the community's concerns in such areas as health, conflict resolution/peer mediation, and the environment. The program's dissemination phase is now under way in several sites. As it is documented and evaluated, it may give rise to yet other innovative patterns of service learning in the academy.

The data cited in this subsection are, of course, not necessarily representative of American higher education. Much more needs to be learned about the broader effect of service-learning on colleges and universities. In what ways does service-learning impact on the overall culture of the campus? How do faculty and student roles change with involvement in off-campus service? Do campuses and communities work together in new and different ways and how does this affect the institution? Most significantly, what can service-learning teach all of the stakeholders—students, faculty, administrators, community members—about learning and about service. We hope that the many models for service-learning that are emerging at postsecondary institutions can be studied in such a way as to yield answers to these and many other questions.

This brief summary of our understanding of the effects of service-learning must conclude with the familiar advice: "further research is needed." It is clear that there is a "field" of service-learning and that this field is supported by a developing body of research. Over the past five years, we have seen rapid growth of interest in service-learning and we fully anticipate that the next five years will yield a deeper understanding of the impact of service and learning.

In Conclusion

Service-learning is becoming a widespread and potent force within higher education and shows potential for becoming a permanent feature at many institutions. Service-learning has widened and deepened our understanding of experiential education in some significant ways. When internships and other off-campus programs began proliferating in the 1980s, the resultant learning opportunities helped to bring the lessons of reality into campus-based learning. Service-learning, with its strong links to social issues, has extended the conceptual basis for experiential education and consequently provided a rich set of connections to nearly all discipline areas. Service-learning constitutes a concrete means for achieving what so many institutions of higher learning promise: the development of students who will become significant actors within their communities and society at large for the betterment of both.

The momentum that service-learning currently enjoys, however, may be short-lived unless a number of significant issues are addressed. Too many programs and program administrators are dependent on "soft" money (in whole or in part) for their continued existence. Faculty who find service-learning to be an effective method for enhancing student learning as well as for engaging students in important social issues often find that their institutions do not reward their efforts when the time comes for promotion and tenure decisions. Happily, there are some notable exceptions, and the number of campuses showing a genuine commitment to service and learning as a powerful combination for the development of students, institutions, and communities is growing each year. One such exception is the Lowell Bennion Center at the University of Utah, which has been instrumental in developing a universitywide policy for officially recognizing faculty involvement in service-learning in its rank and tenure process.

In writing this chapter we have deliberately focused on what is happening to advance service-learning both conceptually and programmatically. We look ahead with guarded optimism, our hope tempered by the fact that programs initiated and sustained by external funds are always in jeopardy. (Memories of the Student Literacy Corps still linger.) Yet our optimism is fueled by having seen so many solid programs grow from well-intentioned volunteerism to closely integrated components of institutional curricula that will be hard to ignore. Service-learning has a place in many mainstream professional organizations. There is a professional journal. There is a growing cadre of service-learning researchers. A vast network of service-learning practitioners has emerged. Service-learning is well on its way to becoming a field within postsecondary education.

Notes

1. Robert Sigmon, *Linking Service with Learning* (Washington, D.C.: Council of Independent Colleges, October, 1994).

2. William R. O'Connell, "Service Learning in the South: A Strategy for Innovation in Undergraduate Education," in *A Resource Book for Combining Service and Learning*, vol. 1, edited by Jane Kendall (Raleigh, N.C.: National Society for Experiential Education, 1990), pp. 594-595.

3. Janet Luce, *Service Learning: An Annotated Bibliography for Linking Public Service and the Curriculum* (Raleigh, N.C.: National Society for Experiential Education, 1988); Jane Kendall, ed., *A Resource Book for Combining Service and Learning*, vols. 1 and 2 (Raleigh, N.C.: National Society for Experiential Education, 1990).

4. Barbara Jacoby, *Service-Learning in Higher Education* (San Francisco: Jossey-Bass, 1996).

5. Dwight Giles, Ellen Porter Honnett, and Sally Migliore, *A Research Agenda for Combining Service and Learning in the 1990s* (Raleigh, N.C.: National Society for Experiential Education, 1991).

6. Jeremy Cohen and Dennis Kinsey, "Doing Good and Scholarship: A Service Learning Study," *Journalism Educator* (Winter 1994): 4-14; G. B. Markus, Jeffrey Howard, and D. C. King, "Integrating Community Service and Classroom Instruction Enhances Learning: Results from an Experiment," *Education Evaluation and Policy Analysis* 15 (1993): 410-419; Thomas Batchelder and Susan Root, "The Effects of an Undergraduate Program to Integrate Academic Learning and Service: Cognitive, Prosocial, and Identified Outcomes," *Journal of Adolescence* 17 (1994): 341-356.

7. Alan Waterman, ed., *Service-Learning: Applications from the Research* (Mahwah, N.J.: Erlbaum, 1997).

8. Dwight Giles and Janet Eyler, "Comparing Models of Service-Learning: A Research Proposal," Proposal submitted to the Fund for the Improvement of Postsecondary Education, Vanderbilt University, 1993.

9. Janet Eyler, Dwight Giles, and Angela Schmiede, *A Practitioner's Guide to Reflection in Service-Learning: Student Voices and Reflection*, Technical assistance guide funded by the Corporation for National Service (Nashville, Tenn.: Vanderbilt University, 1996).

10. M. J. Gray et al., *Evaluation of Learn and Serve America, Higher Education*, First Year Report (Santa Monica, Calif.: RAND, May 1996).

11. Dwight Giles and Janet Eyler, "The Impact of a College Community Service Laboratory on Students' Personal, Social, and Cognitive Outcomes," *Journal of Adolescence* 17 (1994): 327-339.

12. Idem. See also, Scott Myers-Lipton, "The Effects of Service Learning on College Students' Attitudes towards Civic Responsibility, International Understanding, and Racial Prejudice," Doctoral dissertation, University of Colorado, 1994.

13. Janet Eyler, Susan Root, and Dwight Giles, "Service-Learning and the Development of Expert Citizens," in Robert G. Bringle and Donna Duffey, eds. *Service Learning and Psychology* (Washington, D.C.: American Association for Higher Education, forthcoming).

14. Batchelder and Root, "The Effects of an Undergraduate Program to Integrate Academic Learning and Service."

15. Cohen and Kinsey, "Doing Good and Scholarship."

16. Janet Eyler and Dwight Giles, "The Importance of Program Quality in Service Learning," in Alan Waterman, ed., *Service Learning: Applications from the Research.*

17. Myers-Lipton, "The Effects of Service Learning on College Students' Attitudes towards Civic Responsibility, International Understanding, and Racial Prejudice."

18. Eyler and Giles, "The Importance of Program Quality in Service Learning."

19. Christine Hammond, "Integrating Service and Academic Study: Faculty Motivation and Satisfaction in Michigan Higher Education," *Michigan Journal of Community Service Learning* 1, no. 1 (1994): 21-28.

20. Timothy K. Stanton, "The Experience of Faculty Participating in an Instructional Development Seminar on Service Learning," *Michigan Journal of Community Service Learning* 1, no. 1 (1994): 7-20.

21. Robert Serow and Robert Sigmon, "Survey Results: Service Learning at Private Liberal Arts Institutions," *The Independent*, Newsletter of the Council of Independent Colleges, October, 1995, p. 11.

22. Timothy K. Stanton, ed., *The Integration of Public Service with Academic Study: The Faculty Role* (Providence, R.I.: Campus Compact, January, 1990); Jonathan Eisenberg, comp., *National Members' Survey and Resource Guide* (Providence, R.I., Campus Compact, 1990-91); Marshall Miller and Lockhart Steel, *Service Counts: Lessons for the Field of Service and Higher Education* (Providence, R.I.: Campus Compact, 1995).

23. Eyler and Giles, "The Importance of Program Quality in Service Learning."

24. Serow and Sigmon, "Survey Results: Service Learning at Private Liberal Arts Institutions."

25. Eyler and Giles, "The Importance of Program Quality in Service Learning."

26. Kelly Ward, "Service Learning and Student Volunteerism: Reflections on Institutional Commitment," Paper presented at the Annual Meeting of the American Educational Research Association, New York, April, 1996.

Resources for Further Information about Postsecondary Service-Learning Programs

Service Matters: a Sourcebook for Community Service in Higher Education (1994). Published by Campus Compact, Brown University, Box 1975, Providence, R.I. Phone: 401-863-1119.

For program information for Learn and Serve America Higher Education grantees write

Corporation for National Service, 1201 New York Ave., NW, Washington, D.C. 20525. Phone: 202-606-5000.

For information about the Learning and Service Alliance of thirty colleges that will collaborate on service-learning activities as part of the Serving to Learn, Learning to Serve project, write

Council of Independent Colleges, One DuPoint Circle, Suite 320, Washington, D.C. Phone: 202-466-7230.

For a Program Book of project descriptions, including community service grantees, write

Fund for the Improvement of Postsecondary Education, 7th and D Street, SW, ROB-3, Room 3100, Washington, D.C. 20202-5175. Phone: 202-708-5750.

For program information and descriptions and other published and unpublished resources for service learning and experiential education, write

Resource Center for Experiential and Service Learning, National Society for Experiential Education, 3509 Haworth Dr., Suite 207, Raleigh, N.C. 27609. Phone: 919-787-3263.

CHAPTER IX

Service Learning in Teacher Preparation

PETER C. SCALES AND DONNA J. KOPPELMAN

Community service experience for school-age youth is generally viewed favorably, and programs of service learning under school auspices seem to be on the rise. There have been a few voices of dissent, such as students or their parents arguing that required service learning is a violation of the constitutional prohibition against involuntary servitude, an argument found by the courts to lack merit.[1]

It is difficult to determine how many schools or school districts offer service learning and how many require service for graduation. One estimate is that at least some public school districts in about half the states require community service.[2] A Gallup Poll survey of 1,400 youth aged twelve through seventeen reported that 8 percent of the students said their schools required community service, and 21 percent said courses were offered that included opportunities for community service.[3] In a 1990 survey in Pennsylvania, nearly 14 percent of schools gave academic credit for service, double the level of just two years earlier, although most did not require it for graduation.[4]

With the apparent expansion of service learning programs in the schools, a number of questions arise: Are the schools ready? Are current elementary, middle, and high school teachers ready? Will the next generation of teachers be ready? What must be done to ensure that the answers to these questions will be affirmative?

Preparation of Teachers for Service Learning: The Current Status

The many different standards, guidelines, and recommendations affecting teacher licensure and the accreditation of preparation programs have become moving targets as the movement to reform or restructure the public schools has finally included attention to reform

Peter C. Scales is Senior Fellow with Search Institute, Minneapolis, and Adjunct Professor of Psychology at Saint Louis University. He was formerly Director of National Initiatives for the Center for Early Adolescence, University of North Carolina at Chapel Hill. Donna J. Koppelman teaches language arts and social studies in the sixth grade of Chowan Middle School in Edenton, North Carolina.

of teacher development, especially preservice programs. As teacher training institutions consider the preparation of teachers for service learning, questions are being raised about what teachers should know and be able to do in order to collaborate effectively with community agencies in service learning programs.

The certification and accreditation guidelines for programs that prepare middle school teachers, for example, generally acknowledge the importance of school-community collaboration, but offer little guidance as to conditions that foster that collaboration, such as shared values about teaching and learning, about experiential learning, knowledge of youth development, and skills for working with community agencies. Nor is there much agreement about how teacher training can foster those necessary qualities. For example, there are three major sources of standards for the preparation of teachers for middle schools: the guidelines of the National Middle School Association/National Council for the Accreditation of Teacher Education, standards for state certification from the National Association of State Directors of Teacher Education and Certification (NASDTEC), and certification of excellence standards for experienced teachers from the National Board for Professional Teaching Standards. Only standard 11.0 in the NASDTEC "outcomes-based" standards specifically mentions "youth service," stating the expectation that the beginning teacher "organizes, operates, and continuously improves a youth service program." NASDTEC also states that "college students in their preparation programs should be involved in community activities themselves in order to serve as a role model."[5]

Despite such standards, and despite the increasing number of examples of school-community collaboration on a variety of levels, only a minority of teachers are prepared in their preservice programs to establish meaningful connections with community resources when they become practicing teachers.[6] Nearly half of a sample of 439 teachers of grades five through nine in five states said their preparation for "involving community resources" was inadequate or poor.[7] Such minimal preparation prompted one group, in describing how an excellent middle level preparation program should look, to note that teachers need to "draw on diverse community resources to support service learning and community service projects. . . ."[8] It recommended that preservice students "actively engage" in activities that affect youth socially and culturally, perhaps through "a community service internship established outside the school setting, or while working in a youth service agency."[9]

Is there evidence that these kinds of experiences are even being offered to, much less required of, students preparing to be teachers? Are there significant in-service opportunities for practicing teachers to acquire understandings of service learning? The evidence is spotty at best. For example, our spring 1995 ERIC searches with the key words "teacher training for service learning" produced no records. Personal contact was made with numerous organizations, among them the American Association of Colleges for Teacher Education, the Council of Chief State School Officers, the Corporation for National and Community Service, ERIC, the Lincoln Filene Community Service Learning Center at Tufts University, Middle-L (an electronic newsgroup for middle grades educators), the National Helpers Network (formerly the National Center for Service Learning in Early Adolescence), the National Information Center for Service Learning at the University of Minnesota, and the National Youth Leadership Council. We found no data that provide a national overview of how much training teachers are receiving for service learning either at the preservice or in-service level.

While there are several promising models of preservice and in-service training in the literature, it is anyone's guess as to how extensively these or similar approaches are being utilized throughout the country. Our guess is, not much. The single largest source of support for in-service efforts is the School- and Community-Based Program under Learn and Serve America. Of the $30 million in grants awarded in 1994-1995, it is estimated that just $4 to $5 million was used for training and technical assistance.[10] Under the Learn and Serve Higher Education program, a total of $9 million was awarded in fiscal year 1994 to 116 programs, with twenty-one institutions receiving about $2.1 million for activities that included but did not necessarily focus exclusively on either preservice or in-service teacher training for service learning.[11] Thus, at most $6-7 million was allocated for preservice and in-service training combined. Even a recent excellent guide to developing a service learning program, a volume that itself could serve as an outline for in-service or preservice courses, said little about training teachers other than to advise the reader to read "everything you can find on service learning."[12]

Examples of Programs for Preservice and In-service Teachers

Following are some of the most detailed descriptions we found of in-service and preservice preparation in service learning. Most have both an experiential and a reflection component.

According to Root, Moon, and Kromer, one-shot workshops for practicing teachers and placement of preservice teachers in community agencies are the most common techniques used in training for service learning, but neither does much to help translate what is experienced into how to use service learning in the classroom.[13] The authors describe a K-12 preservice and in-service training program at Central Michigan University that had three levels: (1) awareness (one-shot workshops attended by four hundred preservice and one hundred in-service teachers), (2) implementation (four training sessions and a service project, participated in by forty-two teachers), and (3) leadership (level one and two participants who then acted as co-instructors in further teacher training, in which eight teachers participated).

In response to recent education reform legislation in Massachusetts that mentions community service learning as a "preferred teaching methodology," the Lincoln Filene Center at Tufts University offers a program for in-service teachers. Funded in part through a grant from the W. K. Kellogg Foundation for the establishment of a service network among five school districts, the program includes three-day seminars that enable teachers to earn required recertification points. The Center staff has also developed a Leadership Seminar that trains teachers and administrators who are leading efforts to incorporate service learning throughout school districts. In addition, the Center conducts week-long service learning institutes in the summer (funded by the DeWitt Wallace-Reader's Digest Fund). Participating schools must send a team of two students, a teacher, and an agency partner. The Center follows up with the team over the school year as they pilot the service projects. Twelve hours of follow-up are used for staff development, which includes training trainers to take over ongoing in-service programs for teachers. Other technical assistance includes team-building with school and community agency representatives, establishing and maintaining advisory groups of students, teachers, and agency partners, and helping community agencies design job descriptions that are developmentally appropriate.[14]

Five states—Colorado, Indiana, Mississippi, Pennsylvania, and Washington—are attempting to restructure curriculum, accreditation, and teacher licensure to infuse service learning as an effective method of teaching that connects "student development and achievement."[15] Funded by the DeWitt Wallace-Reader's Digest Fund through a grant to the Council of Chief State School Officers (CCSSO), the project provides in-service training to policymakers and educators and assistance in including service learning as an integral part of teacher education. At least one of these states (Pennsylvania) has begun to identify community service (but not necessarily service learning) as a critical area in which high school students must have experience for admission to state colleges. A considerable reworking of practicum experiences appears to have occurred in those states, but far fewer examples of significant change in the preservice curriculum have been identified. CCSSO staff believe the acceptance of community service as a legitimate part of the educational experience is widespread, but that service learning has not yet become a core teaching strategy at either the K-12 or college level.[16]

A Master's degree program at Seattle University involves one hundred preservice students per year.[17] The program includes (1) a twenty-five hour internship either in one of thirteen K-12 schools with a teacher experienced in service learning or with a community agency (interns choosing a community agency must find their own placements), (2) fourteen hours of team-taught classroom instruction in service learning, (3) a service leadership conference attended by peer students, K-12 teachers, and agency representatives, and (4) reflection activities (journals, cooperative learning exercises, papers, discussions). This program evolved from an elective one-credit course in 1991 to integration with a course that by 1994 was required of all education students.

At the University of Iowa part of the elementary education program includes conceptual and experiential activities such as an intergenerational service project called YES (Youth and Elderly in Service), run collaboratively with the local Retired Senior Volunteer Program and the county Big Brothers/Big Sisters program.[18] The service experiences are incorporated into required courses in Foundations of Education and Social Studies Methods, and students also participate in a one-credit practicum that involves working in the Service Learning Program of the Iowa City School District. Cooperating teachers participate in a one-day summer workshop on service learning. An unusual aspect of this program is its facilitating teams of student teachers, cooperating teachers, and agency representatives which develop curriculum plans for how service learning can be included in the student teaching semester.

At Butler University in Indianapolis students in elementary methods courses developed an experimental collaboration to work as Junior Achievement consultants for fifth and sixth graders. The experience of the forty-eight preservice teachers led researchers to conclude that: (1) the manual created by faculty for education students needed to be less of a cookbook and allow for more "practice [for students] in developing their own teaching materials and style"; (2) the faculty needed to highlight the pedagogical implications of community service work; and (3) this kind of experience might be better suited to sophomores than to upperclass students.[19]

Mankato State University in Minnesota has a three-pronged approach to service learning in teacher preparation. Every education major is required to take a course in "Human Relations," during which students must participate in a twelve-week service learning experience. A course in "School and Society" is also required of prospective teachers; a segment of the course is devoted to service learning as a learning method, and students explore such areas as the philosophy, planning, and evaluation of service learning. The third aspect of the Mankato program, a four-credit elective course, provides the most comprehensive preparation in service learning. It involves fifteen preservice teachers in forty to fifty hours of service with community agencies and four hours per week of reflection and discussion. The students also make site visits to nearby communities where service learning is part of the school program, and, as in the University of Iowa program already described, develop recommendations for the faculty on how service learning can best be integrated in the program to prepare teachers for kindergarten through grade twelve.[20]

The Peer Consultant Initiative is training up to six hundred educators and six hundred youth to provide training and consultation on service learning to schools and districts throughout the country. Funded by a three-year Kellogg Foundation grant to the University of Minnesota, and with significant involvement of the National Youth Leadership Council and others, the project also is building the capacity of states to support service learning through training and resources provided with the Council of Chief State School Officers, and through the project funding plan, which calls for states to assume greater responsibility for project financing in years two and three.[21]

Issues in Teacher Preparation for Service Learning

The data and program descriptions above suggest a number of questions that must be addressed to strengthen teacher preparation for service learning. These questions fall into four broad categories: (1) the goals of service learning; (2) the fit of service learning with a philosophy of youth development and education; (3) the operational needs and barriers to a service learning program; and (4) realizing the potential of collaboration.

GOALS OF SERVICE LEARNING

What do school, university, and community representatives see as the goals of service learning? Is everyone using language the same way? For example, in one setting the emphasis may be on service and "moral development," in another on curriculum enrichment, while still other programs may see the development of youth leadership or employment skills as primary goals.

Even if there is some common agreement on the broad goals of service learning, do teachers, administrators, teacher educators, students at both the school and university levels, parents, and community representatives agree on what structures or activities are essential in support of service learning, regardless of the specific goals? Schine describes these activities as follows: (1) the work students do must be challenging and significant; (2) students must have responsibility for planning, doing, and evaluating the activity; (3) they must have a role in collaborative decision making with peers and adults; and (4) there must be opportunities for preparation and reflection.[22]

SERVICE LEARNING AND A YOUTH DEVELOPMENT FRAMEWORK

Does the school, the university, the teacher, or the teacher educator place service learning in a theoretical framework or does service just make sense to them? A broad developmental framework makes the purpose and impact of service more readily understood. For example, Search Institute's studies of more than 275,000 youth in grades six through twelve have produced a framework of developmental assets youth need to succeed. In this framework, service learning may be seen as an experience that will help young people acquire these assets. Helping others is cited as one of the essential elements in positive youth development. Youth involvement in service is directly related to building additional assets the Search Institute study identifies, such as commitment to education, structured use of time, social competencies, and contact with caring adults who provide support and boundaries.[23]

Questions that customarily arise in implementing service learning in the school should be addressed in both preservice and in-service programs. Because it is often a new field for teachers already in the classroom, as well as for those preparing to teach, not only the philosophical basis for service learning but the day-to-day issues and realities involved in service learning should figure prominently in teacher preparation. If potential pitfalls are anticipated in the course or workshop and possible solutions explored, problems that might have become a crisis in implementation can often be prevented or easily resolved. Such questions as determining the nature of the work the students will be doing and how meaningful it really is challenge the program facilitator to plan with care, and to explore the resources and limitations of the community. There is only so much cleaning up of parks that is useful, either to connect students with the community or to serve as a stimulus for academic research, writing, or other skill development. How much will the available work in community agencies—either for K-12 students or student teachers—engage students' minds, stretch their cognitive, emotional, social, or spiritual capacities, and challenge them to play a meaningful role in their families, schools, and communities?

Questions about the reflection component of service learning are discussed here, rather than in the following section on Operational Issues, because such questions also raise fundamental concerns about values and philosophy. The reflection experience, after all, is considered to be the component of service learning that gives it "lasting meaning—as the service providers think about the effect their actions have . . . the line that divides server and served becomes less distinct."[24] Thus, we need to ask what we mean by "reflection." Zeichner says we too often mean thinking about replicating in teaching the findings that research says have been effective, "to the neglect of any consideration of the social conditions of schooling that influence the teacher's work," such as, "how questions of equity and social justice are embodied in their everyday actions and settings."[25] How much are teachers, whether in in-service or preservice settings, encouraged to pursue this deeper kind of reflection?

Most fundamentally, the program facilitators must be prepared to explain how service learning relates to the primary mission of the schools, i.e., academic effectiveness for all students. When this connection is not clearly enunciated important constituencies (parents, some teachers, school boards) may find service learning suspect, not "academic" enough. For example, the University of Minnesota in 1992 began allowing social studies entrance credit for students who had service experiences that were clearly combined with academic activities, but not for courses that were primarily the experience without academic skill building.[26] Similarly, the facilitator must be prepared to ensure that there will be equity of access to desirable service projects among white and nonwhite students, and among poor and nonpoor students. This applies to placements that are part of preservice or in-service training and to students in K-12 school programs.

OPERATIONAL ISSUES

Should teacher training for service learning be required or voluntary? The data suggest that the great majority of K-12 students are not required to have service learning, and almost no jurisdictions require training in service learning of their teachers or prospective teachers. Most teachers do have the option of including service learning in their teaching, however, and so both their preparation and their personal interest is important. Wade studied ten teachers, five from a town without a service learning program and five from a metropolitan area with a long-standing program.[27] She found that all but one teacher cited very positive, long-ago personal experiences with service to others, even though they did not consciously connect those experiences with their current interest in using service learning in their teaching. A second question is: If preservice teachers are to be required to have exposure to service learning, is this best accomplished through special courses or through integration of service learning across the preservice curriculum?

Some of the barriers program facilitators might experience in the operation of a service learning program include the lack of time for working with community resources; insufficient block scheduling to accommodate service learning program needs; the absence of supportive policies and resources for students and teachers; and inadequate school and community support for the learning that students might acquire from nontraditional programs such as service learning.

Teacher training in how to advocate within the building, school system, and community to overcome these barriers is essential. These examples of possible barriers suggest also the need for involvement of administrators and administrator candidates, not just teachers and preservice teachers, in both in-service and preservice training. Some districts have attempted to deal with these obstacles by creating the position of district service learning coordinator. Wade noted that such a coordinator was critical for teachers who do service learning projects to provide help with ideas, coordination, preparation and training, and even transportation.[28] Shumer went further, noting that teachers in a rural Minnesota community felt a service learning coordinator was an "absolute necessity" for success.[29]

In-service and preservice training must reflect the differences among elementary, middle, and secondary grades in the kind of service learning activities that make the best sense. The students are quite different in their developmental needs and capacities. Among other questions for teacher educators to consider are: At what point in the teacher preparation program should service learning be incorporated—early or late? What are the implications for preservice training for service learning of the recent increase in the proportion of "nontraditional" (i.e., older, coming from disciplines other than education) students in college and teacher education programs?

COLLABORATION

"Collaboration" figures prominently in current discussions of school restructuring or systemic reform. Yet most preservice and in-service programs give scant attention to the strategies and practices for establishing sound working relationships between the schools and both formal and informal community groups and agencies. Often the success of a service learning program will depend upon the strength of those relationships. Training programs must help in-service and preservice teachers to learn how to find "good placements"—i.e., agencies or settings where the service learning concept is understood and where the program staff want to give students real responsibility.[30] Field settings are needed that provide meaningful experience and are willing to adapt to the constraints of the teacher preparation program.

Teacher preparation programs can take advantage of opportunities to collaborate on service learning with other university departments or schools, or with other university groups, such as Campus Compact or the Campus Outreach Opportunity League. For example, the University of Vermont's Center for Service Learning involves more than four hundred students from across the campus, not just education students, in course-related community service projects.[31] In-service and preservice programs may collaborate with community resources, especially family support programs, religious organizations, and other youth-serving agencies or programs. For example, churches and synagogues often do service projects and are an underutilized source for training, support, and collaboration.[32] Joint training with community agencies can be explored; most agency personnel need to learn more about "learning" (in which teachers are experts), and most educators need to learn more about youth "service" or "participation" (in which youth workers are well-versed). Training in collaboration is notably absent for professionals who work with youth, not just teachers.[33] But even a project involving mostly in-building people involves a great deal of collaboration, as the following illustrates:

Iris's service learning project at a nursing home involved the school guidance counselor (in preparing the students for interacting with seniors), the music teacher (who taught the students some old time songs to sing to the seniors), the art teacher (who helped the class prepare a craft project to make with the seniors), and the school principal (who videotaped the participants and served ice cream at the last visit of the year). Parents . . . (helped) with transportation or providing snacks or needed supplies and Iris contacted a local bank that contributed funds for project supplies and refreshments.[34]

Recommendations for In-Service and Preservice Training

Ideally, service learning is a marriage between meaningful learning experiences and the responses to community needs. The value of such a program, however, depends on the training of teachers and other leaders in the school environment, and on the intentional inclusion of community resource persons in that training. Preservice and in-service training are interdependent parts of the professional development continuum, and each is equally important if service learning is to become integrated as a core teaching strategy. Teacher training programs at the college level must include structured exposure to service learning programs. This exposure can occur both through required courses and through hands-on experience in local schools with service learning programs.

INTEGRATE SERVICE LEARNING ACROSS CURRICULUM

Rather than designing another course required for prospective teachers, we believe basic principles of service learning should be integrated into existing course requirements. Classes in curriculum, classroom management, educational theory, and subject methods could incorporate service learning as another way to facilitate student learning. As previously discussed, Mankato State University made service learning an integral part of "Human Relations" and "School and Society," two required courses for education students. Prospective teachers exposed to experiences with service learning as a teaching method are likely to emulate these projects in their own classrooms. For example, a service learning project such as preparing lunch at a shelter for the homeless could incorporate many aspects of the mathematics curriculum in a lesson for elementary students. When service learning is incorporated into existing courses, teacher candidates are able to experience its connection to specific subject areas and its appropriateness for various age groups.

In addition, including service learning in more than one course in the teacher preparation program will communicate a message about its importance for teaching and learning. The more a teacher candidate sees examples and applications of service learning, the more comfortable he or she will be with taking a leadership role in similar endeavors. Some schools of education do not have local area schools with service learning programs. A valuable experience would be for a group of prospective teachers to assist in setting up such a program in a cooperating school. Prospective teachers with those experiences are becoming a generation of leaders in service learning programs.

ENSURE EDUCATORS' KNOWLEDGE OF COMMUNITY

Ideally, preservice education has imbued teachers with the importance of getting to know the community in which they work. Preconceived notions about the values, attitudes, and concerns of diverse communities can obstruct effective teaching in general and successful service learning programs in particular. Ideally, in-service training for service learning should begin at least one year before a program is started, and should involve all administrators, teachers, and host community groups who will collaborate. The first step for the in-service program is to ensure that educators have sufficient information about the community and its needs. A useful beginning for this in-service program might be a bus ride that takes educators through all the neighborhoods served by their school. As teachers learn more about the needs of children and families who attend their school, they can design more thoughtful service learning programs. Local agencies, community groups, and parents have special expertise and familiarity with the community and so should be used as resources in the in-service program. Part of the task teachers have is to understand and respect the cultural climate of the community, including religious, racial, and transportation issues in order to know what kinds of services would be appropriate and welcome, and take religious, racial, and transportation issues into consideration. For example, some teachers might not realize that many members of Jehovah's Witnesses feel they cannot accept gifts of any kind; knowing this would affect a project to benefit a group of elderly Jehovah's Witnesses. With preparation, teachers can acquire confidence that they understand the cultures and norms of their community as they undertake service learning activities.

LINK SERVICE LEARNING AND THE EDUCATIONAL PHILOSOPHY

Teachers and administrators together must develop a vision or goal for the service learning program. The success of the program depends in large measure on the degree to which ownership has been built through the process of coming to a common vision. As Mankato State University has developed its program, it has held an off-site retreat two years in succession, involving university faculty, students, and community agency representatives in order to develop this vision and fine-tune the program. Although Mankato's preservice students normally participate in service learning programs that already have been initiated, they too need experience with this planning and visioning stage as part of their reflection activities before participating in the field experience. It is during this real-life and mock planning stage that the participants can devote attention to articulating the fit of the service learning program with the philosophy of education and youth development embraced by the cooperating school and the teacher preparation program. This step offers prospective teachers an additional opportunity to become familiar with their state's curriculum guidelines, and through that connection they can begin to develop their personal theory and approach.

Program facilitators should consider, too, how the service learning experience is connected with other teacher preparation/school reform issues, e.g., teaming, interdisciplinary curriculum development, advisory groups, family involvement. Service learning is an ideal mechanism for incorporating all those elements, but if it is not designed to do so, the activity can then be seen by key constituencies as irrelevant to the "more important" reform or restructuring activities. There may be some potential to deal with these issues through groups such as the Alliance for Service Learning in Education Reform, a consortium established by thirty youth-serving groups and the Council of Chief State School Officers, and now housed at the Close-Up Foundation.[35] As teachers implement service learning in their schools, they need to decide how students will learn about service learning, where they will share their experiences, and who will be their adult advisor. Middle schools have an ideal structure through daily advisor/advisee time. Elementary and high schools need to build time for sharing and reflection into existing courses, or provide separate opportunities for these purposes. Continuity can be encouraged by having students who have done service learning give a presentation to the rising class at its orientation.

IMPLEMENT SERVICE LEARNING DISTRICTWIDE

If a desired outcome of service learning in the schools is producing young Americans who continue to serve their communities as adults, then the service learning program should allow students to become more independent each year. For example, it is a good idea to "link" schools within a district so that as students progress from elementary to middle to high school and beyond, they are becoming more independent in their service. A districtwide commitment to service learning allows a progression of experiences from a project involving the whole building to one involving a single individual.

To promote districtwide commitment, teacher training programs should ensure that teacher representatives from different buildings are included and perhaps linked in the training as peer teams. The inclusion of assistant superintendents and other representatives from the district central office also is critical. These training experiences will pave the way for a service learning progression as students mature. For example, an entire elementary school *building* might work together to serve one agency or cause; each class could meet a different need at various times throughout the year. In the community's middle schools, each *grade* or *team* might provide service for one agency or cause, with advisor/advisee groups responding to different needs. High school students might be placed in community settings according to individual interest, with the school ensuring that peer support is built in by providing that at least two students work with each collaborating agency.

CONNECT SERVICE LEARNING TO THE VALUES AND SKILLS OF THE CORE CURRICULUM

Teachers need to identify the values and skills to be gained from service learning and ensure that they are connected to subject areas. In addition to increased motivation and commitment to academic achievement, educators might reasonably expect an increase in such skills and values as career exploration, leadership, confidence, connection to community, communication, and nurturing a sense of self. Students and host agencies also should be familiar with the values and skills the program is designed to promote. Host agencies in the community should participate in in-service programs for teachers to build a spirit of collaboration. This cooperation is rooted in a shared philosophy, common language, and joint decision making about the program. At the preservice level, one university went even further in thinking about collaboration: a recommendation was made to the University of Minnesota's College of Education that a full teacher preparation program in service learning be organized as a joint venture between the College's Generator Center (a research and practice center for service learning), the College, local school districts, and businesses and community agencies in Minneapolis.[36] This type of collaboration is ideal because it offers advantages for everyone involved.

Connecting service learning to the core curriculum is most readily done in schools and preservice programs with an interdisciplinary commitment and organization. In practice in the middle school, for example, the sixth grade might concentrate on service learning to benefit an environmental agency, integrating its experiences with the curriculum in health, science, mathematics, and language arts. One advisory group might focus on the public health aspects of pollution, another on the scientific and quantitative measurement of levels of pollution, another on how information best gets communicated to lawmakers and the public, and so on.

EXPOSE EDUCATORS TO SUCCESSFUL EXAMPLES

Teachers and preservice students should be exposed to examples of successful service learning programs. They need guidance in the organizational and logistical realities of setting up a program, matching students and agencies, grouping students for support, and integrating service into the core curriculum. Experienced teachers who have not had extensive experience with service learning programs need access to mentors who can guide them on these specifics. Not only should preservice teachers be exposed to a variety of school settings; practicing teachers also should observe successful service learning programs in schools similar to theirs in resources, geographical location, racial composition, and socioeconomic status. These contacts should be ongoing and supportive, as well as conducive to both learning and problem solving.

TEACH THE TEACHERS OF FUTURE TEACHERS

Finally, we must say a word about teacher educators. Just as only a minority of teachers are prepared in such strategies as collaboration with community resources, a necessary component of service learning, so only a minority of teacher educators have themselves been trained adequately in such areas. One study of middle level teacher educators reported that 60 percent had been a teacher educator for eleven years or more, and that 75 percent had not taught for seven years or more at the school level for which they were certified.[37] Given how long ago the majority of teacher educators may have received their own training and how long it has been since most were teaching students at the level of their certification, special efforts need to be made to provide them with continuing education opportunities in community collaboration and service learning.

Conclusion

Search Institute's studies of service learning in religious congregations have lessons for educational settings as well. The Institute found that service has its most lasting impact when five conditions are met. We have paraphrased the conditions to apply to schools and community agencies: (1) the organizations involved (i.e., schools and the agencies where youth provide service) are experienced as warm and supportive places; (2) students have personal experiences with staff that demonstrate care for them; (3) youth are integrated into the workings of the whole organization in which they provide service and not segregated into limited activities; (4) service is treated as an expected and normal part of the school's activities; and (5) the values that support service to and helping of others are reflected throughout the school and community agency, not just in one special class or program.[38]

These conditions reflect a culture of helping, service, and collaboration among peers, between youth and adults, and across institutions in the community. Schools and preservice preparation programs that nurture this kind of organizational culture, and add to it the opportunities and resources for critically thinking about service before, during, and after the service work, are constructing powerful teaching and learning experiences. Research has shown that making this deliberate connection between community service and learning contributes a substantial positive influence to young people's development. Search Institute's studies report that youth who help others as little as one hour per week have half the incidence of negative behaviors such as skipping school, vandalism, and frequent use of alcohol and other drugs.[39]

Educators who want this kind of impact to occur in their institutions and communities need to commit both their own supportive rhetoric and significant professional development resources for in-service and preservice training. Absent that commitment, service learning will remain a strategy used by only a minority of teachers and teacher educators who have essentially taught themselves and persevered in innovating despite significant political and operational obstacles. That is a difficult way to spark a national movement, and a missed opportunity for all youth.

Notes

1. "Court Says High Schools Can Require Community Service," *State Legislatures* 19 (June 1993): 9.

2. Michael Winerip, "Required Volunteerism: School Programs Tested," *New York Times*, 23 September 1993.

3. Meg Sommerfeld, "60% of Adolescents Volunteered in '91, Survey Finds," *Education Week*, 9 December 1992.

4. John A. Briscoe, "PennSERVE: School-Based Community Service," *Inside Education*, Newsletter of the Pennsylvania Department of Education 3 (April/May 1990): 1-2.

5. NASDTEC (National Association of State Directors of Teacher Education and Certification), *Outcome-Based Teacher Education Standards for the Elementary, Middle, and High School Levels* (Dubuque, Iowa: Kendall Publishing, 1993), p. 43.

6. Peter C. Scales, *Connecting Communities and Middle Schools: Strategies for Preparing Middle Level Teachers* (Minneapolis, Minn.: Search Institute, 1995).

7. Peter C. Scales, *Window of Opportunity: Improving Middle Grades Teacher Preparation* (Minneapolis, Minn.: Search Institute, 1992).

8. C. Kenneth McEwin, Thomas C. Dickinson, Thomas O. Erb, and Peter C. Scales, *A Vision of Excellence: Organizing Principles for Middle Grades Teacher Preparation* (Columbus, Ohio: National Middle School Association, 1995), p. 19.

9. Ibid., p. 29.

10. Personal communication with Brad Lewis of the Corporation for National and Community Service, 22 May 1995.

11. Personal communication with Suzanne Mintz of the Corporation for National and Community Service, 23 May 1995.

12. Judith T. Witmer and Carolyn S. Anderson, *How to Establish a High School Service Learning Program* (Alexandria, Va.: Association for Supervision and Curriculum Development, 1994).

13. Susan Root, Arden Moon, and Thomas Kromer, "Service Learning in Teacher Education: A Constructivist Model," in *Integration Service Learning into Teacher Education: Why and How?* (Washington, D.C.: Council of Chief State School Officers, 1995), pp. 31-40.

14. Personal communication with Patricia M. Barnicle, Lincoln-Filene Center, 27 April 1995.

15. Caroline Allam, "One State's Strategy for Change: Improving Student Learning and Teacher Practice through Community Service," *The Generator*, publication of the National Youth Leadership Council (Spring 1992), p. 10.

16. Personal communication with Barbara Gomez of the Council of Chief State School Officers, 25 May 1995.

17. Jeffrey Anderson and Kristin Guest, "Linking Campus and Community: Service Leadership in Teacher Education at Seattle University," in *Integrating Service Learning into Teacher Education*, pp. 11-30.

18. Rahima C. Wade, "Community Service Learning in the Elementary Teacher Education Program at the University of Iowa," in *Integrating Service Learning into Teacher Education*, pp. 41-55.

19. Douglas Roebuck and Arthur Hochman, "Community Service Agencies and Social Studies: A New Partnership," *Social Education* 57 (February 1993): 77.

20. William Olszewski and Darrol Bussler, "Learning to Serve—Serving to Learn," unpublished paper, Mankato (Minn.) State University, 1993.

21. Personal communication with Robert Shumer, Department of Vocational and Technical Education, University of Minnesota, 31 May 1995.

22. Joan Schine, "Community Service: When Theory and Practice Meet," *Educational Researcher* 24 (March 1995): 33-35.

23. Peter L. Benson, Judy Galbraith, and Pamela Espeland, *What Kids Need to Succeed* (Minneapolis: Free Spirit Publishing, 1995).

24. Schine, "Community Service: When Theory and Practice Meet," p. 34.

25. Kenneth M. Zeichner, "Beyond Inquiry-oriented Teacher Education: Rethinking the Practicum in North American Teacher Education" (Paper presented at the Annual Meeting of the Western Canadian Association for Student Teaching, Edmonton, Alberta, February, 1992), pp. 8, 23.

26. Minnesota Department of Education, *Model Learner Outcomes for Youth Community Service* (St. Paul, Minn.: Minnesota Department of Education, 1992), pp. 101-2.

27. Rahima C. Wade, "Contextual Influences on Teachers' Experiences with Community Service Learning" (Paper presented at the Annual Meeting of the American Educational Research Association, San Francisco, April, 1995).

28. Ibid.

29. Robert Shumer, *A Report from the Field: Teachers Talk about Service Learning* (Minneapolis: Center for Experiential Education and Service Learning, College of Education, University of Minnesota, 1994).

30. See Diane Harrington, "Reaching Beyond the Self," *American Educator* 16 (Summer 1992): 36-43.

31. Cynthia Parsons, "SerVermont: The Little Initiative That Could," *Phi Delta Kappan* 72 (June 1991): 768-770.

32. See Peter L. Benson and Eugene C. Roehlkepartain, *Beyond Leaf Raking: Learning to Serve/Serving to Learn* (Nashville: Abington Press, 1993).

33. See Scales, *Connecting Communities and Middle Schools*.

34. Wade, "Contextual Influences on Teachers' Experiences with Community Service Learning," p. 13.

35. Millicent Lawton, "Coalition Created to Promote Youth Service in Reform Efforts," *Education Week*, 25 November 1992; personal communication with Donna Power of the Close-Up Foundation and Alliance for Service Learning in Education Reform, 25 May 1995.

36. Robert Shumer, "Teacher Education and Service Learning," Report to the Department of Vocational and Technical Education, College of Education, University of Minnesota, 30 June 1992.

37. Peter C. Scales, "Strengthening Middle Grade Teacher Preparation Programs," *Middle School Journal* 26 (September 1994): 59-63.

38. Adapted from Benson and Roehlkepartain, *Beyond Leaf Raking*, p. 39.

39. Peter L. Benson, *The Troubled Journey: A Portrait of 6th-12th Grade Youth* (Minneapolis: Search Institute, 1993); Eugene C. Roehlkepartain, *Everyone Wins When Youth Serve* (Washington, D.C.: Points of Light Foundation, 1995).

CHAPTER X

Encouraging Cultural Competence in Service Learning Practice

JANIE VICTORIA WARD

Carol Kinsley captures the common elements which constitute the philosophy of service learning when she describes it as "an educational process that involves students in service experiences with two firm anchors: first, their service experience is directly related to academic subject matter, and second, it involves them in making positive contributions to individuals and community institutions."[1]

The model of service learning as an applied method of education is one that is broad enough to allow a variety of populations to participate and to be served. Some student participants "learn by doing" in projects that focus on local community needs, while others engage with programs that extend to the wider concerns of the global community. Service projects undertaken by school, religious, and social groups can be short- or long-term, and include such activities as the organization of food drives, community clean-up campaigns, tutoring programs, and visits to nursing homes.

Responsibilities and opportunities for prosocial behaviors need to begin at an early age and participants in school-based service learning programs frequently include elementary and high school students. Proctor and Haas present a model that establishes the scope and sequence for school-based service programs. In this model, activities are arranged in hierarchical order with the highest level—the Individual Service Project—integrating and building upon the skills, values, and concepts of the two earlier levels. At the first level, primarily designed for younger children, the school service project is a one-time activity of short duration. At the second level, community service is also a one-time effort, but is designed to serve the neighborhood or entire community. The highest level involves students' continuing commitments of time and energy on a regular basis.[2] Such age-appropriate,

---

Janie Victoria Ward is Associate Professor of Education and Human Services at Simmons College in Boston, Massachusetts.

developmental approaches to service learning, which are designed to provide opportunities for students to develop and apply increasingly sophisticated community service skills and analyses to social problem solving, are highly valuable and worthy of replication.

The process by which students learn to coordinate and integrate academic subject matter with their service component varies with the particularities of the setting. Conrad and Hedin identify six characteristics present in effective service programs: (1) they are valuable and worthwhile to both school and community; (2) they provide opportunities in which young people must be counted upon; (3) they include tasks that challenge and strengthen critical thinking skills; (4) they provide opportunities for students to make decisions; (5) they involve students and adults working together; (6) they provide systematic reflection on the experience.[3] The latter two of these common components, working with adult mentors or advisors and the expectation of personal reflection throughout the process, are particularly noteworthy. Adult advisors serve to encourage, support, guide, monitor, and evaluate. Journal writing, group discussions, and other activities designed to encourage reflection serve to contribute to students' greater understanding of self, of those being served, of social problems, of active citizenship, and of the individual's responsibility to the collective.

Over the past few years volunteerism and community service appear to be capturing the imagination of increasing numbers of America's youth populations. According to the 1992 survey entitled, "Volunteering and Giving among American Teenagers, 12 to 19 Years of Age," published by *Independent Sector*, there has been an increase in volunteer activity. In 1989, 58 percent of youth aged 14 to 19 years surveyed reported volunteering; by 1991, that figure had increased to 61 percent, with most respondents volunteering more hours than they had in the past.[4] Although some research suggests that high school students rarely seek out service opportunities independently,[5] the 1992 *Independent Sector* survey noted that when asked to volunteer teenagers respond positively.

Advocates of service learning suggest that its benefits include an increase in altruism, self-esteem, and efficacy.[6] They call attention to its promotion of prosocial values such as social responsibility and civic involvement through volunteerism. Moreover, service learning proponents argue that through service students can experience the importance of making and keeping commitments to others, as well as learning to work with diverse populations.

Philosophical Underpinnings

The concept of learning through service has strong and enduring roots that emanate from a number of educational, religious, and social welfare traditions. The basic teachings of Judeo-Christian ethics, "love thy neighbor," "do unto others . . .," and the reognition of the importance of putting back into the world more than you take out, provide values and principles upon which community service is based. Educator John Dewey sees implications for education and citizenship development and draws attention to the social orientation that service learning can foster.[7] Moral philosopher Nel Noddings and others see service learning as a means of promoting moral sensibilities as students develop compassion and learn to give of themselves to care for others.[8] After reviewing the philosophies and practices of service learning, Westheimer and Kahne argue that there are two orientations—*charity* and *change*.[9] Thus, service learning activities tend toward two characteristic relationships between the service provider and the recipient: one which emphasizes caring, giving, and compassion (charity) and one that upon critical reflection determines the need for active engagement in political action and social transformation (change). According to Westheimer and Kahne, the differing yet frequently intertwined goals that motivate those who support service learning can be best understood along moral, political, and pedagogical domains. The authors conclude that charity, while important, fails to acknowledge, examine, or respond to structural problems. They write, "Citizenship requires more than kindness and decency; it requires engagement in complex social and institutional endeavors."[10] They warn that enrolling students in short-term service learning projects that have few links to curriculum and/or provide little opportunity for critical reflection on either the nature or the reasons for the services needed serves to minimize the problem and trivialize the helping relationship.

Service Learning at the College Level

Colleges and universities are increasingly participating in the development of service learning programs as they assume the challenge of making community service an integral part of the educational experience. The rationale for community service grows out of "institutional values shared by the academic community."[11] Through this effort, the role of education is expanded as a public trust as the college reinforces its responsibilities to both the community and the students.

This extension of education beyond the walls of the classroom can benefit all parties involved—the university, the students, and the populations served.

Harkavy and Puckett maintain that universities have failed to become as involved in urban revitalization as they should. Rather than shying away from involvement, the authors argue, colleges and universities must reinvent themselves to become once again mission-oriented institutions that advance the idea of academically based community service tied to teaching and research.[12]

Simmons College in Boston, where I coordinate the undergraduate Human Services Program, seeks to build stronger relationships between our institution and the greater Boston community through action-oriented and participatory school-community partnerships. This is achieved through formal and informal means. As we state in our annual catalogue, our undergraduate program offers students a liberal education, which is important in itself, and an appropriate context for professional study, to which the college is equally committed. Most of the college's academic and professional programs offer field work or clinical experiences through which students may explore the nature, opportunities, and implications of a career field. The independent learning requirement is an important component of a Simmons education. There are several forms of independent learning opportunities available in the curriculum, including independent study, internship, and fieldwork.

Simmons College undergraduate students are all women. The majority are white and predominantly working and middle class from racially homogeneous communities with minimal sustained contact with low-income populations or with people of color. Most are young adults who enrolled in college immediately following high school, but many are older women returning to the classroom to obtain a degree after years of professional service and/or family responsibilities.

Informally, Simmons College has established a community service program. It is organized by a small staff of undergraduate volunteers, most of whom are majoring in fields outside of the human services area such as the arts, the humanities, and the sciences. A faculty advisor is on call primarily in a trouble-shooting capacity and the group has a small operating budget. The undergraduates organize and participate in community-based projects which are most often student-initiated, short-term, small, and manageable. Because students tend to participate intermittently, the projects require limited prior preparation and provide minimal opportunities for formal reflection following service delivery. The community service program at our college is organized and administered like many other service programs in colleges, schools, community groups, and religious organizations. The work that these small groups of volunteers achieve is impressive, as is their desire to assist where they are needed in local schools, clinics, and community agencies.

Nonetheless, while the service is admirable, the learning tends to be unstructured, as the educational process is not tied to academic subject matter in any formal manner. To be sure, some students develop and hone specific skills, such as tutoring or counseling techniques. Some gain interaction with populations they never would have met in the absence of these service activities. Many feel good about their service and proud of what they have accomplished. However, the overriding focus on service overshadows concerns about deep learning or social transformation.

Undoubtedly some of the volunteers are perfectly content with their service; they feel the work they are engaged in is worthy and appreciated at the individual and institutional levels. Yet I observe some students who are unhappy and frustrated because the program did not meet their expectations. These dissatisfied undergraduates appear to want more, although most are uncertain of how to bring about their desired ends. This lack of clarity is especially salient when service provision takes place in low-income, ethnic-minority communities which are not familiar to the students, but toward which they often gravitate because of proximity to the college and the fact that students perceive the need for volunteer assistance to be most acute in those communities.

I do not wish to suggest that these students should not work in poor ethnic communities, or that their volunteer assistance is neither helpful nor needed. Instead, I am arguing that I have seen evidence of less-than-helpful practices by volunteer service providers operating from unexamined, preconceived assessments of the community and the characteristics and needs of its residents. Too often in these instances recipients end up getting less out of the service relationship than do the students. While those they serve may gain specific material benefits, such as food, clothing, and other goods, it is less often that recipients of service achieve a sense of personal worth, maintain their self-esteem, or gain the skills to engage in empowerment activities on their own behalf.

While the Simmons School of Social Work is a well-known, highly respected graduate institution, the Simmons College Human Services Program in which I teach is a much smaller and more broadly defined program of study that emphasizes advocacy, family studies, social problem analysis, and social policy rather than focusing on casework and community organization commonly found in social work programs at the baccalaureate and graduate levels. Students with a concentration in human services enroll in core courses which blend the liberal arts with their professional training. All students in human services must complete their independent learning requirement in the form of a senior internship. These internships generally require that students spend a sustained period in the field for at least one full semester. They are closely supervised on site as they assume responsibilities in their preprofessional role. Throughout the internship they have the opportunity and are expected to attend regular progress meetings with their internship advisors and field site supervisors. The senior internship is a service learning activity that provides not only preprofessional training and introduces senior level students to job-specific work skills, but in the process allows them to give something back over the course of the semester. Students have organized food drives, statewide walk-a-thons, and vocational training programs and have coordinated school-based support groups. This internship is a culminating experience for our seniors, offering real-life, active, and effective engagement in community-based settings over an extended period of time. They receive increased responsibility at their worksite over the course of the semester, and they return to the classroom on a weekly basis to reflect systematically upon their experiences, discussing with their peers their frustrations, fears, encounters with obstacles, and their successes.

At the beginning of the semester I ask entering students to write about their past volunteer experiences in community service or other service learning activity. I continue to be moved by the level of concern, commitment, and care expressed in their essays. Many come to college with extensive experience working in soup kitchens, church-related service projects, advocacy groups such as Students Against Drunk Driving, and peer counseling programs. Often it is because of their community work that they are considering human services as a profession. Undoubtedly these are deeply caring, activist-oriented young women of strong moral character, and I marvel at their willingness to devote their time and skills to an overwhelmingly "feminine" profession that is generally underpaid and undervalued in our society.

Two of the core courses in human services have field requirements and by the time these students reach their senior year they have participated over several years in a host of challenging field opportunities such as organizing semiclinical discussion groups for teen mothers, conducting intake interviews with low-income individuals applying for food stamps or mothers applying for assistance under the Women, Infants, and Children (WIC) program, working in day care centers, battered women's shelters, and the like. During the senior internship, faculty work individually with students to design settings that match students' interests and skill levels with worksite needs.

Service in Culturally Different Settings

Often the communities as well as individuals and families who use the services of the agencies and organizations in which we place our students are unlike people and places to which they are accustomed. The settings tend to be in low-income communities of color with which our students have had limited previous engagement. In response to diminishing resources, many social service agencies have suffered cutbacks and layoffs; consequently, local volunteers, particularly those assumed to be well trained and well educated, are being called on to provide more extensive assistance in community and clinic settings. The students are often granted broad flexibility and they are being asked to tutor, counsel, and advise many different kinds of people from a host of life circumstances. Reports from the field state that undergraduates feel underprepared for service in schools, hospitals, and agencies serving diverse populations. Students recognize the need to become more familiar with the practices and the values, attitudes, and beliefs imbedded in other cultures. They make direct requests for a curriculum that emphasizes community and individual empowerment and stresses social action and change—a curriculum that will acquaint them with the complex nature of minority-majority group relations in our society. Moreover, students want to gain the cultural knowledge necessary for competence in delivering human services.

There are several important distinctions that can and should be made among informal student-run community service programs, formal preprofessional programs designed to prepare students for careers in human services, and the formal academically driven service learning programs designed for majors outside of the human services area offered in many colleges and universities. My intent in describing the two service programs in place on our college campus is not to extol one over the other, as each responds to a different set of students' interests and needs. Instead, I hope to share with readers what I have learned from careful observation of college-age participants in community service regarding what students need in formal and informal service learning endeavors in order to feel competent and effective. It is important to note that the students in both programs have much in common. They are very similar demographically, most often from white, middle class, "privileged" backgrounds. They have similar past experiences with service activities, having participated in service programs in their elementary and high schools, churches, and community groups. And they possess both a strong altruistic spirit and a belief in the power of the individual to make a difference in the lives of others. However, the human services majors differ from the students in our community service programs in several important ways. They have expressed a desire to enter human services as a profession and to this end they are willing to do the work to make themselves "change agents" in the process of service delivery. The internship provides an opportunity for students to prepare themselves to shift from a "charity" orientation to a "change" orientation so that they add their charitable, caring, qualities and inclinations to the skills they develop in advocacy and political action. Through in-depth study of social issues from a variety of disciplinary and cultural perspectives, the human services majors recognize that this orientational shift is a difficult, lifelong process with progressive challenges that surface periodically. Most important, these students claim that it is a powerfully humbling experience, one in which they are offered the opportunity to gain greater self-knowledge. Students in informal community service programs with few curricular links, as well as those in formal preprofessional service learning programs, are struggling to become effective change agents. They have made me aware of the troublesome challenges that cultural difference creates for service learning.

Problematic Practices in Service Learning

As a college instructor in human services, I have witnessed unfortunate instances of problematic practices in the design and implementation of service learning programs. Such instances occur particularly when projects are designed to place young adults in low-income, ethnic-minority communities before they are prepared and have had opportunities to become acquainted with the social and political realities confronting the residents' lives. The assumptions held by students about those they help and the nature of the helping relationship are often the source of problematic practices in service learning. In the past few years, changes in the American economy have changed the shape of American poverty. Most of us have been inundated with very clear messages about major social problems and the populations that are the domain of the social welfare system. The poor who receive federal or state financial assistance, particularly low-income people of color, are frequently demonized in the cultural images and rhetoric of our society, depicted as uneducated, unskilled, irresponsible, and unmotivated. Shaped in part by the messages they have received, students often perform their service in low-income, ethnic-minority communities from a judgmental deficit model, believing that those they serve are and should be passive, willing (and grateful) recipients of the students' charitable impulses. This "I give/they receive" orientation to the helping relationship often betrays a "better than/less than" dynamic that impedes the development of real caring relationships in which mutual expectations, responsibilities, and benefits are shared by both those who help and those being helped. No doubt students' self-esteem soars when they feel needed and valued, but it is worrisome that they may be gaining a sense of superiority through the process of making incorrect or inappropriate assumptions about social groups and the nature of the help provided.

As problematic as it is to think all students harbor racial and class bias, it is naive to assume the absence of such attitudes. In their work with college-age students working in urban multicultural community settings, Schram and Mandell found that "it's not easy to change our thoughts about ethnicity because more often than not we aren't even conscious of them. We tend to see what we expect to see."[13] These expectations are framed by socialization processes and shaped by our cultural values, priorities, and role prescriptions. We are all susceptible to the forces of prejudice and ethnocentric bias. But students who wish to perform culturally competent service must, through self-reflection and introspection, resist "cultural encapsulation,"[14] the inability to engage those they serve on any but the service provider's own terms. Much of effective service delivery is about understanding who you are and what you bring to the service relationship. Uncovering unconscious attitudes and unlearning erroneous preconceived notions of self and others can be especially challenging for students who have grown up in middle class, racially isolated settings; an unfortunate artifact of such privilege is that it can distance one from others.[15] Overcoming that social distance requires a critical examination of privilege, social inequality, and minority group membership. Understanding social inequality and its effects upon those who are denied the resources and opportunities that others take for granted establishes a foundation from which students can work toward positive social change and social justice.

Understanding the dynamics of power in interpersonal and societal relationships must be one of the educational objectives of an effective service learning curriculum. Power provides the holder with authority, status, prestige, and influence that can bring about a sense of significance.[16] Students need to appreciate the inherent imbalance of power in the service relationship, recognizing, for example, the nature of the power they possess as it relates to their role (as "expert," "teacher," "trainer") or to their ability to access knowledge, resources, or services that community members may need. Power can be used in any number of ways (for instance, to develop or to control), and thus must be handled mindfully and with care. The dynamic of the passive client/expert outsider may serve to distort students' sense of their participation in the helping relationship; moreover, it may silence the recipient and further impede competent service.

Related to concerns associated with power dynamics is the issue of students' assumptions and expectations regarding their participation in service learning ventures in the urban communities which surround their campus. I have found that students are notably unaware of the history of their college or of the community in which it is located, and know even less about the community's prior relationship to university faculty, administrators, and students. This is particularly important in cities like Boston, where the establishment of collaborative relationships has created painful school-community partnerships in the past. I have personally heard many tales of insensitive, unethical practices that have taken place over the past few decades. University experts, particularly when funding was more available, were reported to have bulldozed their way into low-income communities of color, armed with the latest theory, practice, research study, or group of volunteers. They collected data or organized programs in poor and minority communities primarily for their own ends, ignoring the needs of the community. The people of the communities gained little from the process and often felt cheated, depleted, and betrayed. Because of this unfortunate history, some community residents today still approach school-community partnerships with suspicion and dread and question the usefulness of their cooperation. Students who wish to work in communities that have such histories must be made aware of the past and its influence on service delivery. The work of clarifying for faculty and students the importance of collaboration demands the incorporation of community members' knowledge and advice about issues and priorities that they believe are important and the needs they feel must be addressed. Learning the history of a community and its residents and understanding the historical and present-day social and political realities that create conditions of poverty that impact service provision are critical parts of the service learning process.

Creating Effective Cross-cultural Service Learning Practices

Culture-free service delivery is nonexistent, yet many service learning programs behave as though this is not the case. In my experience as a professor of human services, I have met many college students who have a deep desire to work with the poor and with members of ethnic-minority groups, but I have met few who possess the requisite knowledge to work effectively with culturally different individuals and families. Nor do I expect to find large numbers of these students in my classroom. Cultural competence requires general and specific skills, introduced and developed over a period of time. With effort, creativity, and commitment from college instructors, curriculum developers, community members and, of course, the students themselves, cultural competence can be achieved.

Students and faculty who are serious about effective service learning in culturally diverse communities must strive to contextualize their service, learning all they can about the communities and the individuals they will encounter through class and field work. Course material must provide students with careful in-depth analyses of social problems from multidisciplinary perspectives. The reasons why individuals and families experience particular social problems should be examined, as should existing programs and policies that prevent, alleviate, or may even exacerbate these problems. Students must develop the skills to think critically and solve problems creatively, integrating theory and relevant research with their observations and field experiences.

Part of the preparation that must begin prior to entering diverse communities and continue throughout the experience is engaging in exercises designed to invoke self-awareness. Unpacking the baggage we carry, including the internalized myths we hold about ourselves and others, is crucial cross-cultural work. Locke's model begins with self-awareness.[17] Knowing one's own personal biases, values, and interests, which stem from one's own culture, will greatly enhance students' sensitivity toward other cultural groups.

From there the culturally competent service provider must work to develop a cultural knowledge base. Students should learn the history of the community and of the residents who live there. Whenever possible students should meet with residents formally and informally, visiting homes, churches, and other institutions that have meaning in the lives of community residents. Information should be collected about cultural group values, beliefs, and practices. Locke's multicultural counseling model recommends that service providers examine ten elements relevant to a specific cultural group: degree of acculturation, poverty, history of oppression, language and the arts, racism and prejudice, sociopolitical factors, child-rearing practices, religious practices, family structure, and values and attitudes.[18] Community residents can be enlisted to assist in the collection and interpretation of this information if they feel their effort is respected and valued. The contributions of community residents and those who work closely with community members can be invaluable in uncovering traditional practices and natural social support networks, which are indigenous cultural strengths that support a healthy sense of individual identity and capability.[19] Such attention to strengths, as opposed to focusing attention exclusively on deficits in low-income cultural communities will serve to create a foundation upon which real empowerment at the individual and community levels can take shape.

Charity alone is not enough to address the legacy of inequality in the United States. While care and compassion may motivate students to engage in service learning projects in poor and minority populations, the deep, meaningful, and enduring change in the lives of disenfranchised individuals and communities will take more than episodic gestures of good will and benevolence. At our college, we have discovered that service learning is compromised when undergraduates, placed in low-income, ethnic-minority communities, are allowed to underplay or ignore cultural differences and power dynamics that are inherent in the helping relationship. Service learning programs that expose students, through prior academic study and reflection, to requisite information relevant to the ethnic communities in which they will serve provide a necessary corrective to existing problematic service learning practices. In adopting this curricular strategy we have also learned that contextualized learning promotes powerful learning. Students who are willing to take on the challenge of gaining multicultural knowledge and sensitivity not only come to know and respect the cultural contexts of the communities in which they serve, but also find they are better able to improve their service contributions in ways that are meaningful, transformative, and beneficial to all who are involved.

Notes

1. Carol W. Kinsley, "What Is Community Service Learning?" *Vital Speeches of the Day* 61, no. 2 (November 1, 1994): 14. Others define service learning as "an individual or group act of good will (service) for a person, group, or community, based on planned educational outcomes (learning)." See William Olszewski and Darrol Bussler, "Learning to Serve—Serving to Learn," (Mankato, Minn.: Mankato State University, 1983), p. 2, ERIC ED 367615. In *Education Week* for April 19, 1995, Eli J. Segal highlights the role of responsive citizenship and community involvement through service, academic study, and reflection.

2. David R. Proctor and Mary E. Haas, "Social Studies and School-Based Community Service Programs: Teaching the Role of Cooperation and Legitimate Power," *Social Education* 57, no. 7 (1994): 383.

3. Dan Conrad and Diane Hedin, "The Impact of Experiential Education on Adolescent Development," *Child and Youth Services* 4 (1982): 57-76.

4. *Independent Sector,* "New *Independent Sector* Survey Shows Teen Volunteering and Giving on the Rise," News Release (Washington, D.C.: *Independent Sector*, December 3, 1992).

5. Dwight E. Giles, Jr. and Janet Eyler, "The Impact of College Community Service Laboratory on Students' Personal, Social, and Cognitive Outcomes," *Journal of Adolescence* 17 (1994): 327-339.

6. K. Luchs, "Selected Changes in Urban High School Students after Participation in Community-Based Learning and Service Activities," Doctoral dissertation, University of Maryland, 1981.

7. John Dewey, "Search for the Great Community," in John Dewey, *The Public and Its Problems* (Chicago: Gateway Books, 1946), pp. 143-154.

8. Nel Noddings, *Caring: A Feminine Approach to Ethics and Moral Education* (Berkeley, Calif.: University of California Press, 1984).

9. Joel Westheimer and Joseph Kahne, "In the Service of What? The Politics of Service Learning," Paper presented at the Annual Meeting of the American Educational Research Association, New Orleans, April, 1994).

10. Ibid., p. 19.

11. John E. Moore, "Learning through Service: More Than a Fad," *Liberal Education* 80, no. 1 (1994): 55.

12. I. Harkavy and J. L. Puckett, "Lessons from Hull House for the Contemporary Urban University," *Social Service Review* 68, no. 3 (1994): 315.

13. Barbara Schram and Betty R. Mandell, *An Introduction to Human Services: Policy and Practice*, 2d ed. (Needham Heights, Mass.: Macmillan, 1994), p. 255.

14. Paul Pederson, "The Field of Intercultural Counseling," in *Counseling across Cultures*, edited by Paul Pederson, Walter J. Lonner, and Jurris G. Dragons (Honolulu: University of Hawaii Press, 1976), pp. 17-41.

15. Elaine Pinderhughes, *Understanding Race, Ethnicity, and Power* (New York: Free Press, 1989).

16. John A. Axelson, *Counseling and Development in a Multicultural Society* (Pacific Grove, Calif.: Brooks/College Publishing Co., 1993), p. 163.

17. Don Locke, *Increasing Multicultural Understanding: A Comprehensive Model* (Newbury Park, Calif.: Sage Publications, 1992).

18. Ibid., p. 12.

19. James W. Green, *Cultural Awareness in the Human Services: A Multiethnic Approach* (Needham, Mass.: Allyn and Bacon, 1995), p. 72.

CHAPTER XI

Service Learning and Improved Academic Achievement: The National Scene

MADELEINE M. KUNIN

Service learning, like many good ideas, is not new. I was introduced to the concept in 1985 by Cynthia Parsons, a remarkable woman who told me in no uncertain terms, shortly after I was elected Governor of Vermont, that service learning should be introduced to every school in Vermont. And she made it happen. Her dedication created SerVermont, an initiative to involve all Vermont's children in service learning. Our challenge now is to provide the opportunity to participate in service learning for school children everywhere—not for its own sake but as a key tool for educational improvement.

Nearly sixty years ago a fellow Vermonter, John Dewey, saw the connection between service learning and improving education when he proposed that "schools should be democratic laboratories of learning, closely linked to real community schools."[1] Dewey's affirmation about the mutual enterprise of "living and learning" has long generated both admiration and controversy. Some argue that effective schooling must first put curricular emphasis on the acquisition of basic skills. Others reply that this is not enough. For learning to be truly worthwhile, it must develop values of right and wrong, foster the development of problem-solving skills, and provide hands-on learning experiences, as well as teaching the basics.

This conclusion is gaining strength today as parents, employers, and teachers seek two parallel goals: to imbue students with a sense of basic values, and to reinvigorate the learning process so that all children will achieve the high academic standards required for life work in the twenty-first century. The evidence is mounting that service learning, integrated into a vigorous academic learning environment, produces both results.

On May 15, 1996, Secretary of Education Richard Riley and Harris Wofford, chief executive officer of the Corporation for National Service,

Madeleine M. Kunin was Deputy Secretary in the U.S. Department of Education when this chapter was prepared. She is currently the U.S. Ambassador to Switzerland.

announced the results of a RAND/UCLA study of service by college students.[2] The results were positive in all respects. The researchers were surprised, in light of recent surveys that have shown a decline in civic and political engagement among high school students, that students were so upbeat about community service, and that community organizations were equally enthusiastic with the students' contributions. The report concluded that students who engaged in community service showed greater academic achievement and evidenced greater citizenship than their peers who were not involved in such service. Commenting on the report, Secretary Riley said "Engaging the college student in service appears to represent a powerful educational tool for rekindling students' interest in becoming more responsible citizens."

To create responsible and knowledgeable citizens is our primary charge. No doubt each generation has felt challenged by this major task and has debated how to prepare the next generation adequately for the future. But it appears that in our time we face some special challenges. As we approach the end of the twentieth century we cannot be satisfied with educating a percentage of the population to high academic standards; we must educate everybody. Those with a limited education are denied the opportunity to be self-supporting and contributing members of society. Unlike previous generations, they need to work with their heads as well as with their hands to earn a secure living.

As we strive to educate all students to their highest potential, the definition of a "good education" is constantly being upgraded. The level of knowledge and skills which any individual has will determine his or her well-being. Our ability to make education available widely and equitably will dictate what kind of society and nation we are to become.

This is not an impossible task. What historian Daniel Boorstin has called "the genius of American politics"[3]—our ability as a diverse people to carry out the obligations of self-government—will enable us to continue to reinvent education. But our ongoing capacity to do so depends also upon our capacity to continue to create an informed and politically engaged population. To what extent are we up to the task, or, to put it bluntly, how good or bad is the condition of American education today?

A perusal of education statistics can support almost any answer to this question, depending on where one looks. *A Nation at Risk*, issued in 1983 under the leadership of Education Secretary Terrel Bell, concluded that "if an unfriendly foreign power had attempted to impose on America the mediocre educational performance that exists today, we might well have viewed it as an act of war."[4] This report mobilized governors, mayors, parents, and school officials to take action. If we take the report as a benchmark, where do we stand?

The results are mixed, but in some areas dramatic changes occurred. For example, one of the key recommendations of the report was that high school students take tougher courses. Progress on this front has been impressive. High school students are taking more challenging courses, including a greater number of courses such as algebra, geometry, trigonometry, and calculus, as well as chemistry and physics. The percentage of high school students taking such courses has moved from 14 percent to 52 percent since the report was issued, a truly impressive change.[5] One tangible result of this more stringent curriculum is that mathematics and science scores in the United States have gone up. For 17-year-olds, for example, the gain between 1982 and 1992 was roughly equivalent to one year.[6] Other good news is that the gap in achievement between minority students and white students is narrowing and more students are completing high school than ever before.

But clearly all is not well in American education today. The sobering truth is that any gap between minority and white students is unacceptable and every high school dropout is a sign of failure. While the overall statistics on students' achievement are encouraging, there are tremendous variations from school to school, community to community, and state to state. The differences between "good" schools and "bad" schools are stark, and often the differences are dictated by the wealth or poverty of the children who attend those schools.

We cannot be satisfied until we can provide an excellent education to every child in America. That is why the compelling evidence from schools and communities across the country about the educational benefits of service learning merits our serious attention. We must begin to concentrate on what works in one community and learn how to transplant it to another. It is often said that there is an answer to every problem somewhere in America. Our challenge is to make those answers available everywhere, and make success more the norm than the exception.

The Role of the Federal Government

The hard and exciting work of school improvement will continue to take place predominantly at the local and state levels. However, the federal government is an important partner in this shared effort. Its responsibility is to foster the dissemination of "ideas that work" so that communities can learn from one another, and to provide funding to help level the uneven playing field of public education. The most effective tools to "spread the word" are the President's use of the bully pulpit and his power to convene.

From the outset of his administration, President Clinton used the bully pulpit as well as the budget to place top priority on the major service learning initiative: AmeriCorps. In the face of severe budget cuts he refused to sign a budget bill that did not include continuation of this program, which started with 22,000 students in 1994 and is scheduled to reach 30,000 students in 1997. When he inaugurated his national service initiative in a speech at Rutgers University on March 1, 1993, the President said:

> National Service will be America at its best—building community, offering opportunity, and rewarding responsibility. National service is a challenge for Americans from every background and walk of life; it values something far more than money. National service is nothing less than the American way to change America.
>
> It is rooted on the concept of community: the simple idea that none of us on our own will ever have as much to cherish about our own lives if we are out there alone as we will if we work together.

The President then recalled the legacy of the Peace Corps created by President Kennedy:

> At its height, the Peace Corps enrolled 16,000 young men and women. Its legacy is not simply goodwill and good works in countries all across the globe, but a profound and lasting change in the way Americans think about their own country and the world.

Today, AmeriCorps and a sister program (Learn and Serve America), which encourages service learning in school and college curricula, dedicate two-thirds of their programs to education. I have encountered some of the young volunteers in some of the poorest schools in America, where they provide both help and hope.

The President and the Secretary of Education also have the power to bring people together, to work in partnership with groups on a daily basis in providing opportunities for service learning. An example of this power to convene was evident at a national conference on school reform and national service held in Washington, D.C. in June

1995. Several hundred educators, parents, and community leaders representing nearly every type of school and neighborhood in the United States came together for three days of reflection and mutual encouragement. In recognition of this historic meeting, Secretary Riley and Eli Segal, chief executive officer of the Corporation for National Service, publicly signed a "declaration of principles." In the words of that document, "Improving Our Schools and the Challenge of Citizenship,"[7] they committed their agencies and colleagues to six principles that describe "what's best in our American tradition of self-help and community spirit." Acknowledging that "no single formula for school improvement will fit every local community's needs," Riley and Segal articulated the fundamental principle of President Clinton's approach to effective education reform: "We believe it is important to emphasize the common enterprise of school improvement and the national service movement. Service learning is the bridge."

Strategies for the improvement of education will continue to be vigorously debated in a democratic society, but some areas of consensus are emerging as evidenced by the recent Education Summit with Louis Gerstner, chief executive officer of IBM, and the nation's governors. The President's call for high academic standards was widely applauded. Public support for standards is high, but the problem of getting agreement on them is more complex. Voluntary national standards have been promulgated by nongovernment organizations; some have been widely accepted, such as those for mathematics, arts, civics, and science. The standards for history and English have been more controversial.

But the idea of standards continues to gain momentum because it is a commonsense assumption that in order for children to achieve, we must define what they need to know and then determine how to measure whether or not they know it.

Service learning complements the emphasis on high academic standards when it is appropriately integrated into the curriculum. The added value of service learning is twofold: it is hands-on, community-based learning, and it helps instill the fundamental value of service to others.

As the late Ernest Boyer argued in 1995, "Knowledge unguided by an ethical compass is potentially more dangerous than ignorance itself."[8] Boyer's argument has multiple features, but central to it is the idea that students are not simply the recipients of the knowledge that their parents and teachers provide. Students ought to be active participants in their own learning. And learning has a moral dimension.

Finding ever more effective ways to help students become responsible for their own learning is one goal of genuine education reform. As Boyer recognized, this kind of learning has the further advantage of making clear that knowledge has consequences for the quality of our community life.

What Is Service Learning?

What exactly is service learning? Frank Newman, President of the Education Commission of the States, observed at the National Conference on Service Learning, School Reform, and Higher Education, that the fundamental challenge to both education reform and the larger service community is that "We have to get better at finding the right words to talk about what we're doing. We use a lot of terms—restructuring, systemic change, reform—but these words don't mean much to people. We haven't found the simple straightforward terms that we can use to explain education reform. The same is true of service learning."[9]

How, then, might we take up Newman's challenge?

We can begin with the description offered by the National Service Learning Cooperative: "Service learning is a teaching and learning method that connects meaningful community service experience with academic learning, personal growth, and civic responsibility."[10]

The authors of *Standards of Quality for School-Based and Community Learning*, a report issued in 1995 by the Alliance for Service Learning in Education Reform, suggest that "service learning connects young people to their community by placing them in challenging situations where they associate with adults and accumulate experiences that can strengthen traditional academic studies."[11] This general statement is followed by a declaration of eleven "standards of school-based and community-based" curricular and pedagogic practices. Perhaps most significant among these criteria for identifying and nourishing effective programs of service learning are those which emphasize the active role that students themselves should play in the development of service learning activities, and the insistence that service activities must be fully integrated into the daily academic life of schools by requiring students to reflect in a structured way about the service work in which they engage.

These two principles—the active role of students and the necessity of rigorous academic content—appear in every serious attempt to develop service learning programs. The "Principles of Good Practice for Combining Service and Learning," issued in 1989 at Wingspread by the National Society for Internships and Experiential Education, stated: "Service, combined with learning, adds value to each and transforms both."[12]

These are the overarching definitions, but as Barbara Gomez of the Council of Chief State School Officers observed, "The meaning of service learning will continue to be defined in different ways."[13]

The connection of service learning to fundamental education reform is becoming more evident. For example, in a report issued by the Association for Supervision and Curriculum Development, Judith Witmer and Carolyn Anderson note that "by treating young people as resources for community problem solving . . . service learning has the revolutionary potential for transforming schools. . . . It requires new thinking about education, about what happens in and out of the classroom. . . . It requires that you question the very core beliefs of your school, for it begins with [asking] what do we agree is important for students to know, to be able to do, and to value?"[14] As one writer observed in commenting on a seminal study by Anne Lewis, "Service learning refers both to a type of program and to a philosophy of education."[15]

In a 1996 survey sponsored by the American Alliance for Rights and Responsibilities, Suzanne Goldsmith found that among the 130 largest public school districts in the United States more than 45 percent have service requirements for graduation at one or more high schools in their districts, that 78 percent of schools with required service programs link the service to required academic classwork, and that 95 percent of students engaged in service learning projects or coursework have had significant responsibility for planning their projects and curricular calendars.[16]

Equally important has been the response of the communities in which students have undertaken their service learning experience. Eighty-nine percent of school administrators surveyed praised community and service learning for helping students take more responsibility for their academic learning. And 88 percent of parents whose children take part in service learning activities have indicated that their youngsters' overall schooling experience has been enhanced. Particular commendation has been given to programs where the community service projects are closely tied to the development and use of academic skills. In a typical response, Judy Gordon of the Orange County School District in Orlando, Florida, said, "We've seen a tremendous increase in kids' grades and social skills." Goldsmith reports that "when students plan and evaluate their service projects and reflect on their experiences, service learning can provide a uniquely effective means of developing personal and civic responsibility, self-esteem, and significant improvements in academic problem solving."[17]

Examples of Service Learning

Service learning activities use real-life situations to advance both the acquisition of basic skills and the development of good citizenship. Two examples are given here to illustrate how service learning can help students integrate their academic training with preparation for high-skill jobs and careers.

Service learning projects may reach far beyond a single community, as the Illinois Rivers Project illustrates. With support from Southern Illinois University at Edwardsville, the National Science Foundation, the U.S. Army Corps of Engineers, local school boards and the Illinois State Board of Education, teachers in over 180 high schools in Illinois, Iowa, Indiana, Minnesota, and Wisconsin established the Illinois Rivers Project. Emphasizing the curricular goals of improving teaching and learning in basic subjects like chemistry, earth science, biology, and cultural geography, students worked throughout their junior and senior high school years to monitor the quality of the waters that run through the larger Mississippi basin of their region. Conducting scientific research, using oral history techniques such as interviews, studying local courthouse records, integrating the acquisition of science skills with the study of civics and policymaking, students took an active part in the life of their communities. At the Jerseyville Community High School, students' research first identified the existence of raw sewage that had been illegally dumped into nearby Elsah Creek by many of their own neighbors. After independent scientific confirmation of their results, the students worked with local community and elected leaders to establish an effective new quality water sewage treatment system. Problem solving in mathematics and science among these students showed marked improvement.

An initiative taken by a consortium of middle schools in the inner-city community of West Philadelphia demonstrates the capacity that service learning curricula have for integrating academic achievement and the development of occupational skills. With help from the University of Pennsylvania, several local hospitals, the U.S. Departments of Labor and of Health and Human Services, the Pennsylvania Department of Education and Labor, and with support from the DeWitt Wallace Reader's Digest Fund, the Lilly Endowment, the Philadelphia

Urban Affairs Coalition, and many other local groups and citizens, a communitywide commitment has been made to transform a conventional middle school into a comprehensive community school carrying the banner of genuine education reform into the daily lives of students, teachers, and parents. At the John P. Turner Middle School, service learning practitioners have found a way to implement a "school within a school" whose academic curriculum emphasizes the study of health issues and the professional and vocational careers that arise from an academically challenging exploration of these issues. Evidence shows that the efforts of these sixth to eighth graders have significantly improved their basic skills in mathematics and reading. Their hands-on work experience with participating local hospitals and related health and community organizations is paving the way for a wide range of postsecondary education and career opportunities.

The number and variety of examples nationwide is encouraging. In a report issued jointly in 1995 by the American Youth Policy Forum, Jobs for the Future, and the National Association of Secondary School Principals, Susan Goldberger and Richard Kazis summarize the lessons that can be learned if more schools and communities forge a partnership between education reform and service learning. "Through engagement in specific [and] often messy problems, students can sharpen and deepen their academic and analytic skills . . . [thus] providing all students with the opportunity to develop intellectually through work on practical projects. A school can be a place to join hand and mind."[18]

Helping to Advance the Partnership

What role should the U.S. Department of Education have in this difficult work? Shortly after his confirmation Secretary Riley offered his vision about the nature and the proper limitations of that role: "Our job is to help spark creativity and innovation at the school level, but real leadership must come from teachers, principals, and parents in individual schools. Neither top-down nor bottom-up reform alone is sufficient; both 'ends' must work on what it means for students to learn and achieve at high levels."

That statement guides the work of the U.S. Department of Education. We developed major education reform initiatives like GOALS 2000, the School to Work Opportunities Act, and the reauthorization and transformation of the Elementary and Secondary School Improvement programs by committing ourselves to working with community and education stakeholders across the country to advance the twin causes of excellence and opportunity for every child in America. None of these initiatives would have succeeded without their help and strong bi-partisan support.

Themes such as "family involvement," "venture capital," "local partnerships," "accountability," and "public school choice" have been the common strands of a shared agenda as the Department works with schools and school districts. Our responsibility is to encourage and assist local educators and communities to set high standards of achievement for all their students.

We have observed that the most successful strategies for educational improvement get implemented when all the key partners are at the table, including parents, the private sector, community members, students, and teachers. Service learning is no different. Its success or failure in any community depends heavily on engaging the entire community in its development.

Although tight budgetary constraints are real, services and programs in the U.S. Department of Education and the Corporation for National Service are available to support local efforts. Americorps and grants from Learn and Serve America fund school-based and community-based service learning programs for youth of school age and require collaboration with community organizations.

In FY 1995, the Corporation for National Service supported 128 Learn and Serve America school-based and community-based grants, totaling $40 million and providing service opportunities to over 750,000 young people. Service learning is also compatible with GOALS 2000, which requires that students leave grades 4, 8, and 12 having demonstrated competency in challenging subject matter appropriate at each of those levels as well as their capacity to become effective citizens.

The Improving America's Schools Act of 1994, under Title I, provides a variety of resources to help local schools address the learning needs of disadvantaged students. Section 1114, for example, encourages schools to utilize "innovative teaching methods which may include applied learning and team teaching strategies" to advance the attainment of high academic skills by all students.

Funding guidelines for teacher training (Title II) or the integration "of high quality academic and vocational learning" (Title I, Section 1502) have encouraged schools to leverage local partnerships at the school and community level. The emphasis has been to help schools focus on students' results in learning. GOALS 2000 was designed specifically to focus on school improvement and local innovations.

Both GOALS 2000 and the School to Work Opportunities Act were purposely designed without any regulations.

The Clinton Administration and a number of national organizations have focused a spotlight on education and service learning. Communities in every corner of the nation are joining them in making a strong commitment to improving education. The beneficiaries of this shared strategy will be a future generation better educated and better prepared to participate fully in the life of their communities. As Mather Luther King said, "Everybody can be great because everybody can serve."

The editor gratefully acknowledges the assistance received from Diana Phillips and Saul Benjamin, both of the U.S. Department of Education, in the final stages of preparing this chapter for publication.

Notes

1. John Dewey, *Democracy and Education* (New York: Collier, 1962), p. 17.

2. Maryann Jacobi Gray et al., *Evaluation of Learn and Serve America, Higher Education: First Year Report* (Santa Monica, Calif.: Rand, 1996).

3. Daniel Boorstin, *The Genius of American Politics* (Chicago: University of Chicago Press, 1954), p. 3.

4. National Commission on Excellence in Education, *A Nation at Risk: The Imperative for Educational Reform* (Washington, D.C.: U.S. Government Printing Office, 1983), p. 5.

5. National Center for Education Statistics, *The High School Transcript Study* (Washington, D.C.: National Center for Education Statistics, U.S. Department of Education, 1982, 1987, 1990, and 1994).

6. National Center for Education Statistics, *The Condition of Education, 1995* (Washington, D.C.: National Center for Education Statistics, U.S. Department of Education, 1995).

7. Richard Riley and Eli Segal, "Improving Our Schools and the Challenge of Citizenship," Joint statement at conference on service learning, Washington, D.C., June 22, 1995.

8. Ernest Boyer, *The Basic School: A Community for Learning* (Princeton, N.J.: Carnegie Endowment for Advancement of Teaching, 1995), p. 179.

9. Frank Newman, "Foreword," in *Learning Is the Thing: Insights Emerging from a National Conference on Service Learning, School Reform, and Higher Education*, Report of a conference sponsored by the Education Commission of the States and the National Youth Leadership Council (Roseville, Minn.: National Youth Leadership Council, 1994).

10. Suzanne Mintz and Goodwin Liu, *Service Learning: An Overview* (Washington, D.C.: Corporation for National and Community Service, 1994), p. 12.

11. Alliance for Service Learning in Education Reform, *Standards of Quality for School-Based and Community Learning* (Alexandria, Va.: Close Up Foundation, 1995), p. 2.

12. National Society for Internship and Experiential Education, "Principles of Good Practice for Combining Service and Learning," Special Report of a Wingspread Conference, Racine, Wisconsin, May 1989, p. 1.

13. Cynthia Brown and Barbara Gomez, eds., *The Service Learning Planning and Resource Guide* (Washington, D.C.: Council of Chief State School Officers, 1994), p. vi.

14. Judith Witmer and Carolyn Anderson, *How to Establish a High School Service Learning Program* (Alexandria, Va.: Association for Supervision and Curriculum Development, 1994), p. 12.

15. Anne Lewis, *Facts and Faith: A Status Report on Youth Service* (Washington, D.C.: Commission on Work, Family, and Citizenship, W. T. Grant Foundation, 1988), p. 26.

16. Suzanne Goldsmith, *RE: Rights and Responsibilities* (Washington, D.C.: Alliance for Rights and Responsibilities, February, 1996).

17. Ibid.

18. Susan Goldberger and Richard Kazis, *Revitalizing High Schools: What the School-to-Career Movement Can Contribute* (Washington, D.C. and Boston, Mass.: American Youth Policy Forum, Jobs for the Future, and National Association of Secondary School Principals, 1995.

CHAPTER XII

The Role of the State

GEORGE A. ANTONELLI AND RICHARD L. THOMPSON

What is the state's role in service learning programs? How can states influence the numbers of students participating while ensuring that the service learning experience is beneficial? How can states ensure that teachers and others who have direct contact with students have the knowledge they need to guide service learning experiences? These are among the questions addressed in this chapter.

In exploring answers to these questions, we emphasize one key concept that is central to the issue of the state's role in service learning. We believe it is in the compelling interest of the state for students to be involved in service learning because they will be better citizens for their involvement. The level of support by the state may vary, depending on economics and philosophy, but the state's commitment to service learning should not vary.

North Carolina's Involvement in Service Learning

North Carolina was one of the first states where service learning was viewed as a resource for youth. In 1969, the North Carolina Internship Office was established as a service learning effort. The program had three goals: to increase university and college student involvement with public needs and opportunities; to increase the utilization of off-campus North Carolina as a learning environment; and to provide opportunities for students to be exposed to and develop a service learning lifestyle. Over twenty-five years later, the program is still operating and placing students in service learning experiences. In the early 1980s, the Governor's Office of Citizen Affairs worked with young people to identify service learning programs across the state. Also in the early 1980s, the State Board of Education endorsed granting academic credit for service learning activities. More recently in North Carolina, two offices, the Governor's Office of Citizen Affairs

---

George A. Antonelli is Associate Vice President for Student Services and Special Programs in the General Administration of the University of North Carolina. Richard L. Thompson is Deputy State Superintendent for the Public Schools of North Carolina.

and the State Department of Public Instruction, have collaborated to foster service learning in the public schools. The Governor's Office of Citizen Affairs took the lead in designing a plan for volunteerism in North Carolina, following the passage of the National and Community Service Trust Act of 1993.

As a part of the development process for "Communities Building Communities" (North Carolina's state plan for community service and service learning) and to promote awareness of the importance of service, eight regional summits were held across North Carolina. Approximately eight hundred participants, including three hundred young people, developed the plan for Communities Building Communities and participated in setting the state's priorities. This plan has given rise to new public-private partnerships, the development of networks of community-based agencies, and a growing awareness of the need for people in the state to help each other. Again and again, citizens identified the promotion of collaborative projects and the need to build a statewide infrastructure for volunteer and service efforts as priorities. According to the plan, "At a basic level, North Carolinians recognize that service makes a difference in people's lives, both for those that are served and those that are serving."

The vision of Communities Building Communities is multifaceted. The plan includes:

- increasing volunteerism among North Carolinians of all ages and experiences as a vehicle for community problem solving;
- promoting strong interagency and community collaboration to maximize resources to meet community-defined needs;
- providing recognition and support of individual volunteer efforts and successful or promising private sector initiatives and public-private partnerships which address community-defined needs;
- utilizing local, state, and federal resources to reinforce and expand quality volunteer service programs as well as to initiate new programs;
- stimulating increased community awareness of the impact of volunteer service on local communities and the public and private sectors;
- supporting the development of citizenship and leadership skills among community members, especially youth and traditionally underserved populations;
- allowing for dissemination and exchange of information about model service and volunteer programs and best practices through networks, meetings and publications;

- developing and implementing at all levels service learning programs which actively involve participants, schools, and agencies in community problem-solving efforts;
- assessing service program and agency needs for training and technical assistance and making such assistance available as needed;
- monitoring quality and sustainability through information and evaluation systems.

In education, top priorities were to increase the rate of literacy among school-aged youth, adults, and families, and to provide more service learning opportunities that translate into job skills for young people. North Carolinians also viewed service projects as a way to address community needs in rebuilding neighborhoods, in protecting and improving the environment, in health care, and in the control and prevention of crime.

North Carolina is not alone in its recognition of the benefits of service learning. While not all states have made their commitment as explicit as the plan for Communities Building Communities, state education agencies, teachers and administrators, legislators and community service agencies in every region of the country are viewing service learning as a promising approach. Meaningful participation in the home, school, and community forges bonds between the child and these three domains. When these bonds are strong, the young person is unlikely to do anything that would threaten them. The implication for schools is that service can be not only a learning experience, but a protective factor in young people's lives. Young people who are given responsibilities behave responsibly. The student who has opportunities for meaningful service becomes a better prepared citizen; thus, the impetus for states to focus more attention on service learning for the common good of the state.

State Supports for Service Learning

From President George Bush's Points of Light project to President Clinton's AmeriCorps, national leaders have used the presidential platform to promote service learning. But there are decisions and commitments that must be made at the state level, and it is in the self-interest of the states to impart to students and citizens the importance of service learning. In addition, many of the obstacles that stand in the way of implementing sound programs can be effectively removed, or reduced, at the state level.

While it is true that service learning has in recent years become more generally accepted, its place in the schools is still frequently questioned, if not opposed, by a public anxious about its schools and about the country's young people. The state can play a pivotal role in allaying that anxiety by informing parents, state and local officials, and the citizenry at large about the purposes and content of service learning. The State Department of Education can take the lead in establishing a climate of support for service learning, educating state leaders (those in business and the professions, legislators, and other elected officials) about the importance of service learning, enunciating policies that promote service learning in schools and communities. Service learning is a form of experiential learning, and because experiential learning is not widely understood, the public (parents, public officials, taxpayer groups, and others) needs to be informed about the role of service learning in the curriculum and its relationship to the goals of the public schools. State endorsement is further demonstrated when legislation in support of service learning is enacted.

As is true of any innovation, if critical questions can be resolved early, the program's chances of success and of being sustained are increased. There are the everpresent questions around funding, the place of service learning in the state's education goals, the need for specialized teacher training, and the role of the private sector. In addition, planners must ask who, at the state, county, district, and schoolhouse levels, will assume responsibility for leading the service learning efforts, and to what extent will parents or guardians be involved. Other issues have surfaced in several states and districts as service learning becomes more widespread: Will course credit be given? Will the state mandate or only encourage service learning? How will state, county, and local government roles overlap or complement each other?

Answering these and other important questions that will undoubtedly arise is a key step for a state in determining the role of service learning. Gaining the support of stakeholders, from legislators to students, is critical. In California, Senate Bill 2147 allows public schools to establish pilot service learning projects, but provides no funding for implementation. Proposed legislation (April, 1996) would establish and fund service learning programs in public schools and offer credit to participating students. The State Department of Education has introduced the "Superintendent's Challenge Initiative," which sets forth standards for service learning in a sequence, for kindergarten through grade five, grades six through eight, and high school. The Initiative includes examples of age-appropriate activities. At this writing, the state has recognized fourteen "challenge districts," which are at various stages of implementation.

The Minnesota legislature approved a bill allowing school districts to offer service learning opportunities with the option to grant participants credit toward graduation. Participation is optional, and funding in a particular school district comes from a special tax levied in that district.

Undoubtedly the state with the strictest mandate for service learning is Maryland. A 1992 bill in that state's legislature required all public high school graduates, beginning with the class of 1997, to perform seventy-five hours of community service. The Maryland State Board of Education requirement says that all students must complete seventy-five hours of service, including preparation, action, and reflection, prior to graduation. School districts choose between a seventy-five-hour requirement to be completed sometime between grades six and twelve or the development of a plan to incorporate service into the school curriculum.

If a statewide initiative in service learning is to be effective, policymakers must, usually in collaboration with regional or local education agencies, develop clear descriptions of the roles of the players. Some issues of responsibility or accountability can be most effectively addressed at the state level. Funding, program evaluation, and mandatory vs. voluntary service are among the concerns that will benefit from consideration and/or action at the state level. Some states have found creative ways to link federally funded programs such as School-to-Work and the Learn and Serve portion of the National and Community Service Trust Act, or Goals 2000. Thanks to the passage of the National and Community Service Trust Act, forty-seven of the fifty states now have a service learning coordinator. (At last report, the remaining three states chose initially not to apply for funding from the Corporation for National Service.)

One key to the success of a program intended to provide opportunities for students to serve and to learn is training. In order for their service to be meaningful and truly useful, students must know how to serve, and their teachers must be able to help them acquire the skills they will need. The state has a significant role in providing training for students and teachers. As a major presence in teacher preparation and certification, the state can exercise its influence to encourage and support training in service learning. In New York, with seven hundred school districts, the State Department of Education role is primarily that of provider and supporter of training and technical assistance. In addition to public funds for Learn and Serve, as well as a grant under the Eisenhower initiative in support of programs that "enhance teaching and learning," the W. K. Kellogg Foundation, with supplementary funding from the state, has provided a grant for development of a corps of "peer consultants" responsible for establishing regional networks of Learn and Serve grantees, potential grantees, and others interested in promoting service learning in Kindergarten through grade 12.

In Oregon, the State Department of Education staff views service learning as a strategy with potential to strengthen education practice across age groups, disciplines, and abilities, and is the primary strategy for the state's federally funded School-to-Work initiative. In yet another application, students eligible under Title I funding have opportunities through service learning to test their skills in community settings. Also in Oregon, House Bill 3293, passed in 1989, required the State Department of Education to establish guidelines for service learning in the state's public schools. The program is not mandatory, but the guidelines include awarding participants credit towards graduation.

THE STATE AS ADVOCATE AND CONVENER

How can states best assist in and encourage service learning? We would argue that the role of state departments of education, universities, and other state agencies is to advocate for service learning. The state department also acts as convener, the agency that brings groups together to find the common ground that is necessary for service learning to work and work well.

In its role as advocate, the state department can educate state leaders (legislative, other elected leaders, business leaders) about the importance of service learning; it can establish policies that encourage service learning in schools and communities, and encourage education, social service, and other agencies to work together in collaborative projects. The importance of the state's influence in teacher preparation has already been discussed, and as service learning's advocate, the state should urge teacher preparation programs to include service learning as a component of training. In addition, the state should recognize service learning efforts of teachers, community leaders, and others. The state can publish materials about integrating service learning in the curricula, adopt policies that encourage service learning, and provide speakers for legislative committees, youth legislative assemblies, teachers' groups, and other meetings where education issues are addressed.

As convener, the state can mediate the collaborative relationships critical to the success of service learning. There are numerous reasons for collaboration, but first and foremost may be the fact that collaboration is the best way to deliver services to those who need them. Linking agencies to one another in ways that allow them to share information and expertise is beneficial to those in need and maximizes the use of limited funds and personnel. Issues of "turf" are common among education, health, and community service agencies. These issues are often fed by the distribution of federal funds in communities. For example, maternal and child health in most communities has long been served by the local public health department. The rising number of pregnant teenagers and young mothers in public schools led to the provision of services at the school level. Schools and health departments in many areas have begun to collaborate to provide these young women and their babies with the services they need.

States that have designated a statewide service learning coordinator have made a significant move toward developing a coherent approach to service learning. Not only does this move pave the way for combining funding streams, but it will facilitate the gathering and dissemination of information. The state office for service learning then becomes the logical resource for program developers and practitioners—a clearinghouse with information about model programs and materials, and a catalyst for developing networks and sustaining communication among these individuals as well as evaluators, policymakers, and researchers. A clearinghouse can serve, too, to identify potential support and prevent wasteful duplication. Some states provide funding in support of service learning, but in this time of limited resources, the state role will include working with local authorities to gain funding from local government and corporate sponsors for service learning models.

Coordinating a clearinghouse, providing technical assistance, coordinating recognition of individuals and programs, and conducting evaluations of model programs are all ways the state can act as convener. The state may choose to fund or partially fund programs, provide in-kind space and other services, collaborate with universities or other groups, or establish the clearinghouse in conjunction with other service efforts. Chief among the functions of a service learning clearinghouse are to aid in data collection and dissemination and to provide training and technical assistance. Clearinghouses provide a single source from which individuals can obtain information on such topics as model programs, resources, organizations, consultants, and conferences.

Funding for these clearinghouses is often a mix of private and public funds. In North Carolina, a state university with a strong history of encouraging service learning operates a clearinghouse open to all state residents. North Carolina Central University (NCCU) in Durham has made a commitment to help teachers, service agencies, and students with service learning projects. In addition, it has joined the Campus Compact, a national agency of five hundred colleges and universities devoted to increasing the presence of service learning on state campuses. NCCU is forming a State Compact with the University of North Carolina at Chapel Hill and Bennett College as the anchor schools. Furthermore, it should be noted that Elon College, in North Carolina, has an outstanding service learning program in its own right.

Finally, through the service learning clearinghouse and in other areas concerned with youth, the state can model service learning by involving young people as advisors or members of boards and other groups that are representative of the people of a state.

States have a role to play in funding for service learning. Efforts are underway nationally to procure state funding to support service learning. Experience indicates that community service programs cannot sustain themselves over the long term without a diversified funding base. Experience also shows that it is difficult to put a dollar figure on service learning projects because most of the projects are based on local needs and must be tailored to meet those needs.

Federal, state, and local governments provide grants and, in many cases, operate programs in many of the areas typically addressed by service learning projects. Projects that affect senior citizens may be funded by federal or state funds through senior centers. Environmental projects may be supported by local groups that are concerned about the environment. Service learning may be viewed as a way to prepare young people for careers, as a drug prevention method, as a means of keeping schools safe, and as an education reform effort. Just as states often direct teacher training programs to cover various emphases in their programs, providing funds for and requiring course work in service learning is an appropriate role for states in promoting service learning.

Direct payment in support of service learning programs may be a route some states are not willing to take, but there are other ways to demonstrate commitment, for example, recognizing the worth of young people and of those who work with them. In North Carolina, two students serve as advisors to the State Board of Education. Through attendance at monthly meetings and participation in discussion of issues, the students show policymakers that young people can make a difference. Young people who have participated in service learning projects often make the best spokespersons before legislative committees and at conferences.

States can honor teachers, students, administrators, and community service agencies engaged in service learning. Awards luncheons, certificates, proclamations, press conferences, and public service announcements are relatively inexpensive ways to recognize those who make service learning work and to raise the profile of service learning in the state. One additional role for states is to help evaluate service learning efforts to ensure that students are gaining from the experiences. Universities, state education departments, and other agencies generally have evaluation sections that can study service learning programs. Evaluation is essential in justifying the expenditures of funds at all levels. A local program will gain credibility when the state shares in the evaluation.

POLICY IMPLICATIONS OF STATE INVOLVEMENT

Convening a gathering of key groups is one way to begin discussion of service learning. Legislators, state and local government agencies, state departments of education, teachers, administrators and other educators, students, parents, and community agencies are among those who should be involved in making decisions about service learning. Key issues in determining a state's role in service learning are the needs of local communities, the vision for students as determined by local communities, the budget and other resources at the state's disposal, and the philosophical outlook of the governor and legislators.

Teacher training must be a primary concern for states in considering the implementation of service learning. Training for prospective teachers and those who already are employed must be addressed before service learning is implemented statewide. Collaboration is critical to the training model since institutions of higher education, local school districts and schools, education associations, and state educators are all likely to be involved in training.

North Carolina and other states already have in place professional development programs that may be good avenues for training in service learning. North Carolina's Teacher Academy provides intensive one-week summer training experiences for teachers at sites around the state. The North Carolina Center for the Advancement of Teaching, a residential facility, offers training in many areas of education and other topics. The Principals Executive Program and the Principal Fellows Program offer training to school leaders. Many other programs already exist and can be tapped to offer training in service learning.

In North Carolina, an approach to teaching teachers and prospective teachers to use technology offers an effective model for professional development in service learning. Consortia composed of public schools and community colleges and centered around higher education institutions have been established to coordinate training in regions of the state. This model is a cost-effective means for states to ensure that teachers have the skills they need to integrate service learning into their teaching.

Another model makes use of local experts. While staff development often seems based on the premise that the experts all live out of town, actually there is often an "expert" in an adjoining classroom or right down the hall. Also, teachers who attend training in areas of interest to staff can become experts in how the information applies at their building level.

Training provided by teachers for other teachers may be more efficient than that provided by an outside consultant because they are already working within the school's schedule. Perhaps most important of all, peer teachers often have automatic credibility and will present information from a practical point of view. Moreover, ongoing support for new ideas and programs is readily available when the expert is in the classroom down the hall or in a nearby school. Teachers who might be reluctant to try something new, may be willing to take risks when support is close by. Finally, staff development by teachers for teachers, particularly within the same building, can promote rapport and teamwork. Within a school district, it can promote linkages among teachers at the same grade level or in the same subject area when those teachers may not have had the opportunity to work together on other efforts. The state's role in promoting peer teaching may be to tie such efforts by teachers to rewards or bonus salary structures, just as teachers receive bonus pay for assuming certain other duties.

Another critical issue for teachers and school administrators is time—time for training, time to administer service learning, time to work with outside agencies, and time to ensure that the service learning experience is meaningful to students. Service learning may be perceived as one more thing that must be incorporated into what teachers do during the six or so hours of the school day. As a rule, it is the local education agency that deals with the allocation of teachers' time, but the state, in incorporating service learning into its policies, can validate the use of professional time for service learning activities.

PROVIDING MODEL PROGRAMS AND POLICIES THAT LOCAL DISTRICTS CAN ADAPT

Effective service learning models are those that are incorporated into what is already taking place during the school day. Service learning projects actually add value to many subject areas, rather than taking anything away from these subjects. Science students study environmental projects in their community and use the results to lobby for actions. If a project involves working with people with disabilities, students learn in class about the limitations and the capabilities of those being served in order to interact successfully with them. If students are working on flower gardens around the school, the project is linked to their study of horticulture. Students design their own projects for extra credit or as part of an assignment. Students conduct a needs assessment in the community around the school to find out what needs are not being met and then design service projects to meet those needs. All are examples of service learning integration.

Teachers and administrators must have time to develop new service learning programs and to formalize programs that individual teachers have often carried out without adequate support. Teachers also need time to develop new projects, to build and strengthen partnerships with community organizations, and to discuss service learning with other staff. Administrators must have time to deal with organizational and legal issues, including transportation, schedules, liability, and other issues. States can offer scheduling models that address the need for more time during the school day. Many states, including North Carolina, are changing laws and policies to give local teachers and administrators more flexibility in scheduling and programming that should enhance the ability to plan.

The prevalence of emphasis on local control and site-based management at the school and school district level may explain why few state legislatures have passed bills regarding service learning. Instead, nationwide, many service learning programs have been implemented by actions of state school boards, local school boards, and individual school decisions. Individual school districts and individual schools across the country also have mandated service learning projects. Maryland was the first state to mandate service learning. The effectiveness of the legislation has yet to be tested since the class of 1997 is the first to which it applies.

The issue of mandatory versus voluntary service evokes strong opinions among policymakers, those who work with youth, and young people themselves. In a Resource Sheet published by the National Service Learning Cooperative, Nancy Murphy cites some of the reasoning on both sides. For example, proponents of mandatory service suggest that if young people are not required to perform community service, they may not choose to participate in service projects on their own. They ask, "If states and local districts can mandate participation in English, mathematics, and other subjects, then why not service learning?" Murphy notes that arguments against mandated service range from practical to philosophical to constitutional. The rationale for opposition to compulsory service includes the suggestion that service learning interferes with other academic learning time, and that time spent on service learning outside the school day interferes with extracurricular activities.

Parents in Bethlehem, Pennsylvania, claimed that mandatory service is a form of involuntary servitude and a violation of the Thirteenth Amendment to the U.S. Constitution. The lawsuit was dismissed on the basis that mandatory service does not violate students' Thirteenth Amendment rights. In a similar lawsuit in Chapel Hill, N.C., the right of local boards of education to require community service was upheld.

Some state boards of education have developed policies encouraging service learning. For example, in 1989 the Pennsylvania State Board of Education adopted a Resolution on Student Community Service, stating that "students are an important and often underutilized resource for solving pressing public problems such as illiteracy, school failure, underachievement, and isolation of elders." The Board's resolution further stated that "[P]rograms of community service should be an integral part of education at all levels and strongly urges schools, colleges and universities to institute or strengthen community service programs so that every student is encouraged to serve and participate in volunteer services."

Conclusion

States do have a role to play in encouraging service learning. This role is seen primarily as one of convener in bringing together those who can make service learning work and as advocate to create an awareness of the benefits of service learning and to initiate the training, support, and other collaboration that must be in place for service learning efforts to succeed. The ultimate goal is service and learning to create a better citizenry for today and tomorrow.

CHAPTER XIII

Service Learning as a Vehicle for Youth Development

SHEPHERD ZELDIN AND SUZANNE TARLOV

What is school-based service learning? There is little consensus. For some, it is a reform initiative aimed at making schools more responsive and relevant to young people. For others, service learning is an instructional strategy, a means for improving the academic achievement, citizenship, and community membership of young people. For others, it is a program that integrates meaningful work in the community with rigorous course work and structured reflection.[1] For still others, it is all of the above.

However it is defined, service learning and arguments in support of it have not gained wide acceptance among school administrators, public officials, and community workers. Consequently, it is often viewed as an "add-on," not an integral part of the school curriculum. The confusion in definition also impedes professional development efforts. Without clearly defined exemplary practice in service learning it is difficult to train staff effectively.[2]

The need for a better understanding of what service learning can provide for young people is the focus of this chapter. In particular, we propose that this understanding can be enhanced if service learning is viewed from the perspective of youth development. Such a perspective can offer insights about key aspects of development in youth, suggest how activities in a service learning program can contribute to that development, and help youth make a successful transition into adulthood.

When this chapter was written, Shepherd Zeldin was Director of Research and Planning in the Center for Youth Development and Policy Research at the Academy for Educational Development in Washington, D.C. He is now Executive Director of Funds for the Community's Future, also in Washington, D.C. Suzanne Tarlov was Program Officer in the Center for Youth Development and Policy Research at the Academy for Educational Development. She is now Manager of Development and Communication at Funds for the Community's Future.

Connecting the Outcomes of Service Learning to Youth Development

A first step in defining service learning is to articulate outcomes that it seeks to promote among young people. Service learning is typically connected to academic learning and citizenship. When youth speak, however, it becomes clear that service learning promotes a much wider range of outcomes.[3] They report that they have learned to solve problems, to conduct independent study, and to express themselves. Some will say that they have learned to interact productively with people different from themselves and that they learned to work as a team. Others report how their experience has helped them prepare for a job or a career. Still others refer to their personal growth, explaining that they have learned how to take care of themselves or get a job done under stressful conditions. While they do not often report growth in civic competence, they may say that they became more intimately connected with someone or something—their peers, the elders to whom they have read, the park that they cleaned, or the adults who guided and taught them.

These views of young people who have engaged in service learning programs are consistent with research that emphasizes the need of youth for a broad range of abilities in preparing for adulthood. Most young people are not likely to acquire this full set of abilities unless they also develop a positive identity characterized by a sense of personal well-being and a sense of connection and commitment to others.

The Center for Youth Development and Policy Research was established at the Academy for Educational Development in 1990. Its goal is "to transform concern about *youth problems* into public and private commitment to *youth development.* At the core of the Center's framework for youth development are three basic tenets: *problem-free is not fully prepared*—preventing high risk behaviors is not enough; *academic skills are not enough*—young people are engaged in the development of a full range of competencies (personal, social, vocational, health, civic); *competence, in and of itself, is not enough.* Skill building is best achieved when young people are confident of their abilities, contacts, and resources, and are called upon by their communities to use their skills."[4]

Figure 1, prepared at the Center for Youth Development and Policy Research, lists the type of outcomes young people need to acquire if they are to move successfully through adolescence into young adulthood. The list reflects the views of specialists in several disciplines and is supported by the findings of research.[5] We believe that most advocates

ASPECTS OF IDENTITY: Young people demonstrate a positive identity when they have a sense of personal well-being, and a sense of connection and commitment to others.

- **Safety and Structure:** a perception that one is safe in this world on a day-to-day basis, and that some events are predictable.
- **Self-Worth:** a perception that one is a good person who can and does make meaningful contributions.
- **Mastery and Future:** a perception that one can and does "make it" and has hope for success in the future.
- **Belonging and Membership:** a perception that one values, and is valued by, others in the family and surrounding community.
- **Responsibility:** a perception that one has control over one's own actions, is accountable for those actions and for their consequences on others.
- **Spirituality and Self-Awareness:** a perception that one is unique and is ultimately attached to families, cultural groups, communities, higher deities and/or principles.

AREAS OF ABILITY: Young people demonstrate ability when they gain knowledge, skills, and attitudes that prepare them for adulthood.

- **Physical Health:** the ability and motivation to act in ways that best protect and ensure current and future health for oneself and others.
- **Mental Health:** the ability and motivation to respond affirmatively and to cope with positive and adverse situations, to reflect on one's emotions and surroundings, and to engage in leisure and fun.
- **Intellectual:** the ability and motivation to learn in school and in other settings; to gain the basic knowledge needed to graduate high school; to use critical thinking, creative problem-solving and expressive skills; and to conduct independent study.
- **Career:** the ability and motivation to gain the functional and organizational skills necessary for employment, including an understanding of careers and options and the steps necessary to reach goals.
- **Civic and Social:** the ability and motivation to work collaboratively with others for the common good, and to build and sustain caring relationships with others.
- **Cultural:** the ability and motivation to respect and respond affirmatively to differences among groups and individuals of diverse backgrounds, interests and traditions.

FIGURE 1
Youth outcomes: Accomplishments expected of young people

Source: AED/Center for Youth Development and Policy Research.

of service learning would agree that activities in such programs can make a significant contribution to the achievement of these developmental outcomes. In this sense, the outcomes listed in figure 1 could be thought of as the goals of service learning. Although they are implicit in most writing about service learning, there is an advantage in making them explicit.

Challenges. While there are political reasons for defining its goals in terms of academic learning, that approach does not acknowledge much of what service learning can accomplish with young people. A first challenge, then, is to *articulate the broader goals of service learning.* By linking service learning activities directly to youth development and to preparation for young adulthood, advocates will be in a better position to craft messages that persuade school officials and community leaders to support these broader aims.

A second challenge is to *use developmental outcomes as a foundation for planning.* Unless expected outcomes are specified, practitioners have little guidance when making day-to-day decisions and they are less likely to maintain a focus on developmental needs as well as on academic needs of young people.

A third challenge is *to work for modification of existing accountability systems* so that the broader goals of service learning are incorporated in standards of success. Service learning practitioners, as well as the schools in which they work, may then be held accountable for a broader range of outcomes.

Locating an Empirical Foundation for Service Learning

It will also be necessary to offer a stronger research-based justification for service learning. As it stands, "the case for community service receives provisional support from quantitative, quasi-experimental studies and even more consistent affirmation from the reports and testimony of participants and practitioners."[6] There is certainly a need for systematic evaluations of service learning programs. Until such evaluations have been completed, it will be useful to consider research on adolescent development, where some of the findings are relevant for service learning.

An important task is to identify the specific ways through which service learning helps young people acquire the outcomes listed in figure 1. To do so, the staff at the Center for Youth Development and Policy Research have been asking youth, youth workers, and educators to identify the key day-to-day experiences that promote the healthy development of young people. We have also been collaborating with a group of scholars to address this issue by reporting original research and synthesizing past research.[7]

Among these sources we find remarkable agreement that young people need a variety of services, many of which are provided by families, schools, and various community organizations. Equally important, however, is the need for developmental "opportunities" and "supports" such as those shown in figure 2. Opportunities, as used here, refer to the ongoing possibilities for young people to (a) be involved in active learning, (b) make decisions and contributions, (c) take on new and progressively more complex roles and responsibilities, and (d) engage in part-time or volunteer work. Opportunities have the greatest influence when they are perceived by young people as challenging and relevant. Supports are the ongoing relations through which young people become connected to others and to community resources. Supports can be emotional, motivational, and strategic, and they have the greatest influence when they are provided by diverse adults, peers, and social networks.

Two conclusions can be drawn from our work. First, it is apparent that providing young people with developmental experiences is an effective strategy for preventing problem behavior and for encouraging achievement in school and elsewhere. Second, developmental opportunities and supports can have influence whether they occur in families, schools, youth organizations, or social networks. Legitimate opportunities and supports, therefore, should be offered in all settings in which young people live. A high-quality service learning program can be one such setting.

A challenge to advocates, therefore, is to *show how research has demonstrated that developmental experiences of the type provided in service learning can be effective in promoting the healthy development of youth.* Advocates should see that this information is conveyed to practitioners as well as to school administrators and the community. Another challenge is to *examine systematically service learning programs in the context of other ongoing experiences in the lives of young people.*

Building Opportunities and Supports into School-based Service Learning

Three important phases of a service learning project are (1) preparing and planning for the project, (2) engagement in and completion of the project, and (3) analysis, reporting, and making new applications

OPPORTUNITIES FOR INFORMAL INSTRUCTION AND ACTIVE LEARNING

- *Exploration, Practice, and Reflection:* The chance to actively learn and build skills, and to critically test, explore, and discuss ideas and choices.
- *Expression and Creativity:* The chance to express oneself through different mediums and in different settings, and to engage in both learning and play.

OPPORTUNITIES FOR NEW ROLES AND RESPONSIBILITIES

- *Group Membership:* The chance to be an integral group member (e.g., family, school, youth organization), by fully taking on the responsibilities of membership.
- *Contribution and Service:* The chance to have positive influences on others through active participation in formal or informal community- and family-based activities.
- *Part-time Paid Employment:* The chance to earn income and to be a part of the work force, when such work is done within a safe and reasonably comfortable setting.

EMOTIONAL SUPPORT

- *Nurturance and Friendship:* To receive love, friendship, and affirmation from others, and to be involved in caring relationships.

MOTIVATIONAL SUPPORT

- *High Expectations:* To receive high expectations from others, including the opportunities, encouragement, and rewards necessary to meet high expectations.
- *Standards and Boundaries:* To receive clear messages regarding rules, norms, and discipline, and to be involved in discussing and modifying the boundaries as appropriate.

STRATEGIC SUPPORT

- *Options Assessment and Planning:* To receive assistance in assessing one's options, and to be involved in relationships characterized by coaching, feedback, and discussion.
- *Access to Resources:* To receive assistance in gaining access to current and future resources through involvement and connections to people and information.

FIGURE 2
Opportunities and supports: Experiences that promote the development of young people

Source: AED/Center for Youth Development and Policy Research.

of the learnings from the project. Moreover, in order for the service to be meaningful for the students, it is important that reflection should occur throughout the project. Advocates must be prepared to provide evidence from research on adolescent development that illustrates how exemplary service learning provides the opportunities and supports essential to youth development.

In the preparation and planning component of many service learning programs students are typically involved in the selection of projects. They are thus provided with opportunities for self-directed learning and creativity and for participation as a valued group member. For example, in the Community Service Program in Springfield, Massachusetts, students began by conducting an inventory of community needs and then reached consensus with their peers and the school staff on service projects to be undertaken. Also in Springfield, at the Chestnut Street Middle School, teachers and community representatives introduced students to a number of service projects and discussed why they were important. Students were then encouraged to select a project and they were given a few days to think about their choices before making a commitment. At the National Indian Youth Leadership Project in Gallup, New Mexico, a summer camp offers an opportunity for students to learn valuable skills to use in identifying and planning projects to implement in their home communities during the school year.

From a developmental perspective it is not simply the project itself that is important; how decisions are reached is also important. Youth need to be given ample time to do the necessary research, have discussions with their peers, formulate and express their positions, and test the pros and cons of different options. Throughout this component, the staff should ensure that all young people have choices and varied roles and that they understand the high expectations that will guide their involvement. At the same time, the staff should provide the necessary supports to help youth find their own meaning in the project and to "bond" as a team. Regardless of which projects are selected, whether individual placements or collective actions, periods of reflection help young people to consider the alternatives, reach closure, and appreciate the processes used to make decisions.

The second component—the service experience itself—also presents possibilities for developmental experiences. The chance to contribute to community is a powerful opportunity, but the opportunities for choice, active learning, and reflection, combined with the provision of supports are key features in designing service learning programs. At the Oakland (California) Health and Bioscience Academy, for example, students are required to undertake one hundred hours of internships. They report to their group about their placements as well as about what they have learned about themselves through the experience. This type of expression is difficult for many youth. Hence practitioners are challenged to offer the ongoing support necessary for achievement. Sometimes youth give formal presentations, sometimes they role play, and sometimes they communicate their experience through poetry.

Reflection is a vital strategy for helping young people discover meaning for themselves in the service experience. From a developmental perspective, young people should be allowed to express their learning in a variety of ways. Ongoing guidance from adults, provided by the service learning staff as well as by adults at the placement site, is also important. When emotional and strategic supports are explicitly embedded within the service experience, young people will gain affirmation and establish connections with community resources that too often are missing in their lives.

During the third component of service learning, young people are typically engaged in formally analyzing, reporting, and making new applications of their learnings. At this time, they have opportunities to reflect on the complete experience, test conclusions, and disseminate their findings. From a developmental perspective, the "new application task" is critical. At Liberty High School in Washington state, for example, many students are motivated to learn how to analyze the chemical and biological indicators of environmental health because this knowledge is essential to the team's collective goal of increasing public awareness of threats to the community. Similarly, because youth are doing "real work" in their placements in the Kalamazoo (Michigan) School District's Education for Employment Program, they are motivated to attend career preparation classes to learn how to address the practical issues that they confront on a weekly basis.

Creating opportunities for students to continue their efforts after the program is completed allows youth to go on learning at their own pace and foster a sustained sense of citizenship. At the Freedman School in Springfield, Massachusetts, young people returned to the retirement home to surprise an elder on her eighty-eighth birthday. In 1988, a student in the National Indian Youth Leadership Program mentioned earlier suggested replanting peach trees every year in the Canyon de Chelly to make up for destruction wrought by Kit Carson in the canyon, and the replanting has continued ever since. At the Meyzeek Middle School in Louisville, Kentucky, eighth grade students have applied their learning to medical and disaster relief and nutritional programs in their communities by offering presentations in the form of symposiums.

At its best, service learning provides opportunities and supports to young people throughout all components of a project. It is important for advocates to communicate examples that challenge practitioners to offer in each phase of a project a rich array of opportunities and supports that will promote youth development.

Community-based Youth Organizations as Partners with School-based Service Learning Practitioners

School-based practitioners should recognize that they have many strong allies in the youth development field—organizations that young people attend voluntarily. The most visible are the national youth-serving organizations such as the Boys and Girls Clubs of America; Girls, Incorporated; Cooperative Extension. But there are just as many community-based organizations—neighborhood youth and community centers, parks and recreation departments, religious institutions, family support programs—that have a powerful influence on the daily lives of young people.[8]

At their best, community organizations are explicitly in the business of promoting youth development, and they have the expertise to engage particularly those young people who are alienated from schools or have few connections to community members and institutions. Especially in low-income and immigrant communities, these organizations can fill gaps resulting from the limitations of schools and other social institutions. Community organizations have maximum flexibility in scheduling since they are constrained neither by the fifty-minute class period nor by established age groups. Because the development of these organizations has often been rooted in communities and neighborhoods, their organizational cultures more closely represent that of the youth they serve, as compared with schools and other public sector agencies. Similarly, leadership in these organizations tends to represent more closely the racial, ethnic, and cultural backgrounds of participants in their programs. Together, these characteristics allow community organizations to make opportunities and supports accessible to many young people who do not consistently receive them elsewhere.[9]

Community youth-serving organizations have much in common with school-based service learning programs. Many offer the central components of service learning, although they may be called something different. Youth plan the projects, the service experience is typically complemented with formal instruction, and such efforts always include innovative strategies for individual and group reflection. For example, the Boys Choir of Harlem in New York City sponsors concerts and other events for residents in poor neighborhoods, and the staff uses musical instruction as a way of teaching life skills and fostering a sense of achievement, persistence, teamwork, patience, and self-reliance. Most youth organizations expect young people to become involved in the community as part of "membership" in the group. Youth as Resources, a national program sponsored by the National Crime Prevention Council, provides small grants to young people to design and carry out community-oriented projects of their own choosing, and systematic efforts are made to link these experiences to formal or informal instruction.

At their core, community organizations are also about citizenship and community membership. At El Puente Academy for Peace and Justice in New York, participants learn the many skills of community education and advocacy, using them, for example, in organizing sustained campaigns against a proposed incinerator in their neighborhood and helping to build bridges among different cultural groups in the community.

Like practitioners in school-based service learning programs, community youth organizations attend to supports as much as to opportunities. They realize, as Ianni has demonstrated,[10] that young people from troubled families or disadvantaged neighborhoods crave the support that comes from structure or predictability in their lives. It is for this reason that community organizations strive to ensure that all youth receive ongoing respect and reassurance from staff. Activities are designed to build friendships among members. Motivating young people through high expectations and setting clear standards for behavior is also a critical aspect of youth organizations, as illustrated by the Jesse White Tumbling Team in Chicago. In order for tumblers to perform for the community, they must adhere to strict rules and regulations which include no drinking, smoking, swearing, dropping out of school, or being unkind to neighbors. And, finally, community organizations provide strategic supports to young people in low-income neighborhoods. Whether providing young people with a mentor, introducing them to potential employers, or helping them locate and complete a college scholarship application, community organizations use innovative strategies to link young people to existing community networks.

Challenges and strategies. The focus on opportunities and supports connects school-based service learning programs and community-based youth organizations, making both unique among public and private service providers. It is unfortunate, therefore, that information gaps and suspicions too often characterize relationships among schools and community organizations. Neither the schools nor the community organizations have the resources to provide high-quality service learning for all young people. Ongoing communication and collaboration, therefore, are necessary. The challenge is to bridge the gaps between organizations that have a similar mission. Service learning practitioners in schools can address this problem by inviting youth workers to share their expertise with school staff. Additionally, collaborative sponsorship of programs can be initiated by school-based practitioners.[11]

In addition to program initiatives, it will be useful for school and community practitioners to engage jointly in public education and staff development. Disseminating strategies of best practice is one approach. But school and community youth organization staffs will ultimately have to confront the fact that many stakeholders—including local leaders and school officials—too often question the ability and motivation of youth, especially those labeled "high risk," to engage fully in service learning. This stereotype is reflected in the selection of programs that we offer high risk youth and, more subtly, in the ways that we interact with them.[12] The need to engage in sustained public education for adults is readily apparent. Without such efforts, it is doubtful that the values of youth "service," "contribution," and "involvement" will be fully integrated into future school or community policies.

Increasingly, youth organizations are coming together in localities to form "networks for youth development" or "communitywide professional development systems."[13] These coalitions are concerned with promoting youth development among all young people in the community. To that end, they focus on adult education, engaging local planning bodies and community leaders in discussions and providing them with opportunities to visit exemplary programs to highlight their messages. Further, the coalitions seek to share expertise and limited resources by engaging organizations in joint training and professional development programs.

A challenge to school and community-based advocates of service learning will be to ensure that schools are included in these networks. Currently, schools are not adequately involved, although there are exceptions. At the Children, Youth, and Family Council in Philadelphia, for example, teachers participate on the advisory board that assesses community training needs. At YouthNet in Kansas City, Missouri, school administrators serve on a committee that sets the direction of the coalition and develops training programs. And the Professional Development Institute in New Haven, Connecticut, is training school security staff in youth participation and youth development. Communitywide networks have the potential, through their collective capacity, to raise issues, provide forums, disseminate information, offer training, and generate support for service learning and youth development. This work would be enhanced by the active involvement of schools. The challenge to advocates from all sectors, therefore, is to form, support, and participate in such networks.

Concluding Statement

Because of its focus on preventing youth problems rather than promoting youth development, society continues to set low expectations for young people. Service learning, in contrast, sets high expectations for young people, not only for classroom accomplishments, but also in terms of active engagement and contribution to community.

It is curious, therefore, that service learning has not been fully endorsed by educators, the general public, or policymakers. This failure is not simply one of poor marketing; it is a lack of attention to integrating practice with explanatory language and argument. Our conclusion is that service learning advocates have failed to coalesce the strong theory and supporting research into a simple language that is convincing to relevant audiences. Equally important, the lack of clarity makes it difficult, if not impossible, to implement consistently effective staff development programs in service learning.

Advocates for school-based service learning have natural allies among community-based youth-serving organizations. Indeed, these organizations recognize that youth development is best served when young people's lives are not fragmented and when the edges or boundaries between school, neighborhood, and community overlap or disappear. The challenge will be to build bridges among schools and community organizations. In the long run, it will be most useful to create and support communitywide networks and training systems that bring service learning not simply to the "believers," but to all adults, regardless of where they work, who are seeking new strategies for helping young people make the transition from adolescence to young adulthood.

Notes

1. See Joe Nathan and Jim Kielsmeier, "The Sleeping Giant of School Reform," *Phi Delta Kappan* 72, no. 10 (1991): 738-742; Joan Schine, *Young Adolescents and Community Service* (Washington, D.C.: Carnegie Council on Adolescent Development, 1989).

2. National Youth Leadership Council, *Learning Is the Thing: Insights Emerging from a National Conference on Service Learning, School Reform, and Higher Education* (Roseville, Minn.: National Youth Leadership Council, 1994).

3. Virginia Anderson, Carol Kinsley, Peter Negroni, and Carolyn Price, "Community Service Learning and School Improvement in Springfield, Massachusetts," *Phi Delta Kappan* 72, no. 10 (1991): 761-764; Harry Silcox, "Abraham Lincoln High School: Community Service in Action," *Phi Delta Kappan* 72, no. 10 (1991): 758-759; Dan Conrad and Diane Hedin, "School-Based Community Service: What We Know from Research and Theory," *Phi Delta Kappan* 72, no. 10 (1991): 743-749.

4. Center for Youth Development and Policy Research, *Overview* (Washington, D.C.: Center for Youth Development and Policy Research, Academy for Educational Development, 1992).

5. Karen Pitman and Michele Cahill, *A New Vision: Promoting Youth Development* (Washington, D.C.: Academy for Educational Development, 1992).

6. Conrad and Hedin, "School-Based Community Service."

7. Shepherd Zeldin and Lauren Price, "Creating Supporting Communities for Adolescent Development," *Journal of Adolescent Research* 10, no. 1 (1995): 6-15; Shepherd Zeldin, *Opportunities and Supports for Youth Development* (Washington, D.C.: Academy for Educational Development, 1995).

8. Karen Pitman and Marlene Wright, *Bridging the Gap: A Rationale for Enhancing the Role of Community Organizations in Promoting Youth Development* (Washington, D.C.: Academy for Educational Development, 1991); Carnegie Council on Adolescent Development, *A Matter of Time: Risk and Opportunity in the Nonschool Hours* (New York: Carnegie Corporation, 1993).

9. Samuel Whelen and Joan Wynn, "Enhancing Primary Services for Youth through an Infrastructure of Social Services," *Journal of Adolescent Research* 10, no. 1 (1995): 88-110; Milbrey McLaughlin, Merita A. Irby, and Juliet Langman, *Urban Sanctuaries* (San Francisco: Jossey-Bass, 1994).

10. Fritz Ianni, *The Search for Structure* (London: Free Press, 1989).

11. For examples, see Schine, *Young Adolescents and Community Service.*

12. Linda Camino, "Understanding Intolerance and Multiculturalism: A Challenge for Practitioners, but Also for Researchers," *Journal of Adolescent Research* 10, no. 1 (1995): 155-172.

13. Center for Youth Development and Policy Research, *Best Practices of Community-Based Training Systems for Youth Workers* (Washington, D.C.: Academy for Educational Development, 1995).

CHAPTER XIV

Looking Ahead: Issues and Challenges

JOAN SCHINE

In the Foreword to this volume, Harold Howe asserts that service learning "has more to do with becoming a mature adult than any academic exercise; and it is at least the equal of academic effort in building an understanding of others, the capacity to be an effective citizen, and the promise of leading a balanced life in an increasingly complex world." Implicit in this statement is an assumption about the purposes of the public schools and about their mission: If our children are to become competent adults and effective citizens, if they are to be prepared to meet the challenges that lie ahead, then public education must seek to combine rigorous academic instruction with an equally rigorous and demanding experience of learning through service to the community.

Both elements, Howe argues, are essential. "Service learning will have to become an integral part of the school curriculum rather than the extracurricular activity it too often is." Madeleine Kunin echoes that view in chapter 11 of this book, suggesting that service learning does indeed bring "added value" to the curriculum, and that it ought not be considered an "add-on."

What are the conditions that will make it possible for service learning to become an integral part of schooling in America? What are the impediments? How significant is the debate over mandated versus voluntary service? What is the role of service learning in curriculum reform? The importance of "structured reflection" is stressed repeatedly, but is there a common understanding of the term? These are among the questions that the authors of this Yearbook raise, and that we must continue to consider as we contemplate the problems and possibilities for service learning in the years just ahead. There are practical considerations as well: Is there a particular age or grade level when it is most appropriate to introduce service learning in the curriculum? Can current scheduling practices accommodate service learning? How can

---

Joan Schine serves as a consultant on service learning and educational reform. She was the founding Director of the National Center for Service Learning in Early Adolescence.

schools and community agencies establish strong collaborative relationships to facilitate service learning? What costs will incorporating service learning add to the school budget? Finally, and fundamentally, is there a common understanding of the term itself?

A decade has passed since the late Ernest Boyer, then president of the Carnegie Foundation for the Advancement of Teaching and an early supporter of youth service and service learning, suggested five principles of school-based service that he hoped would prove helpful to administrators considering the addition of service learning to the curriculum. These principles and Boyer's comments on them are reproduced here:

> *First, a service program begins with clearly stated educational objectives.* A service program is rooted in the conviction that schooling at its best concerns itself with the humane application of knowledge to life. Service is concerned with helping others, but, above all, it is concerned with improved learning. It is about helping students to discover the value of the curriculum, and to see that, in the end formal learning must be considered useful not just economically but socially as well.
>
> *Second, a service program should be carefully introduced and creatively promoted.* . . . Thoughtful people differ, not over the notion of service, but whether it fits in the program of formal education. . . . A cautious beginning is not inappropriate.
>
> *Third, service activity should be directed not just to the community but also toward the school itself.* We urge that the notion of service focus more directly on the school itself, through tutoring, of course, but also perhaps through other tasks so students begin to discover what it takes to make a school work and accept a more active and responsible role.
>
> *Fourth, service activity should be something more than preparation for a career.* Students . . . may derive profound satisfaction from their direct contacts with those who benefit from their help, and from knowing they are participating in something worthwhile. These values are important in life whether [or not] one's service is ultimately related to a career.
>
> *Fifth, students should not only go out to serve; they also should be asked to write about their experience and, if possible, discuss with others the lessons they have learned.*[1]

Definitions and Goals

In the years since Boyer set forth these principles, descriptions and definitions of service learning have proliferated. While all share some common elements, there are differences—some minor, others significant—in emphasis and vocabulary. In 1990, Jane Kendall, at that time the executive director of the National Society for Internships and Experiential Education, found 147 different definitions of the term "service learning."[2] It is scarcely surprising, then, that writers in this volume, while unanimous in their support of service learning, see in it a variety of attributes. For example, while Gene Carter's discussion of service learning in chapter 5 underscores its role in revitalizing the curriculum, Haynes and Comer stress in chapter 6 the place of service in contributing to a school climate that is characterized by a sense of community and caring. The Shoreham-Wading River program, on the other hand, as Winifred Pardo describes it in chapter 7, derived its initial impetus from a conviction that "the service experience could make a vital contribution to a young person's development and to the health and life of the larger community."

While the goals of service learning cover a wide range, there is some agreement as to its philosophy and structure. The National Helpers Network, Inc. (formerly the National Center for Service Learning in Early Adolescence) describes service learning succinctly as "the pairing of meaningful work in the community with structured reflection."[3]

The Alliance for Service Learning in Education Reform (ASLER) says simply that "service learning is a method by which young people learn and develop through active participation in thoughtfully organized service experiences."[4]

The language of the National and Community Service Trust Act of 1993 describes service learning as "an educational experience

- under which students learn and develop through active participation in thoughtfully organized service experiences that meet actual community needs and that are coordinated in collaboration with school and community;
- that is integrated into the students' academic curriculum or provides structured time for the students to think, talk, or write about what they did and saw during the actual service activity;
- that provides students with opportunities to use newly acquired skills and knowledge in real-life situations in their own communities; and
- that enhances what is taught in school by extending students' learning beyond the classroom and into the community and helps to foster the development of a sense of caring for others."[5]

One may quarrel with a definition that consigns service learning to the role of a "method" or a means to an end, and we may wish that the

National and Community Service Trust Act had made it clear that "educational experience" is not confined to the schoolhouse. Program developers, practitioners, policymakers, and legislators will devise their own interpretations; nevertheless, common elements emerge: meaningful service, active participation, reflection, and learning.

It is evident that programs of service learning embrace a variety of goals and objectives. In addition to the obvious one of meeting community needs, the goals may include career exploration, citizenship education, acquiring or improving "basic skills," reconnecting alienated youth with the community, enrichment of the academic curriculum, promoting altruism and creating a "culture of caring," or even providing the impetus (and a model) for school reform. Service learning is indeed a promising program, but it is not the wonder drug of schooling, destined to create a brave new world of public education. The capacity of service learning to encompass a variety of goals constitutes both promise and peril. Like many earlier initiatives that failed to fulfill their promise, service learning could founder under the weight of unrealistic or grandiose expectations.

Conditions for Success

The programs that are most likely to survive and grow are those that have examined the range of possible goals in terms of the philosophy of a particular school or school district and the needs of that particular population. They are selective in setting goals and have identified clear benchmarks against which to measure their achievement of these goals. Planners anticipate the pitfalls they may encounter. The very energy and commitment that will make a program come to life may cause its adherents to overlook what is perhaps the most critical factor in determining whether the project will succeed or fail: enlisting the support of the school community—the administration, staff at all levels, parents, and students—and the community at large. Not only the agencies where students will serve, but the media, the clergy, and the public should be kept informed, and, where possible, included in the planning.

In today's climate of concern about public expenditures, the question of costs will need to be addressed early and directly. Winifred Pardo declares that at the Shoreham-Wading River Middle School cost containment was not a problem. This enviable circumstance can be ascribed to the school's longstanding commitment to service learning and community involvement; service has been viewed as integral to the curriculum from the school's opening day. But in most school districts, questions regarding cost will arise. Teacher time must be counted an expense. There may be transportation costs. A small fund should be set aside for materials and for celebration of the students' achievements. There will be unexpected contingencies, especially at the start. Some successful initiatives have been able to combine funds from a number of sources such as federal grants under the School-to-Work initiative, the Office of Juvenile Justice and Delinquency Prevention, Learn and Serve America, and grants from the private sector, including foundations. The amounts will not be great at the local level, but the need for some funding should be acknowledged. In introducing any innovation, it is wise to avoid surprising the public.

Meeting Real Needs

As Janie Ward points out in chapter 10, some volunteer service providers "[operate] from unexamined, preconceived assessments of the community and its residents' characteristics and needs; . . . often in these instances recipients end up getting less out of the service relationship than do the students who serve." Program operators need to recognize that while every community has its share of unmet needs, and virtually every individual, regardless of age, can make some contribution, the service that will be truly welcomed is the one that the community has identified as needed.

In the same vein, the connection between classroom learning and the service activity must be evident to the learner, so that each enriches the other. Many claims have been made in the name of personal or social growth; frequently, a potpourri of objectives is subsumed under the rubric of youth development. Goals in this area should be clearly stated, and progress toward these goals subject to ongoing scrutiny. Few areas of growth are more difficult to measure, and, as Richard Lipka suggests in chapter 4, there is scant information about long-term outcomes.

Mandatory or Voluntary?

If service learning is indeed a powerful resource in education, why not make it a requirement in every school? This question has inspired some of the most vehement discussions among practitioners and proponents of service learning, among students and parents, and among others who comment on the current state of education. One state

(Maryland) requires seventy-five hours of community service for graduation or an alternative program devised by the local district and approved by the state Superintendent of Schools. Maryland's class of 1997 will be the first to graduate with this requirement in effect.

The American Alliance for Rights and Responsibilities surveyed the 130 largest school districts in the country to gather information on required service. Among the respondents (72 percent of the districts contacted) there was wide disparity in the structure of the service requirement. There are significant differences in expectations and program content among states, among school districts, and even among schools within a single district. In spite of the efforts of advocates of service learning to distinguish between them, the terms "community service" and "service learning" are often used interchangeably. The definitions of service learning cited earlier illuminate the distinction. Performing community service is ordinarily a positive experience for the participant. It *may* also be a learning experience, but only when a reflective component is part of the whole does community service become service learning. Many schools encourage "one-shot" voluntary service activities, such as a holiday luncheon for senior citizens, a holiday party at a day care center, or a drive to raise funds or to collect food. Through these experiences students will occasionally develop a heightened awareness of community needs and a commitment to service. But if school-based learning is to realize its potential for enriching the curriculum, serendipitous learning is not sufficient. A "reflective component" must be an intrinsic part of the whole.

In Florida's Dade County, the number of hours of service required is not specified, but the district's policy stipulates that "the project should be meaningful and require a commitment of time on the part of a student. Students must keep a service Activity Log and complete a summary of their project(s)." Chatham County (Georgia) requires students to perform five hours of community service per year. Cincinnati and Corpus Christi, in sharp contrast to this approach, include service in required social studies classes.[6]

Objections to mandatory service include claims that it constitutes "involuntary servitude" and that only voluntary service is truly meaningful. In Maryland, just before the legislature approved the community service requirement for high school graduation, the president of the State Teachers Association protested that "it would dilute the efforts of high schools to exact more rigorous academic performance from students,"[7] a point of view shared by proponents of "back to basics." Questions have been raised, too, about the quality of service that reluctant participants will provide, and about whether some students, unwilling or unskilled, may even do more harm than good.

On the other hand, those who support making community service mandatory argue that many students who would benefit from participating would be unlikely to volunteer. They suggest, too, that as long as service is voluntary or an elective, the message to students is that it is less important than the many activities that constitute the required program. In a letter to the editor of the *Washington Post*, Ernest Boyer responded to the furor over the Maryland legislation. He wrote,

> It seems especially inappropriate to reject community service because it is "not voluntary." Schools are not centers of volunteerism. They are places where our children are asked—required—to complete programs that prepare them for life: economically, civically, and morally. A service requirement is as justified as a requirement in math or science or physical education if it helps contribute to these essential ends.[8]

Service is seen by its advocates as an "equalizer." Males and females, athletes, honor students, immigrants with limited English proficiency can participate as equals. Students whose paths might never cross in the ordinary course of their school lives can come to know and respect each other on the proverbial "level playing field."

Some scholars, such as Chester Finn and Gregg Vanourek of the Hudson Institute, criticize making service learning (which they refer to as "mandatory voluntarism") a requirement and in doing so reveal their ignorance of the distinctions made between service learning and other programs such as experiential education, community service, and character education.[9] If scholars like Finn and Vanourek can so misconstrue the nature and purposes of service learning as part of the curriculum, then advocates for service learning will need to devote considerable effort to informing parents, legislators, and the public about the purposes and processes of service learning. In particular, the distinction between service learning and community service must be made again and again.

At its Annual Conference in April, 1993, the Association for Supervision and Curriculum Development, an international association that counts superintendents, principals, supervisors, teachers, school board members, and higher education faculty among its members, adopted a resolution in support of "required student service learning programs for students of all ages." It is worth noting that the ASCD resolution, unlike the legislative mandates, specifies "service learning" rather than simply "community service." This is more than a matter of terminology; it is a significant distinction. Service learning by definition involves more than the service task. The real issue is not so much the substance of the task as the way it is approached; the meaning derives from carefully designed opportunities for student preparation and reflection. As Lipka suggests in chapter 4, the "blend of theory and practice, thought and action provides the necessary ingredient to bring together the cognitive and affective dimensions which result in authentic learning."

Efforts to infuse service learning into the existing curriculum have multiplied in recent years. Where this is accomplished successfully, the issue of mandatory versus voluntary service becomes moot. When, for example, activities like producing oral histories, interviewing older adults and documenting local history and customs are integrated into the social studies or language arts class, the curriculum and the community are both enriched. Similarly, when a study of the water supply leads to testing the rivers and streams of the community and reporting the results to the state department of environmental protection, students easily understand that their study of science has immediate application and, in addition, learn something of the functions of government.

The service requirement has already survived legal challenges in the courts of New Jersey, Pennsylvania, Maryland, New York, and most recently (July 1996) in Federal District Court in North Carolina. Nevertheless, the debate over requiring service is still open. Convincing arguments can be made for each position. Many thoughtful individuals are concerned about overburdening an already crowded school schedule; others are seeking to define the limits of the school's responsibility. Whatever one's philosophical view, there are practical considerations. For example, if service is required of all students in areas where service opportunities are few or transportation is a problem, making a good match between student and service placement may be difficult. In urban settings, there is the question of scale: finding enough suitable placements accessible to the school, in reasonably safe locations, may be a deterrent to enabling all students to participate. Less tangible, but equally critical, are issues of "quality control." Does collecting canned goods at Thanksgiving fulfill a community service requirement? Is sixty hours of service over four years as meaningful as thirty hours in a single semester? Are some kinds of service especially suitable for certain age groups? Are there cultural norms to be considered in placing young people in service roles in our multicultural society?

The Need for Research

The legitimacy of school-based service learning, whether required, integrated into the curriculum, or an elective course, will no doubt continue to be debated for some time. The questions cited here are only some of those that schools and colleges will need to address in the future. They highlight the need for in-depth research on student and community outcomes, and for objective evaluation of existing initiatives. In 1990, Harold Howe issued a call for more rigorous research about the impact on youth participants:

> Statewide or citywide youth service endeavors have started in a number of places. Formal evaluations of several of these undergird strongly their value in terms of useful accomplishments for dollars invested. Less is known about the long-term impact of youth service on the lives of the young.[10]

As is frequently the case with innovative programs, planners and program leaders have tended to allocate scarce resources to program development rather than to research. The credibility of service learning will be measured in terms of demonstrable benefits, with emphasis on students' achievement and acquisition of skills. The development of the field must be guided by meticulous evaluation and research.

In September of 1995 the W. K. Kellogg Foundation sponsored the Service Learning Summit, convening thirty-nine individuals from a variety of disciplines "to review and discuss the impact of service learning and ways to increase our knowledge of impact and improve practice."[11] Five studies currently under way were described. The largest of these is the Learn and Serve K-12 Evaluation conducted by Brandeis University's Center for Human Resources and by Abt Associates. A three-part study, it is examining impact on program participants, on the communities, and on the institutional impact of school-based service learning programs funded by the Corporation for National Service. Other current studies, such as that of the Search institute, focus on the impact of exemplary service learning programs on achievement. Another study is looking at the impact of the Active Citizenship Today (ACT) program on "such outcomes as civic and community-related knowledge and skills, attitudes toward civic participation, involvement in civic and community service activities." The ACT study is also exploring the program's impact on participating teachers, an area of particular interest when service learning is viewed as a vehicle for overall school reform. While there has been considerable discussion of the effects of participation in service learning programs on teaching styles and teacher morale, it is difficult to find reliable data on such effects. The evaluation of Calserve, the California Learn and Serve programs, explores the manner of implementation of service learning and the effect of mediating factors as well as other basic questions relating to impact. A study of the Early Adolescent Helper model focuses on effects of participation in service learning in early adolescence and on "how impact is related to program characteristics and the types of service students perform."

These five studies are a fraction of the research projects now planned or under way. Clearly, the service learning field has started to attend to the need for systematic research and evaluation. Nevertheless, at the close of the Service Learning Summit, the participants proposed next steps. "The group felt that the most critical next step and the only strategy to receive a majority of votes is to fund research and evaluation studies to measure the effects of various models of service learning programs."[12]

A Sequential Approach

Up to this time, service learning opportunities have been provided at a particular grade level or grouping, most often at the high school and more recently at the middle school. Involving students in varied experiences over several years, as is the case in the Shoreham-Wading River Middle School described by Pardo, has been the exception rather than the rule. Alec Dickson, one of the early proponents of youth service, the founder of Great Britain's Voluntary Service Overseas, and president of Community Service Volunteers, suggests that we must look beyond the somewhat isolated service experience and discover ways to develop a sequential approach, just as we do in other areas:

> What I fail to see in many school-based programs of service learning is provision for growth. If it is math or chemistry or French, then students at [age] fifteen will be tackling questions commensurate with their age and grade. The worst thing that could befall us would be if students were to grow bored with the patterns of social involvement that we present them with.[13]

The risk of boredom can easily be avoided if service learning is viewed in a developmental context. In such an approach the students would progress from relatively simple group projects that emphasize service within the school and even within the classroom in the early years, through an increasingly complex sequence as they learn the skills of service and are able to assume greater responsibility for initiating, planning, and completing projects. Over time, when service learning activities are designed to build on the skills and understandings acquired in earlier experiences, the students will become increasingly competent in service roles. With skilled adult leadership they will also become more comfortable and competent in the process of reflection, so that the learning is internalized and habits of critical thinking and problem solving are reinforced. When service learning is seen as a cumulative, multiyear component of the school program, not only will it be connected with the traditional academic disciplines, but its potential for developing skills needed for future employment will be realized. The Boston Public Schools have taken a step toward a multiyear approach to service learning with the development of a Comprehensive School Plan. This plan affirms the continuing centrality of service learning in the curriculum and every school will be expected to include service learning in its program.

The Core Values

Surveys and polls consistently show that parents, educators, and others concur that the schools should convey "core democratic values." Enlarging the scope of service learning from the primary grades through the high school years will encourage a growing understanding and internalizing of these values as young people assume some of the responsibilities that are the privileges and obligations of membership in a democracy.

Although in some quarters the mention of values education occasions debate, most educators are aware that there is no such thing as a "value-free" curriculum. Moreover, a 1994 study of almost 1200 Americans' views on public education reveals that "people want schools to teach values, but they especially want schools to emphasize those values that allow a diverse society to live together peacefully."[14]

Values education, character education, civic education, and service learning, while not synonymous, share many goals and concerns. While some practitioners in these fields emphasize individual behavior and attitudes and others stress group values, all accord the school a significant role in transmitting personal and societal values. All include, although in very different ways, the effort to teach "core democratic values." They are, however, frequently viewed as competing for time in the school schedule, as well as for scarce resources. Realizing that both tangible and human resources are and will continue to be limited while needs continue to grow, advocates in these areas must consider carefully the consequences of such competition. They will need to find new ways to collaborate, especially as the inventory of "what students are expected to know and do" grows ever longer.

Making Common Cause

It is not difficult to understand and even sympathize with the concern for "turf" that program developers and staff exhibit in their search for support, but this posture can be harmful. For example, Don Eberly, a longtime champion of youth service, notes that a Wingspread Conference on "National Youth Service: A Democratic Institution for the 21st Century" was held in July, 1991, just before the Commission on National and Community Service was to become operational. Although the participants were able to reach consensus on several principles they believed should inform a national youth service program, they "spent too much time carving out their respective claims to a piece of the national service pie—all very politely, of course—and too little on the future of national service."[15] If service learning programs and the array of related initiatives are to realize their potential in school reform, concerns for the "purity" and ownership of discrete programs will need to be replaced by collaboration and mutual support.

In Summary

There is still much to learn about the process and the effects of service learning. Public perceptions of a fraying social fabric, the disintegration of community, and the alienation of youth have kindled interest in activities or strategies that show promise of reconnecting youth to society. Employers are concerned about securing a work force of competent individuals—workers who are conscientious, literate and responsible, able to follow directions, equipped with skills for the economy of the 21st century. Many employers therefore look to service learning as a way of developing the attitudes and skills needed for success in the world of work. Those who believe that the mission of public education is to prepare our youth for productive and contributing citizenship see service learning as a promising strategy.

In this last decade of the century, then, schools across the country face new and growing demands. Not only are they charged with ensuring that their students master the basics, but they must prepare a diverse population of young people for "the information age," equipping them as well with sophisticated skills that not long ago were unheard of at the precollegiate level. They must in addition deal with a rapid rise in school-age population, and with the obligation to provide for a growing number of students with special needs. They must search for ways to assimilate new waves of immigrants, and prepare all students for the responsibilities of citizenship in a democracy. Moreover, the problems of urban areas do not disappear at the schoolhouse door. "Almost three-quarters of Americans (72 percent) say 'drugs and violence' are serious problems in schools in their area."[16] Finally, while struggling to meet these growing demands, schools across the country are faced with shrinking budgets.

No wonder, then, that there are those in the education community and in society at large who resist adding service learning to an already crowded agenda. The challenge for advocates of service learning will be to demonstrate that, rather than being one more burden, service learning can address some of these issues and contribute substantially to ameliorating the problems our schools and our society face.

Notes

1. Ernest L. Boyer, "Foreword," in Charles H. Harrison, *Student Service: The New Carnegie Unit* (Lawrenceville, N.J.: Princeton University Press, 1987).

2. Seth S. Pollack, "Higher Education's Contested Service Role: A Framework for Analysis and Historical Survey," in Haas Center for Public Service, *To Strengthen Service Learning Policy and Practice: Stories from the Field* (Stanford, Calif.: Haas Center for Public Policy, Stanford University, 1996).

3. Susan Poulsen, *Learning Is the Thing: Insights Emerging from a National Conference on Service Learning, School Reform, and Higher Education* (Roseville, Minn.: National Youth Leadership Council, 1995).

4. Alliance for Service Learning in Education Reform, *Standards of Quality for School-based Service Learning* (Chester, Vt.: SerVermont, 1993), p. 1.

5. Commission on National and Community Service, *What You Can Do for Your Country* (Washington, D.C.: Commission on National and Community Service, 1993). This definition has been adopted by the Corporation for National Service, the successor to the Commission.

6. American Alliance for Rights and Responsibilities, *A Brief Sample of Community Service Requirements in Public Schools around the U.S.* (Washington, D.C.: American Alliance for Rights and Responsibilities, 1995).

7. Jane R. Stern, "Service or Servitude?" *School Youth Service Network* 3, no. 2 (Spring 1992): 1. Published by the Constitutional Rights Foundation, Los Angeles, Calif.

8. Ernest L. Boyer, "Public Service for Students?" in Letters, *Washington Post*, 8 March 1992.

9. Chester E. Finn, Jr. and Gregg Vanourek, "Charity Begins at School," *Commentary* 100, no. 4 (October 1995): 46.

10. Harold Howe, "Teen-Age America: Myths and Realities," *Adolescence* 9, no. 1 (1990): 9. (Family Resource Coalition Report).

11. Dale A. Blyth and Candyce Kroenke, eds., *Proceedings from the Service Learning Summit*, September 9-10, 1995 (Minneapolis, Minn.: Search Institute, 1996), p. 3.

12. Ibid., p. 24.

13. Alec Dickson, personal communication, May 1, 1991.

14. Jean Johnson and John Immerwahr, *First Things First: What Americans Expect from the Public Schools* (New York: Public Agenda, 1994), p. 24.

15. Don Eberly, *National Service from 1988 to 1996: A Personal Perspective* (Raumati Beach, New Zealand: The author, 1996), p. 9.

16. Johnson and Immerwahr, *First Things First*, p. 10.

Questions for Further Study

1. Both preservice and in-service teacher training programs are being reviewed and revised. To implement service learning, a teacher must not only have specific skills and training but also needs to have knowledge of the community beyond the school. How can schools of education prepare teachers for conducting programs of service learning? What experiences must be included in the teacher education program?

2. Service learning is a form of action learning. Historically, few teacher training programs have given more than passing attention to the methodology or content of action learning. How can teachers already in the classroom be helped to explore and employ this approach? How can they acquire the knowledge and skills needed to implement service learning successfully?

3. In the foreseeable future the high school graduate will need sophisticated knowledge of technology and accessing information previously demanded only of a limited number of experts. In the face of a knowledge explosion and of the growing importance of technology in education, how can we justify taking time in the school day for service to the community? What evidence exists, and what further information is needed, to support the legitimacy of including service learning experiences?

4. College and university staff in general have been more resistant to the introduction of service learning than their K-12 colleagues. What are the causes of this resistance? What are the legitimate applications of service learning at the college level?

5. In some quarters there is pressure to make service to the community a requirement for high school graduation. Is it possible to accommodate such a requirement and maintain the integrity of service learning as distinguished from community service? If service learning is to be incorporated in the school's offerings, whether as a separate requirement or a component of regular class work, how can parents and the community at large be involved? What supports or obstacles can be anticipated? What information is needed in advance?

6. Within the school reform movement there are strong arguments for "personalizing" education. This approach is often coupled with discussions of how best to "match" content with the developmental needs of the child. What is the role of service learning in responding to these needs?

7. Many K-12 educators see service learning as a way to instill the values of caring, compassion, and responsibility to the community. Ought the schools be expected to teach values? What evidence is there that engaging in service learning reinforces the "core democratic values"? Will teaching values through service learning bring the school into conflict with parents or the community at large?

Resources in Service Learning

Campus Compact (postsecondary)
Brown University, Box 1975
Providence, R.I. 02912
(401) 863-1119

Campus Outreach Opportunity League (COOL) (postsecondary)
1511 K Street NW, Suite 307
Washington, D.C. 20005

Corporation for National Service
1201 New York Ave., NW
Washington, D.C. 20525
(202) 606-5000
For K-12 information:
Learn and Serve America, Ext. 136
For higher education, Ext. 117

National Association of Partners in Education (NAPE)
209 Madison St.
Alexandria, Va. 22314
(703) 836-4880

National Helpers Network
245 Fifth Ave., Suite 1705
New York, N.Y. 10016-7641
(212) 670-2482

National Service Learning Cooperative Clearinghouse
R-290 Vocational & Technical Education Building
1954 Buford Ave.
St. Paul, Minn. 55108
(800) 808-7378

National Society for Experiential Education
3509 Haworth Drive, Suite 207
Raleigh, N.C. 27609-7229
(919) 787-3263

National Youth Leadership Council
1910 West Country Road B216
Roseville, Minn. 55113
(800) 366-6952

Search Institute
700 South Third St.
Minneapolis, Minn. 55415
(800) 888-7828

Thomas Jefferson Forum
Tufts University
Lincoln Filene Center
Medford, Mass. 02155
(617) 627-3858

Youth Service America
1319 F Street, NW, Suite 900
Washington, D.C. 20004
(202) 296-2992

Name Index

Subject Index

INFORMATION ABOUT MEMBERSHIP IN THE SOCIETY

Membership in the National Society for the Study of Education is open to all individuals who desire to receive its publications. Membership dues for 1997 are $30. All members receive both volumes of the current Yearbook.

For calendar year 1997 reduced dues are available for retired NSSE members and for full-time graduate students *in their first year of membership*. These reduced dues are $25.

Membership in the Society is for the calendar year. Dues are payable on or before January 1 of each year.

New members are required to pay an entrance fee of $1 in addition to the annual dues for the year in which they join.

Members of the Society include professors, researchers, graduate students, and administrators in colleges and universities; teachers, supervisors, curriculum specialists, and administrators in elementary and secondary schools; and a considerable number of persons not formally connected with educational institutions.

All members participate in the election of the Society's six-member Board of Directors, which is responsible for managing the affairs of the Society, including the authorization of volumes to appear in the series of Yearbooks. All members whose dues are paid for the current year are eligible for election to the Board of Directors.

Each year the Society arranges for meetings to be held in conjunction with the annual conferences of one or more of the major national educational organizations. All members are urged to attend these sessions at which the volumes of the current Yearbook are presented and critiqued. Members are also encouraged to submit proposals for future Yearbooks.

Members receive a 33 percent discount when purchasing past Yearbooks that are still in print from the Society's distributor, the University of Chicago Press.

Further information about the Society may be secured by writing to the Secretary-Treasurer, NSSE, 5835 Kimbark Avenue, Chicago, Illinois 60637.

RECENT PUBLICATIONS OF THE NATIONAL SOCIETY FOR THE STUDY OF EDUCATION

1. The Yearbooks

Ninety-fifth Yearbook (1996)

Part 1. *Performance-Based Student Assessment: Challenges and Possibilities.* Joan B. Baron and Dennie P. Wolf, editors. Cloth.

Part 2. *Technology and the Future of Schooling.* Stephen T. Kerr, editor. Cloth.

Ninety-fourth Yearbook (1995)

Part 1. *Creating New Educational Communities.* Jeannie Oakes and Karen Hunter Quartz, editors. Cloth.

Part 2. *Changing Populations/Changing Schools.* Erwin Flaxman and A. Harry Passow, editors. Cloth.

Ninety-third Yearbook (1994)

Part 1. *Teacher Research and Educational Reform.* Sandra Hollingsworth and Hugh Sockett, editors. Cloth.

Part 2. *Bloom's Taxonomy: A Forty-year Retrospective.* Lorin W. Anderson and Lauren A. Sosniak, editors. Cloth.

Ninety-second Yearbook (1993)

Part 1. *Gender and Education.* Sari Knopp Biklen and Diane Pollard, editors. Cloth.

Part 2. *Bilingual Education: Politics, Practice, and Research.* M. Beatriz Arias and Ursula Casanova, editors. Cloth.

Ninety-first Yearbook (1992)

Part 1. *The Changing Contexts of Teaching.* Ann Lieberman, editor. Cloth.

Part 2. *The Arts, Education, and Aesthetic Knowing.* Bennett Reimer and Ralph A. Smith, editors. Cloth.

Ninetieth Yearbook (1991)

Part 1. *The Care and Education of America's Young Children: Obstacles and Opportunities.* Sharon L. Kagan, editor. Cloth.

Part 2. *Evaluation and Education: At Quarter Century.* Milbrey W. McLaughlin and D. C. Phillips, editors. Paper.

Eighty-ninth Yearbook (1990)

Part 1. *Textbooks and Schooling in the United States.* David L. Elliott and Arthur Woodward, editors. Cloth.

Part 2. *Educational Leadership and Changing Contexts of Families, Communities, and Schools.* Brad Mitchell and Luvern L. Cunningham, editors. Paper.

Eighty-eighth Yearbook (1989)

Part 1. *From Socrates to Software: The Teacher as Text and the Text as Teacher.* Philip W. Jackson and Sophie Haroutunian-Gordon, editors. Cloth.

Part 2. *Schooling and Disability.* Douglas Biklen, Dianne Ferguson, and Alison Ford, editors. Cloth.

Eighty-seventh Yearbook (1988)

Part 1. *Critical Issues in Curriculum.* Laurel N. Tanner, editor. Cloth.

Part 2. *Cultural Literacy and the Idea of General Education.* Ian Westbury and Alan C. Purves, editors. Cloth.

Eighty-sixth Yearbook (1987)

Part 1. *The Ecology of School Renewal.* John I. Goodlad, editor. Paper.

Part 2. *Society as Educator in an Age of Transition.* Kenneth D. Benne and Steven Tozer, editors. Cloth.

Eighty-fifth Yearbook (1986)

Part 1. *Microcomputers and Education.* Jack A. Culbertson and Luvern L. Cunningham, editors. Cloth.

Part 2. *The Teaching of Writing.* Anthony R. Petrosky and David Bartholomae, editors. Paper.

Eighty-fourth Yearbook (1985)

Part 1. *Education in School and Nonschool Settings.* Mario D. Fantini and Robert Sinclair, editors. Cloth.

Part 2. *Learning and Teaching the Ways of Knowing.* Elliot Eisner, editor. Paper.

Eighty-third Yearbook (1984)

Part 1. *Becoming Readers in a Complex Society.* Alan C. Purves and Olive S. Niles, editors. Cloth.

Part 2. *The Humanities in Precollegiate Education.* Benjamin Ladner, editor. Paper.

Eighty-second Yearbook (1983)

Part 1. *Individual Differences and the Common Curriculum.* Gary D Fenstermacher and John I. Goodlad, editors. Paper.

Eighty-first Yearbook (1982)

Part 1. *Policy Making in Education.* Ann Lieberman and Milbrey W. McLaughlin, editors. Cloth.

Part 2. *Education and Work.* Harry F. Silberman, editor. Cloth.

Eightieth Yearbook (1981)

Part 1. *Philosophy and Education.* Jonas P. Soltis, editor. Cloth.

Part 2. *The Social Studies.* Howard D. Mehlinger and O. L. Davis, Jr., editors. Cloth.

Seventy-ninth Yearbook (1980)

Part 1. *Toward Adolescence: The Middle School Years.* Mauritz Johnson, editor. Paper.

Seventy-eighth Yearbook (1979)

Part 1. *The Gifted and the Talented: Their Education and Development.* A. Harry Passow, editor. Paper.

Part 2. *Classroom Management.* Daniel L. Duke, editor. Paper.

The above titles in the Society's Yearbook series may be ordered from the University of Chicago Press, Book Order Department, 11030 Langley Ave., Chicago, IL 60628. For a list of earlier titles in the yearbook series still available, write to the Secretary, NSSE, 5835 Kimbark Ave., Chicago, IL 60637.

2. The Series on Contemporary Educational Issues

This series has been discontinued.

The following volumes in the series may be ordered from the McCutchan Publishing Corporation, P.O. Box 774, Berkeley, CA 94702-0774. Phone: 510-841-8616; Fax: 510-841-7787.

Academic Work and Educational Excellence: Raising Student Productivity (1986). Edited by Tommy M. Tomlinson and Herbert J. Walberg.

Adapting Instruction to Student Differences (1985). Edited by Margaret C. Wang and Herbert J. Walberg.

Choice in Education (1990). Edited by William Lowe Boyd and Herbert J. Walberg.

Colleges of Education: Perspectives on Their Future (1985). Edited by Charles W. Case and William A. Matthes.

Contributing to Educational Change: Perspectives on Research and Practice (1988). Edited by Philip W. Jackson.

Educational Leadership and School Culture (1993). Edited by Marshall Sashkin and Herbert J. Walberg.

Effective Teaching: Current Research (1991). Edited by Hersholt C. Waxman and Herbert J. Walberg.

Improving Educational Standards and Productivity: The Research Basis for Policy (1982). Edited by Herbert J. Walberg.

Moral Development and Character Education (1989). Edited by Larry P. Nucci.

Motivating Students to Learn: Overcoming Barriers to High Achievement (1993). Edited by Tommy M. Tomlinson.

Radical Proposals for Educational Change (1994). Edited by Chester E. Finn, Jr. and Herbert J. Walberg.

Reaching Marginal Students: A Prime Concern for School Renewal (1987). Edited by Robert L. Sinclair and Ward Ghory.

Restructuring the Schools: Problems and Prospects (1992). Edited by John J. Lane and Edgar G. Epps.

Rethinking Policy for At-risk Students (1994). Edited by Kenneth K. Wong and Margaret C. Wang.

School Boards: Changing Local Control (1992). Edited by Patricia F. First and Herbert J. Walberg.

The two final volumes in this series were:

Improving Science Education (1995). Edited by Barry J. Fraser and Herbert J. Walberg.

Ferment in Education: A Look Abroad (1995). Edited by John J. Lane.

These two volumes may be ordered from the Book Order Department, University of Chicago Press, 11030 S. Langley Ave., Chicago, IL 60628. Phone: 312-669-2215; Fax: 312-660-2235.